DEEP CHANGE

DEEP CHANGE

CREATING SPACE FOR MEANINGFUL
TRANSFORMATION

KEES DORST

THE MIT PRESS   CAMBRIDGE, MASSACHUSETTS   LONDON, ENGLAND

The MIT Press
Massachusetts Institute of Technology
77 Massachusetts Avenue, Cambridge, MA 02139
mitpress.mit.edu

© 2025 Massachusetts Institute of Technology

All rights reserved. No part of this book may be used to train artificial intelligence systems or reproduced in any form by any electronic or mechanical means (including photocopying, recording, or information storage and retrieval) without permission in writing from the publisher.

The MIT Press would like to thank the anonymous peer reviewers who provided comments on drafts of this book. The generous work of academic experts is essential for establishing the authority and quality of our publications. We acknowledge with gratitude the contributions of these otherwise uncredited readers.

This book was set in ITC Stone and Avenir by New Best-set Typesetters Ltd. Printed and bound in the United States of America.

The graphic representations of the models that appear throughout this book are created by Sulayka Janssen.

Library of Congress Cataloging-in-Publication Data

Names: Dorst, Kees author
Title: Deep change : creating space for meaningful transformation / Kees Dorst.
Description: Cambridge, Massachusetts : The MIT Press, [2025] | Includes bibliographical references and index.
Identifiers: LCCN 2025010305 (print) | LCCN 2025010306 (ebook) | ISBN 9780262553742 paperback | ISBN 9780262385442 epub | ISBN 9780262385459 pdf
Subjects: LCSH: Organizational change | Creative thinking
Classification: LCC HD58.8 .D67 2025 (print) | LCC HD58.8 (ebook) | DDC 658.4/06—dc23/eng/20250721
LC record available at https://lccn.loc.gov/2025010305
LC ebook record available at https://lccn.loc.gov/2025010306

10 9 8 7 6 5 4 3 2 1

EU Authorised Representative: Easy Access System Europe, Mustamäe tee 50, 10621 Tallinn, Estonia | Email: gpsr.requests@easproject.com

CONTENTS

1 BEYOND CRISIS 1

2 WE ARE NOT SOLVING OUR PROBLEMS ANYMORE 7

3 FRAME CREATION 29

4 CREATING CHANGE IN ORGANIZATIONS 71

5 PARADIGMS 93

6 SOCIETY IN TRANSITION 125

7 HOW: THE STUDIO 159

8 DELIVERING DEEP CHANGE 197

EPILOGUE: THERE'S ONE MORE THING 209

APPENDIX 1: WHY INNOVATION FAILS 211
APPENDIX 2: THE METASTUDIO 217
APPENDIX 3: PUBLIC SECTOR INNOVATION 221
APPENDIX 4: THEME ANALYSIS 229
APPENDIX 5: STUDIO PRINCIPLES 237
APPENDIX 6: MASTERING DEEP CHANGE 245
APPENDIX 7: MAKE YOUR OWN COLOR OF CHANGE 249
ACKNOWLEDGMENTS 251
NOTES 253
BIBLIOGRAPHY 265
INDEX 275

1

BEYOND CRISIS

To be in accord with the time, you are told to . . .
—The *I Ching*[1]

1.1 TOWARD NEW PRACTICES

The epigraph that opens this chapter is the phrase used at the beginning of every prophecy in the *I Ching*, the ancient Chinese *Book of Changes*. It wisely encourages the seeker of advice to shape their actions in a way that is well-aligned to the field of conflicting forces in the problem situation, the environment and the challenges ahead. Unfortunately, we seem to be living in a time of persistent misalignment. As we do our best to fix the problems that come our way, it often feels like we are just plugging holes with "solutions" that never resolve anything. On the contrary, every fix brings up a plethora of new issues that have to be dealt with. We find ourselves running from crisis to crisis.

What is the matter here?

In this book, we will argue that this is a twofold challenge.

First, there is a fundamental mismatch between our normal ways of approaching problems and the nature of the very open, complex, dynamic, and networked challenges facing us today. We will delve into this much more deeply in chapter 2, but the upshot is that in our complex, networked world the basis of normal problem-solving (cause-and-effect reasoning, in which *one thing* leads to *another*) goes out the window: doing *one thing* sets off a network of reactions that are hard to predict. Hence, if you approach such open, complex, dynamic, and networked problem situations via everyday problem-solving you end up confused, running around in circles, and just getting more and more stuck. In this book, we will see that when problem-solving doesn't work anymore, we need a different logic: start with the underlying human values, reframe, and create space for meaningful transformation. To be in tune with the times, we really need to think and act very differently.

And second, the *scale* of the challenges we face is dramatically increasing. In the coming ten years, there will have to be sweeping changes to how we deal with energy (toward zero emissions), with care in society (in face of the aging population), with nature and biodiversity (preserving the basis for our very existence), with infrastructure, with finance, and the list goes on. There is a rising awareness that deep change is needed in all these sectors—on a "systems level," as they say—but we seem to be incapable of getting that done. Yet shaping these transitions is the big challenge of our time.

In this book, we will see that while these two challenges—the need to deal with new open, complex, dynamic, and networked problems and the need to shape transitions—are very different in origin, they share a common nature and can be approached through the same logic and set of practices. Through these practices, we can not only reframe problem situations (creating new ways forward), but also inform organizational change (by synchronizing top-down and bottom-up reframing) and spark sector-level transformation (by creating and adopting new paradigms). To support these practices, we propose a new type of innovation infrastructure, a "studio," that creates the space for ongoing, deep, and meaningful transformation. By bringing together these studios, we can shape the transitions we need.

1.2   THIS BOOK IN A NUTSHELL

We start on our journey in the next chapter, by bootstrapping: We first need to understand more about our current way of thinking, and then take a good, deep look at other logics before introducing a reasoning pattern that is much more suited to the challenges we face (chapter 2). Then we will encounter a set of practices that embodies this logic and translates it into practical steps, and we will explore how these practices can work on a project level (chapter 3). We will then consider how these practices play out in and across organizations (chapter 4), how they can be used to change the paradigms in a sector (chapter 5), and how they can be taken to a societal level, to lead transitions (chapter 6). The *studio model* introduces the infrastructure to support these new practices on a continuous basis, creating the space for meaningful transformation (chapter 7). Yet the quality of deep change ultimately doesn't come from a theory or a model, but from us as people, seeking to deliver deep change (chapter 8).

Here are some pointers to open the book, before we get underway:

- The backbone of the book is formed by twenty-four inspiring case studies and many real-world examples. They will take us through the new thinking and introduce practices to achieve impact. They show how we can escape the old thinking that was creating the issues, and build paths to deep change—time and time again:

Alcohol-related violence in an entertainment district was suppressed through tough law and order measures
   ... UNTIL ...
   seeing the situation through the lens of a music festival led to the creation of an environment that supports a vibrant nightlife. (see § 4.1)

People who did not pay their amenities bills in time were sent reminders for ever-increasing amounts, and then a debt collector to demand the money they didn't have
   ... UNTIL ...
   the water company realized that if people in such financial strife cannot afford the basic amenities they need help, not prosecution. (see § 6.5)

The professional systems to support health and well-being were struggling to cope with the demand for services
   ... UNTIL ...
   citizens organized themselves to support the people in need of care in their neighborhood. (see § 6.5)

In the face of an environmental crisis caused by intensive agriculture, the ministry was struggling to bridge the divide between farmers and nature
   ... UNTIL ...
   the long-term vitality of the region was put center stage in the discussion, creating a common ground to deal with differences. (see § 6.2)

- Each chapter starts with a question or challenge, introduces some model(s) to make sense of the situation, and then moves to cases to see

how this works out in practice. These cases in turn lead to reflections, models, and more questions. The chapters together sketch a logic, a consistent worldview, an underlying mentality, and a set of practices, methods, and tools that works across projects, organizations, sectors, and societal transitions.
- This book builds on earlier work that was published in the MIT Press book *Frame Innovation*, taking the thinking much further to show how creative framing practices can be used to inform organizational change, support sector-level change and create a framework for societal change. To start, we will briefly go through some material (in chapters 2 and 3) that a reader of the earlier book might recognize—but now building on ten years of additional learning and insights.
- While this book is based on original research, it is not academic in tone. Rather, it seeks to transform the findings of the academic research into practices, for action and impact. To anchor the thinking back to where it originated, we refer to the underlying studies and discussions that are captured in academic papers. To pinpoint these, I have to refer to my own work a bit more than I would normally do—for which I apologize in advance.
- This book is a proposition. The main conclusions are brought together in the studio model, in chapters 7 and 8. These conclusions are based on twenty-plus years of work by a growing community of practitioners and researchers (see the acknowledgments). Over the years, we have generated much more material than can be included in these few pages, executing literally hundreds of projects and learning many lessons from each. This book concentrates on properly presenting the backbone of the thinking, with some peeks into the many practices and workshop techniques we have developed over the years (the flesh on the bones).
- Finally, by way of an outline, the following points take you through the line of reasoning in this book and give a taste of what is to come in the next chapters:

"A problem can never be solved using the same thinking that created it." (§ 3.2)

Changing the normal is the hardest thing. (§ 5.2)

A best practice is what worked in the past. (§ 2.1)

When the problem situations you are dealing with have become more open, complex, dynamic, and networked, you will have to become open, complex, dynamic and networked yourself. (§ 2.1)

In complex problem situations, there are no solutions: Forget problem-solving. Rather, create interventions that bring the whole system to a better state. (§ 2.3)

The future belongs to the quickest learner. (§ 2.5)

A learning loop only works when it is complete; otherwise, nothing is learned. (§ 7.2)

A frame is a way of looking, thinking, and acting. (§ 3.2)

To create a new frame, we need to go back to the deep human values at play, then rebuild the world from there. (§ 3.3)

Value sits only in the lifeworld of people. (§ 6.4)

Projects don't change the world. (§ 4.1)

To effect change, we have to synchronize top-down and bottom-up movements in an organization. (§ 4.2)

A system changes when all layers start to move. (§ 5.3)

The new paradigm is always worse than the old one. (§ 5.1)

Shaping transitions is the great challenge of our time. (§ 1.1)

In transitions, there is no problem ownership. (§ 6.3)

We live in a time of parallel transitions: If we are not careful, it will always be the same people left out. (§ 7.4)

If it doesn't work for society, it doesn't work at all. (§ 7.5)

The aim is to create organizations and systems that have a deep inner vitality. (§ 6.4)

To create space for deep change, we need a lab, an academy, a podium, and a temple. (§ 7.1)

It is only real when it makes you feel alive. (§ 8.1)

2

WE ARE NOT SOLVING OUR PROBLEMS ANYMORE

"If seven maids with seven mops
Swept it for half a year,
Do you suppose," the Walrus said,
"That they could get it clear?"
"I doubt it," said the Carpenter,
And shed a bitter tear.
—*Through the Looking Glass*[1]

2.1 OPEN, COMPLEX, DYNAMIC, AND NETWORKED

Problems are obstacles in the flow of life. We want to get on with things, but something is holding us back—so the natural reaction is try and get rid of this barrier as soon as possible. We normally use an action we have learned, that is in our repertoire, to react to the problem and make it disappear. That is what a real solution does. To quote the philosopher Ludwig Wittgenstein, reflecting on his way of dealing with philosophical issues: "We are aiming at . . . complete clarity. But this simply means that the philosophical problems should completely disappear. The real discovery is the one that makes me capable of stopping philosophy when I want to."[2] If this succeeds, the obstacle is passed and we can probably hardly remember it having been there at all (reflection-in-action[3]). But sometimes this is hard, and we don't get past the obstacle. Then we need to stop and think, take the problem seriously, and study what actually is the matter in the problem situation in order to find other—less obvious—ways forward. The first experience of the problem then becomes a gateway to exploring the counterforces, tensions, and underlying paradoxes that cause the problem situation. Through this exploration, we learn, thus building up experience that extends the repertoire of responses at our disposal.

But in this day and age, a new category of problems has emerged for which our normal ways of problem-solving don't seem to work anymore. It is fundamentally different from what we have seen before. In today's networked world, we have created webs of inspiration, expression, connection, and reflection. But in creating these great new links and opportunities (the "good stuff"), we inadvertently networked our problems (the "bad stuff") too. We have made them more *open, complex, dynamic, and networked* than ever before. And that creates all kinds of difficulties for our normal ways of thinking. To elaborate on this, point by point:[4]

An *open* challenge is one in which the border is unclear and often permeable. Normally, when we start out solving a problem, we conveniently draw a mental circle: On the inside are the things we need to think about, and on the outside are those that will be ignored (the context). But in our hyperconnected world, there is no such thing as a context anymore. You just don't know what should be inside the active problem space and what can safely be left outside. This can even shift over time: Aspects of the problem situation or stakeholders that could initially be ignored may need to be brought in later, as the problem space moves and expands (see § 7.3). This makes thinking about these problem situations hard, and it introduces a lot of uncertainty. In this book, we will see how an innocent (and understandable) mistake in setting the problem boundary can cause immense problems later on as the situation develops.[5]

A *complex* problem situation consists of many elements, with many relationships among them, and also interdependencies between these connections. This makes the behavior of the whole thing difficult to predict: a small local action can lead to a chain of unexpected effects. The properties of such a truly complex problem situation are unknowable, even through exhaustive analysis. Therefore, such complex problem situations (*systems*) require a completely different approach from complicated problem situations.[6] Complicated systems have many elements and relationships, but those are knowable and can be mapped, so the outcomes of an action can be predicted. In contrast, when dealing with true complexity, you basically have to "kick" the system to see how it responds; the response will show which of the relationships and interdependencies are actually important, and which other ones can safely be ignored for the moment. The true structure of the problem situation then emerges from such interventions (for an example, see § 5.3).

A *dynamic* problem changes over time, with the addition of new elements and the shifting of connections (e.g., shifting priorities, shifting boundaries of the problem situation). To deal with such wildly dynamic problem situations, the problem solver cannot isolate themselves but must be in constant contact with the developing problem landscape while they work out what to do (see § 6.2).

The *networked* nature of today's problem situations means that you cannot isolate and "own" the problem anymore (by closing the problem space; see the earlier discussion). Nor can you "own" the solution. Both the challenges we face and the solutions we create are networks in themselves (§ 7.4).

Often, a complex problem situation doesn't show its true nature, and we are tempted to go about our business in the normal way. Problem-solving is what we have learned to do from an early age, and we pride ourselves to be good at it. But in the face of such open, complex, dynamic, and networked problem situations, conventional problem-solving thinking will fail, no matter how well conceived and executed. These open, complex, dynamic, and networked problems require a different approach. We must shift our thinking.

Case Study: The Complexities of Farming

At this point, a case study will help give a sense of what it means to deal with an open, complex, dynamic, and networked problem situation. This particular problem situation plays out in Holland, and it concerns the urgent need to address an environmental crisis by transitioning from intensive (industrial-scale) farming to local, circular, nature-friendly agriculture (for more on the background to this problem, see § 6.2). On the face of it, this may seem a fairly straightforward problem to solve: We know that large-scale intensive farming (producing large volumes at a low cost) is causing severe environmental problems in such a densely populated country, so it makes sense to look at types of agriculture that have a higher added value, have less volume, and are less polluting. Why don't we just do it? Instead of moving forward, a crisis has emerged that has been exacerbated by the fact that people have tried to deal with this open, complex, dynamic, and networked problem situation as if it was merely a complicated problem to be fixed.

They have underestimated the *openness* of the problem arena. There are real questions about where to start and who to involve. For instance, if you want to stimulate local circular farming practices, you could concentrate on farmers and the agricultural sector, but one of the issues that puts pressure on the farmers' business models these days is that land value is increasing. It is pushed up by the need to build new housing for a growing population, and the need to use the land for the production of renewable energy. These developments, far removed from the agricultural domain, put a huge pressure on potential business models for sustainable farming. These farms can only be profitable when the consumer is happy to pay more for their food when it is sustainably grown. Apart from a niche market, this is not yet part of the general culture. This means we need a culture shift, and educating the public becomes an important part of the transformation.

The *dynamics* of these market factors make it very hard for the farmers to plan; any major shift toward sustainable practices will involve a major investment, which will need to be earned back in a reasonable time.

So the problem is deeply *networked*, with many issues and parties that would not even see themselves as being connected at all. In this case, the supermarkets that are used to negotiating sharply with the farmers over the price they pay for the produce will have to be part of the solution.

And we haven't even begun to describe the *complexity* of this challenge. This problem area has direct relationships with public health, food security and food accessibility, the sustainability of the agricultural sector, developments in the use of rural space, education, food culture, water management, and more. It is directly connected the worldwide food system and the pressures that is under to address the forces of a growing world population, climate change, the loss of biodiversity, and so on.

It must be clear by now that these issues cannot simply be solved by any one party (there is no single, identifiable "problem owner"). An almost endless list of stakeholders with conflicting demands and sometimes incompatible ways of thinking will sooner or later have to be involved in this transition. In the end, this is a societal problem, and creating progress in this space requires the involvement of all of society.[7] Later in this book (§ 6.2), we will see how conventional problem-solving has not only failed, but made this particular problem situation much worse. You will also see how, through a deep understanding of the tensions and paradoxes underlying the problem situation, new strategies can be developed to shift the agricultural system toward a better state.

Organizations have huge trouble dealing with these open, complex, dynamic, and networked problems, and the new types of challenges they bring. When facing uncertainty, they tend to hold on to "best practices" and "evidence-based strategies." But by definition, a best practice is something that worked in the past; in adopting it, there is an assumption that the problem situation is stable, so we can apply it again and get to the same results. In a world that is rapidly changing, there is absolutely no guarantee that this holds true.

In the end, the only way forward for organizations that have to function in a brave new world of open, complex, dynamic, and networked problem situations is by mirroring this environment. They will have to become more open, complex, dynamic, and networked themselves.

The advent of more open, complex, dynamic, and networked problem situations also hits home in our personal lives. We live in a media environment replete with rhetoric around technological progress, one that tells us we should be happily hyperactive beings running around in a constant state of excitement and flow.[8] But often, the reality of living in a world of open, complex, dynamic, and networked problem situations feels more like struggling through mud. The day-to-day experience of these problem situations is one of confusion: When everything is connected, there are so many things to take into consideration that it becomes harder and harder to progress. The inherent uncertainty of these problem situations can lead to indecision, restlessness, and stress. We live in a tangled web.

2.2 A BRIEF ANATOMY OF COMPLEXITY

But how can we develop new practices to deal with the complexity that is there and devise a new way to approach these complex problem situations? First, we need to develop a close understanding of complexity itself. This requires a quick dip into the huge field of complexity and systems theory—focusing first on the structure of complex problems and then on the dynamics of complex systems.

While working at IBM, David Snowden worked on a framework to help leaders choose their strategies for dealing with various types of problems (later, this became known as the Cynefin model). His framework distinguishes four types of complex problem situations—simple, complicated, complex, and chaotic—and suggests different ways of responding to them.

In a *simple* problem situation, the relationship between cause and effect is obvious to all. The appropriate strategy is *sense > categorize > respond*, based on best practices. One might say that to the competent person this type of problematic situation hardly registers as a problem at all, in normal life—for example, a doctor sees a patient that clearly has the flu, routinely prescribes the appropriate pills, and sends the person to bed.

In a *complicated* problem situation, the relationship between cause and effect requires analysis or some other form of investigation and/or application of expert knowledge. The appropriate actions are *sense > analyze > respond*, with a reference to what is seen as good practice in the field. This is what we will call (normal) problem-solving in this book (see § 2.4). Note that this is in no way easy: The complicatedness of the problem situation and the knowledge and skills required to deal with it can stretch us right to the edge of our abilities. A good example of complicatedness would be an aircraft: All the elements of the plane's systems (hydraulic, electric, fuel, sensors, digital systems like stability control and autopilot, etc.) are known and their behavior is essentially predictable, but the whole machine is incredibly complicated. Note that the systems' behavior can be predicted because the systems are separated, made to function without interdependencies or interference between the systems—and that accidents often occur when this interference happens, despite best efforts to keep the systems separate.

In a truly *complex* system, the relationship between cause and effect is such a tangle that it effectively can only be perceived in hindsight. Hence, the best way to tackle a complex problem situation is by forcing this hindsight up front, as it were, by acting upon the system: *probe > sense > respond*. Insight into the behavior of the system will emerge from this practice. Note that in this case, in contrast to the simple and complicated systems discussed previously, this approach starts with probing rather than analyzing. This is important as it requires a quite a different mentality from the problem solver. Some people seek to reduce ambiguity and find safety in analysis and numbers, but in the case of a complex systems, this is the wrong way to go.

In the case of a *chaotic* system, there only is a very general sense of the possible relationship between cause and effect at an overall system level—if at all. There is nothing much to gain by extensive analysis; the appropriate way forward is *act > sense > respond*, then see whether patterns emerge. (Note that there is an issue with this category: In the case of real chaos, there will be no patterns at all; as soon as there is a pattern, we would call it *complex*. Chaos is a negative notion, defined by a lack of something—in this case, a pattern—rather than a positive property.)

Case Study: The Train to Nowhere

Often, complex problems are misdiagnosed as being complicated. Take, for instance, the planning process for a high-speed train.[9] Such planning problems are notoriously difficult (the term *wicked problems* was coined by Rittel and Webber in the context of urban planning[10]). In such a big and complicated engineering project, there needs to be an early decision about where the tracks should cut through the landscape. The first approach is often to take this on as a complicated problem, by analyzing the problem situation and creating a solution that is technically optimal. But what to do then if the proposed track, which is optimized in a technical sense, is questioned for other, social and environmental reasons? We suddenly move from the closed and ordered world of a complicated problem into the realm of real complexity. In this complex world, there is a mismatch between the general good that a high-speed could bring (for society and the economy) and the enormous local impact such a train line has, affecting the quality of life of people that find themselves living along the track—people that probably don't have much to gain from the line at all. Tackling this problem situation is possible if and only if we take its full complexity on board. An approach of "thinking complexly" would begin by listening closely to the people concerned in order to understand the value systems at play. In this case, a way forward was found by looking at the local problems in terms of quality of life and creating probes to see how this quality of life can be achieved in novel ways in order to compensate for the impact of the train. What definitely doesn't work is what the government did: repeating the common mistake of adopting the "complicatedness" strategy of commissioning more research to analyze the problem situation. The assumption is that once we know everything about the problem situation, we have somehow "solved" it. But more research is the last thing needed here. This is not a crisis of knowledge, but a crisis of practice.

Let's go one step deeper into understanding complexity. The dynamics of complex systems can be described in terms of different four types of *balance*:[11] stable, dissipative, on the edge of chaos, and experiencing a state change.

A *stable* system behaves in an (almost) linear way to disturbance. It is in equilibrium or near equilibrium, and its order is hardly disturbed by outside influences. The dominant order is clear, and the system behavior is predictable.

The trouble starts with a *dissipative* system: the forces that push it out of balance have more influence, making the system behave in a nonlinear, cyclical way; the system most likely displays a pendulum movement around a balanced state. The system does display increasing instability with disturbance, and this means that small causes can already have large consequences. The push and pull of forces mean that the behavior of the system at any specific point in time is increasingly hard to predict.

When this balancing system is overwhelmed, it can move to the *edge of chaos*. Here, behavior is unpredictable and nonlinear. This can be the start of a new order; that is, a new type of balance can arise. At the edge of chaos, you will often see a dual structure: a troubled dominant upper stream, and an undertow of the new order forming.[12] This is the result of a system that is trying to cope with in an increasing number of critical incidents (much like a paradigm that starts to run out of predictive value[13]). The dynamics of these near-chaotic systems is unpredictable: A large number of small shifts (in an evolution) or a small number of bigger shifts (revolutions) can occur. Both of these are hard for organizations to cope with, as their ways of problem-solving normally deal with small and singular disturbances.

Then a system can enter a *state change*, a nonlinear jump. Getting to the limit of what the old order can deal with creates complete disequilibrium and the collapse of the upper stream, in combination with a breakthrough of the undertow as the new dominant order. The elements of the system are reconfigured to reflect a new order.

This is a highly idealized description of a change process; later in this book, we will come back to and critique this framework (see § 5.2 and 6.3).

Case Study: The Rise and Fall of the Village Shop

Let's explore how this model of four types of balance and disequilibrium can help further the understanding of a complex societal issue: for instance, the rise and fall of the village shop.[14]

The stable system: Traditionally, every village with more than a couple of hundred inhabitants would have its local shops, such as the grocer, the butcher, the baker, and so on. Over the years, these specialized shops disappeared, with typically only a local self-service supermarket remaining. Supermarkets were economically viable because they catered for a stable local clientele, and they were valued as part of the social fabric of the village.

The dissipative system: But times started to change again. While the older generation of villagers (the loyal customers) was disappearing, new houses were built and new people (young families, commuters) moved to the village. With a growth in car ownership and increased mobility, the new people lived, worked, and also shopped in a much wider radius than older customers, and often did their major shopping at cheaper supermarkets that sprung up at the fringes of bigger towns and cities in the area. The village streets got quieter. The local supermarket put on special events and sales, expanding its assortment to cater to the needs of a much more varied population.

The edge of chaos: There came a point at which people used the village shop only as a fallback, a place to go only if you had forgotten to buy something in town. The village shop was seen as expensive, and as sales dropped, it had to limit the assortment of goods for sale. Buying these goods in small quantities made it hard to get good wholesale prices. The village shop grew quieter and slipped into debt.

The state change: By now, the shop was in imminent threat of closure—and indeed, many such shops have closed over time. In the end, it is not the commercial value but the community value of these shops that can lead to their rescue. In some villages, shops are now successfully run by volunteers as a community project. And some of these are quite enterprising, moving to a new commercially viable business model by specializing in local produce (with subscription models for standard grocery shopping, efficient local delivery, etc.). In other areas, local government has been rethinking how to replace the community value of the village shops in a different way. Historically, these villages didn't have shops at all but were serviced by traveling markets once a week. There have been efforts to reestablish these "market days." They serve as a focal point for the community while supporting less-mobile villagers in getting their grocery needs.

You can also use the Cynefin framework to make sense of this case study. In the dissipative state of the change process, the proprietor of a village supermarket might diagnose a fall in sales as a simple problem: Just lower the prices, and you will sell more. But these discounts only work in a stable environment while the proprietor is actually in a truly complex problem situation; there are many hidden factors at play. The changes in demographics and mobility mean that the discounts will not have the desired effect of increasing sales, but they will impact the profit margin on the items sold—therefore exacerbating the problem. This can drive a person to despair.

In a general sense, the complex systems framework captures the dynamics (the rise and fall) of the village shop phenomenon quite well. The description highlights some lessons on the nature of complex systems that we will build on going forward. (1) The original system was under threat as the elements in the system (inhabitants) changed and the system border expanded. It opened up, disturbing the "closed world"[15] that the village shop was so well adapted to. (2) Note that in this case study, the way forward can be found in increasing, rather than decreasing, the level of complexity—by extending the systems border to arrive at regionally operating markets. (3) There is a fundamental shift in the overall value proposition that underlies the system: What used to be the secondary function of these shops (serving as community hubs) becomes much more important. (4) In systems theory, there is a neat sense of progress: the old structure collapses while a new structure breaks through, one that is more all-encompassing and has a more refined functionality. We cannot be sure that this is true in the case of the village shop; although the flexibility (and therefore the vitality) of the new formula is much bigger than the old one it replaced, it is yet to be seen whether these new forms will create a new balance for long. The forces that created the imbalance are still around, and the behavior of the new system that has been created is yet to be understood.

These observations are bound to spark intuitive recognition in the reader; and the models are helpful in sensitizing us to what is important when approaching truly complex problem situations. It is good to understand the misunderstandings that may occur when people are not on the same page, and the Cynefin framework in particular clarifies the inevitable failure of leadership when the problem situation is misdiagnosed. At the same time, these models do not help create new practices; for that, we need a different approach.

2.3 BEYOND PROBLEM-SOLVING

To start on a different path, it is good to first articulate what we need to throw away—radically—to move away from cherished thinking patterns and practices. We need to (1) forget solutions, then (2) forget problem-solving, (3) forget projects, and then (4) forget heroes. This is quite a list, and it requires an explanation.

First, we have to *forget solutions*. Any attempt at creating "the solution" to "the problem" is futile: In a truly complex situation, problems are never really clearly defined, and there *is no* silver bullet solution that will magically satisfy all the needs and wants of the various stakeholders. The way to achieve progress in a complex situation is to create high-quality interventions to move the whole system toward a more desired state. And this is not going to do away with the complex situation; it cannot be resolved as such (in the same way that a simple problem is "solved"). True complexity is here to stay: the open, complex, dynamic, and networked nature of the problem situation itself is not going to change through our efforts. There is no ultimate balance or stability to strive for; even if we manage to achieve a period of relative stability, we need to keep probing, learning, improving, and sensing again to make sure we understand the dynamic undercurrent that can surface any moment. This is something we have known for millennia: In the *I Ching*, the classic Chinese oracle of change, the wise advice of what to do in a problem situation is followed by an outline of what the next situation that results from your actions is going to be like, and what to do then, and so on. There are always changes, and problem situations transform in an ongoing process. Therefore, in saying that solutions are not on offer, we have to also forget the ideal of a stable state. But as you will see later, this doesn't mean that a measure of stability can't be created through creating dynamic system vitality (rather than through striving for an immutable new structure; see § 6.4).

Case Study: Look at You

For this example, let's look at our bodies as open, complex, dynamic, and networked systems. To make us who we are, a body consists of many interlocking systems (blood, lymphatic, nervous, muscular, skeletal, hormonal) that have a different physical basis (some work by mechanically pumping fluids around, while others are electric, chemical, or mental[16]), and while they could be considered as separate mechanisms, we know they influence each other in predictable and unpredictable ways—including sudden cliffs of chaos that tend to happen not just when one system fails, but when the general vitality across systems has been undermined to the point of a total collapse. Interaction among the systems is also something we experience in a healthy body: We eat when are feeling unhappy, we feel warm when in love, we feel sick to the stomach when fearful. These cross-system interactions mean that support for our health will always need to be holistic rather than a single-system diagnose-and-fix approach. In complex matters of health, forget single solutions; there might be a quick fix (physical system repair), but well-being and vitality have many dimensions.

Next, we need to *forget problem-solving*. In complex problematic situations, problems can never really be clearly defined. The problem interpretation can shift, and the formulation of what we see as the "problem" can be part of the discussion (what can be seen as the problem actually coevolves with our view of possible solutions; see § 3.4[17]). This compromises the direct link between cause and effect. Problem-solving thinking is based on *causality*, the idea that one thing leads to another. In a complex situation, on the other hand, everything is connected in a giant tangle, so one thing doesn't actually lead to another, but instead to many shifts and changes that are hard to foresee. In such a situation, we need to shift our thinking away from looking for *the* solution to *the* problem, because neither really exists. This means that we have to forget problem-solving as we have effectively pulled the rug from under it. When we step away from problem-solving because the assumptions that underlie it don't work, then we have to forget not just direct causality, but also the linear thinking that it implies.

But if solutions don't really exist, and linear thinking doesn't work, that means we need to also *forget projects*. Stepping away from this is hard for some organizations; normally, in situations that require fresh approaches, they are used to creating "innovation projects." But complexity forces us to think in long-term programs instead: Creating change in a complex system requires multiple interventions, which can each consist of many steps. Change then is achieved through influencing the system rather than through implementing a plan to "solve the problem." The case study introduced in chapter 4 will follow the twists and turns of the changes in the entertainment area over fourteen years since the original King Cross project. This gives a rare insight into the way complex systems actually evolve and change in a stream of innovation activities (see § 4.2).

We tend to associate ideas with a "lightbulb moment" and the accomplishment of a single person. In a complex problem situation, that situation is extremely unlikely—so perhaps we also need to *forget heroes*. Innovating in a complex environment often requires a combination of ways of thinking and the practices of many people. This starts with a healthy dose of humility and extremely good listening skills. In her research, Tua Bjorklund has shown that in complex organizations, innovation does not come from "product champions" (as the management literature suggested); instead, it requires a relay race that involves many people across the organization to realize an initiative.[18]

2.4 A DIFFERENT LOGIC

It is easy to say that we need to think differently, but that statement is fairly meaningless if we don't first ask ourselves: How do we reason now? We need clarity on this, as a basis for exploring what thinking differently would look like. We will use a model from formal logic to describe the key reasoning patterns that underpin current reasoning and problem-solving. This then provides a basis for understanding the challenges we face as thinkers and doers—the deeper, fundamental issues that we need to conquer when we create new practices to address open, complex, dynamic, and networked problem situations.

To create clarity, we will have to step away from the world of practice and action for a moment and use a fairly abstract model to think through the fundamental differences between reasoning patterns. We create an abstraction by way of bracketing: When the real-world situation we want to think about is much too complex and chaotic, we want to ignore all unnecessary details (unnecessary, that is, in the context of what we want to achieve). Abstracting is a process of putting things between brackets, of temporarily looking away from them.

Case Study: Abstraction Gone Badly Wrong

Design researchers who have developed methods for designing have often done so by focusing on the *dynamics of design processes*, bracketing everything else that makes up a normal, gloriously messy design situation: the properties of *the designer*, *the design problem*, and *the context*. Their methods then lay out the design process in a sequence of steps—pretending that because these models are purely process-oriented, they can be applied by *all* designers to *all* design problems in *all* design situations. (This is not true: Just because you choose to ignore something, that doesn't mean it isn't important!) However, in bracketing the designer, the problem, and the context, these theorists ignore pretty much everything that is interesting, and also difficult, about designing in practice—thus reducing the usefulness of their methods and theories. The art of design in practice is all about the intricacies of choosing the best actions to take in a concrete design context, depending on the nature of the specific design problem and the abilities of the designer. Abstraction done badly doesn't go there: It stops at creating a theory or model, then presents this to the world as truth. But in real life, those aspects that a theorist conveniently puts between brackets and ignores all come back to haunt us as we try to use their thinking in practice.

This tells us that the clarity that we gain through abstraction inevitably comes at the expense of realism. In the next paragraphs, we will go through four different types of reasoning as if they are separate, but in real life, these are always combined, nested on different levels, and as practitioners, we switch between these with lightning speed. Yet it is useful to stop time for a moment and ponder these types as fundamentally different ways of reasoning, as they are often misunderstood and confused. Later in this book (§ 6.2), we will revisit this abstract model and add more elements to it, making it less abstract, more realistic, and ultimately more useful.

When we step way back and look at a problematic situation at its most abstract, we can see that it consists of (1) various elements, (2) a pattern of relations among these elements, and (3) an outcome. In analytical thinking, this outcome could be knowledge or understanding. In productive thinking, when we set out with an intent to do or make something, to change the world, the outcome is the value that we try to achieve.

This three-way distinction between *elements (what)*, *patterns of relationships (how)*, and *results (outcome / value)* helps us to distinguish four basic reasoning patterns. To understand the differences among these ways of reasoning, we can simply compare different settings of the knowns and unknowns in the following equation:[19]

$$\text{what} + \text{how} > \textbf{outcome}$$

REASONING TOWARD AN OUTCOME: DEDUCTION

At the start of a process of deduction, we know the elements (the *what*) in the situation, and we know *how* they will interact together. This knowledge allows us to reason toward an outcome. For instance, if we know that there are planets in the sky, and we are aware of the natural laws that govern their movement within the solar system (as defined by the laws of gravity), we can predict where a planet will be at a certain time. The calculations to support this prediction can be very complicated, but in the end, reasoning deductively toward that prediction is not problematic. This outcome can be translated into a forecast, which can be checked through observation. In terms of our simple equation, the starting position for deductive thinking looks like this:

$$\text{what} + \text{how} > \text{???}$$

Deduction makes us feel safe: If and when we know all the elements of the problem situation and how they hang together, then we can confidently deduce the outcome. This is rationality at its most unassailable. In professional practice, this type of thinking expresses itself in the belief that we can produce "logical" strategies and blueprints, or the claim to base ourselves on "best practices" and "evidence-based interventions." But this gold standard of pure logic can only be achieved in a closed world, in which we are absolutely sure we know *all* the elements of the problem situation and *completely* understand all the relationships at play beforehand. In the real world, this never happens[20]—and when it does, we are talking about quite uninteresting, mechanical, routine reasoning.[21] In practice, all problems are messy. Yet it is tempting to claim that we have used deduction in dealing with a problem; this claim to pure rationality is so strong that we don't even have to defend the result. It is "logical," after all.

REASONING TOWARD NEW KNOWLEDGE: INDUCTION

Matters are more complex in the next reasoning pattern, induction. We leave the closed world of deductive reasoning to enter a more open, creative space:

$$\text{what} + \text{???} > \textbf{outcome}$$

At the start of the reasoning process, we again know all the relevant elements in the situation, and—if we again take the planets as an example—we know the outcome of their interactions in the sense that we can observe their movement across the night sky. But suppose we do not yet know the laws of gravity, the pattern of relationships that governs their orbits. We can't logically deduce such a law from observations alone. But we can observe the movement of the planets and think deeply about the underlying patterns that could potentially cause this behavior. The formulation of laws that explain this behavior is always a creative act, where the pattern of relationships is dreamed up and proposed (as a hypothesis). We test the hypothesis by trying it out, using it to predict future outcomes. When it doesn't quite fit (the feedback loop through observations doesn't give us the result we were hoping for; there is not a complete fit between the prediction and the real outcome), then we go back and tweak the hypothesis, and try again. This process of hypothesizing and trying out is the basis of progress in science. When the accepted theory doesn't match the observations anymore, a paradigmatic shift may be needed.[22]

In the Middle Ages, the conventional wisdom among astronomers was that the planets and sun were orbiting around the earth. That was an unquestioned truth, borne out by observations and sitting comfortably within the Christian view that God created the universe for humanity: Of course, the earth would then be central. The astronomers of the day didn't have all the elements (not all the planets had been discovered) and had only a simple model to calculate the movement of the planets—yet this theory was good enough to account for the observable phenomena: almost, but not quite. In Kuhn's account of scientific progress, the current paradigm gets to be questioned when the number of exceptions and "special cases" needed to accommodate observations that do not quite fit starts to proliferate. At that point, a new theory is needed to pass the test of Occam's razor ("given two possible explanations, the simpler explanation that covers all observations is the best"). It still came as a shock in 1543 when the Polish astronomer Nicolaus Copernicus (after much trepidation) posited the hypothesis that the earth and other planets orbit around the sun. In this paradigm, the earth was no longer the center of the universe (we will return to this in § 5.1).

Inductive reasoning is also the type of thinking in detective novels: there is (1) a dead body (the *outcome*), and only a limited number of people who could have done the murder (gathered in a train, a scary remote house, an isolated community) as the (2) *what*; these are the elements of the situation. The detective's task is to align the means, motive, and opportunity, uncovering both the value that would be created by the murder (the motive) and *how* the deed was done (means and opportunity). Unfortunately, when Sherlock Holmes was asked by his admiring sidekick Dr. Watson how he manages to solve such a complex murder case, he answered, "It is all deduction, my dear Watson." However, what he is doing is actually induction.

REASONING TOWARD A SOLUTION: ABDUCTION

Now in these two analytical forms of reasoning, we are starting out with facts and take thinking steps to reach/establish knowledge and understanding. We are reasoning from origins to consequences, from cause to effect. But when we want to create valuable new things (be they products, procedures, strategies, situations, etc.), the basic pattern of reasoning is backward: from (intended) effect to the cause-to-be. This reasoning from consequences to their origin initially was rather aptly called *retroduction* by Charles Peirce; he later settled on the term *abduction*, which is now in common use, so that term will be used here as we try to understand the art of thinking backward.

In abduction, we set out to create a new *what*—a new "element" for the problem situation—so that the interactions (*how*) in the system lead to a desired outcome, which creates the intended *value:*

$$??? + \text{how} > \textbf{value}$$

In *first-order abduction*, we know the result, the value we want to achieve through the outcome, and also the how, the pattern of relationships that will help achieve the value we seek. The missing element is the what (a [technical] object, a service, a system), which still needs to be created. In this type of abduction, we don't question the how and thereby exclude the creation of new working mechanisms. This is the reasoning pattern behind problem-solving: creating new solutions (what) by building on a tried and tested how. Causality is not in question. The very sophisticated and complicated reasoning patterns of engineers could be seen as the epitome of this type of reasoning.

In open, *second-order abduction* (also called *design abduction*), the starting point is that we *only* know something about the nature of the outcome, the desired value we seek to achieve. So, the challenge is to figure out what new elements to create, while there is no known or chosen *how* that we can trust to lead to the desired outcome. As these are quite dependent on one another, they should both be developed in parallel. This double creative step requires us to devise proposals for both the *what* and the *how* and to test them in conjunction.

$$??? + ??? > \textbf{value}$$

The fact that there are several unknowns in the equation means that the only way to progress is by proposing a *how* and seeing whether it can be made to work. We call the act of proposing such a hypothetical pattern of relationships *framing*. A frame is a way of seeing the world and thinking about it, leading to a new way of acting upon it (see figure 2.1).

$$\text{what} + \underbrace{\text{how} > \textbf{value}}_{\text{FRAME}}$$

Figure 2.1 A frame is a way of looking at the problem situation that connects the intended *value* with a possible *how*.

Framing is the key to second-order abduction, because the only way to approach an open and complex problem situation is to work backward (from right to left in the equation): starting from the only known in the equation, the desired value, and then adopting or proposing a new frame; the frame implies the new *how*. Once a credible, promising, or at least interesting frame is proposed, the creative practitioner can shift to first-order abduction, envisioning the element (the *what*) that will allow the equation to be completed. Only complete equations with elements (whats), patterns of relationships (hows), and desired outcomes (values) in place can be critically investigated, using the powers of observation and deduction to see if the elements and frame combined actually do create the desired outcome.

Creating and testing these frames and potential solutions is a propositional and iterative process, in which we learn our way toward a resolution. From the outside, this may look like a playful process, and to an extent it is. Unfortunately, this very playfulness means it is sometimes misunderstood and dismissed as mere trial and error—a type of thinking that is not to be taken seriously. But it is a deeply serious, deliberate, and thorough exploration that has its own particular logic that is fundamentally different from the logic used in fields that are predominantly based on analysis (deduction, induction) and problem-solving (first-order abduction). Both first-order and second-order abduction are fundamentally open reasoning patterns: There are always several outcomes possible, so in a sense you never know whether you are right. Actually, there is no right or wrong. Abduction is inherently pragmatic; *truth* and *being right* just doesn't come into it. Quality does, and so does usefulness. This is what the two types of abduction have in common.

There is a fundamental difference between first-order and second-order abduction, which has huge consequences for the types of processes needed to reason in such a way—in approach, methods, and also mentality. The heart of the distinction between first-order and second-order abduction (say, the difference between a problem-solving approach and a design approach) can be illustrated by an example, as in the following case study.

Case Study: Look Behind You

Picture a beautiful old Mediterranean city with a medieval center of little alleyways and sunny squares that attracts floods of tourists in the summer season. Unfortunately, this also works as a magnet for small crime: Tourists are robbed in the street, quite often, and this is giving the city a bad name. The municipality of course wants to prevent these crimes from happening.

The first-order abduction (problem-solving) way to achieve safety and security (the *value*), is to take crime-prevention measures (the *how*). These measures (the *what*) include awareness campaigns and warning signs (e.g., "Pickpockets About"), increased police presence, increased punishment for perpetrators, and so on. These measures can be successful, but they do also scare people, which compromises the good time they are seeking on holiday in this wonderful city. They also inadvertently reinforce the city's bad reputation.

The second-order abduction approach to achieve this same intended value of safety and security is completely different. In questioning how these robberies actually take place, designers realized that one of the scenarios was connected with a very specific situation: When tourists walk through the narrow alleyways of the old city, they are quite safe, but as they come out to a sunny square, they need to orient themselves. Their eyes aren't attuned to the sudden bright light, so they stop. That is exactly the moment when thieves come from behind and grab their bags. It has happened before you even know it. The first solution direction the designers explored picked up on this being framed as an orientation problem—to be improved by communication (the *how*). If they provide clear signs (the *what*) to the tourists, just as they come on to the square, they will know where to go and move on. It turned out that this solution really didn't work very well for tourists that travel in families or groups, as signs provide places for them to stop and decide where to go. There is an awful lot of negotiation going on in holiday trips. In the end, the designers decided to create much smaller signage for pedestrians, dark poles with black signs and small white lettering, positioned in the middle of the square. When you come to the square, even if your eyes aren't attuned to the light, you see that there is information there and you just keep walking . . . and without even knowing it, you are moving out of harm's way. The lettering is quite small, so you have to walk right up to the sign, where you are safe. The *how* in this case is about finding ways to make sure that tourists avoid the dangerous spots they aren't even aware of. The signs (the *what*) are used as an inobtrusive way to position people.

2.5 REFLECTIONS

This foray into logic is the most abstract part of this book. In the coming chapters, we will happily descend from these lofty heights into more practical considerations. The key point here is that when we find ourselves in open, complex, dynamic, and networked problem situations, we only have the *value* to be achieved to go on. In the next chapter, you will see how we can experimentally frame and reframe the situation until we find a way into the problem situation that captures as much of the complexity as possible. Second-order abduction is the only way to deal with open, complex, dynamic, and networked problems.

So, second-order abduction lies at the core of creative practice—in all disciplines. Every discipline has a creative edge, a way to evolve within its ever-changing environment. But especially in disciplines that identify themselves with analysis and problem-solving, this creative practice is often poorly articulated and supported. In the creative disciplines, on the other hand, second-order abduction is the core reasoning pattern. These disciplines have had to develop elaborate practices, methods, and tools to support this pattern. A selection of these practices, methods, and tools will be introduced in the next chapters as we explore the logic needed for addressing open, complex, dynamic, and networked problem situations.[23]

POSTSCRIPT

We started this chapter with a quote from *Through the Looking Glass*, in which the Walrus and the Carpenter bemoan the sorry state of the beach they visit. In this chapter, we considered the open, complex, dynamic, and networked nature of the problem situations we are facing and the need to find a new way forward. Simply getting more maids with more mops is not going to do the trick: We need something else. This realization has been phrased in many ways, on many levels—from alarming UN reports on the state of the world to the idea that in our organizations we need to be "thinking outside the box." But who made the box in the first place? It was us. We need to step away from the kind of thinking that led to these problems. And we need to get on with it. But getting on with what? And how? In the next chapter, we start to show what can be done to navigate the complex issues of our times.

3
FRAME CREATION

Though this be madness, yet there is method in't.
—from Shakespeare's *Hamlet*[1]

3.1 PRACTICES

You will have noticed that one of the central concepts used in these chapters is *practices*. We have leaned on the popular usage of the term, but we need to be more precise and specific now, because this concept is going to play a central role in the development of a new way of thinking in this book. Practices are at the basis of frame creation, and they are used in this book to look differently at organizations (chapter 4) and disciplines (chapter 5)—by understanding them as bundles of practices.

A *practice* is a deliberate and coherent set of activities intended to achieve something. It is a way of seeing, thinking, and acting. We will here focus on the basic models of practices, which represent them as layered, with the layers containing statements on the *what*, the *how*, and the *why*[2] (see figure 3.1). Looking at this from the top down: the first layer is that of the concrete actions, the "doing" of the practice—the *what*. The second layer is more tactical and describes the *how*—that is, the method(s). Then there is a third layer, here rather quizzically described as *why/how*, which describes the *principles*, the strategic approach to achieving the values (the reason this is characterized as *why/how* is that, coming from above, this is the *why* behind the methods, while coming from below, this is the *how*—as in, how to achieve the intended value). The deepest layer describes the values that are embedded in the practice. In seeking to understand these values at the roots of people's practices, you

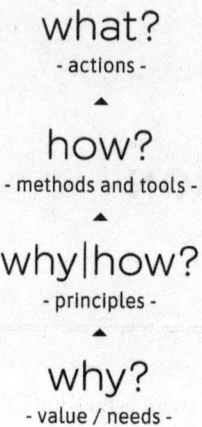

Figure 3.1 The layers of a practice.

dig for them by repeatedly asking "What is this really about?" (Note that this simple model of practices is used here because it provides everything needed to feed the bigger argument of this book. There are many other ways and possibly better ways to model practices, which detail and integrate notions like *intent*, *goal*, and *strategy*.)

Problems tend to present themselves on an action-level: Something is not quite right, and we feel the pressure to act to change an unwanted situation into a better one. This means that more often than not, the first attempts to resolve a problematic situation will be based on the "normal" repertoire of actions, drawn from the existing methods, principles, and value set. This makes perfect sense as this is the most efficient way to go about our business. Expertise and resources are already available, and if these are at hand, then the problem situation can be resolved with both efficiency and at speed. But when that fails to bring the desired results, we have to go back and rethink the approach itself: considering other methods, perhaps looking further afield beyond the confines of the professional framework that was initially used, looking to other disciplines. We seldom go back to the underlying principles and values—yet that is what is needed to deal with complexity (see § 2.4). To create deep change, we need to go to the level of values and principles and dwell there for a while, creatively reconsidering how they could be embodied differently through reframing.

FRAME CREATION

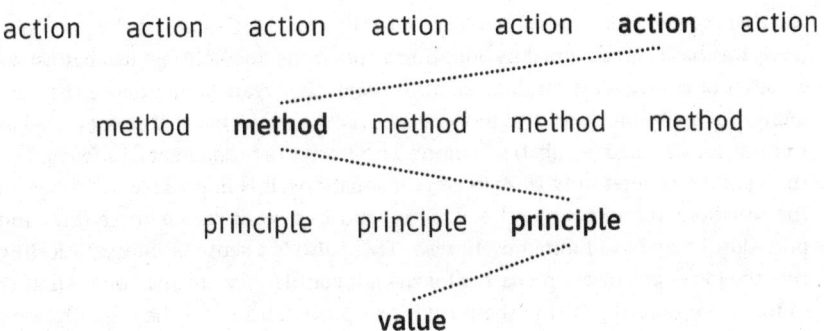

Figure 3.2 The pyramid of practice.

What makes this layered model of a practice interesting is that it opens up possibilities by emphasizing that any value can be achieved in multiple ways, through many different actions (see figure 3.2).

But coming from the top down, the path downward is bound to look deceptively logical: "Of course this is how we do it," as if it is the only way. Practices that are often used successfully can become well entrenched and completely self-reinforcing. But although we might be unaware, they always contain choices about the values we find important, the principles we use to think about them, and the methods and actions we are going to apply. Practices always contain a way of seeing the problem situation. The hidden nature of these embedded choices in practices can become incredibly limiting.

Case Study: On Hierarchy and Reliability

Defense forces are confronted by extremely open, complex, dynamic, and newly networked problems (which they call volatile, uncertain, complex, and ambiguous [VUCA]), and they find themselves quite ham-fisted in dealing with them. Traditionally, these forces are prime examples of a classic organizational hierarchy. This way of thinking is deeply engrained in the structure, processes, and culture (what we will later call the *regime*) of the organization, which in this case is also the whole sector. To even start to think about changing them at a fundamental level, we need to peel back many layers of engrained actions, methods, and principles.

When the top brass was asked what they felt was the central value around which the armed services are organized, they settled on *reliability*. This is not something that anybody can object to—seeing that the defense forces are dealing with life-threatening situations, and that they are handling all kinds of bombs (which they call *devices*). But while it is valid to keep reliability as a core value, on the principles level, this has been actioned by adopting a "planning and control" mechanism as a matter of course. This can be seen all through the organization: hence the hierarchy, the many processes and procedures, and the education that is organized as training for standard (combat) situations. This leads to a fundamental problem: The rules and procedures only work in certain situations. It is impossible to foresee all the situations the forces might encounter, and in new situations these rules and procedures may have limited usefulness. There also is a sense of unease, a feeling that the forces are always preparing for the last conflict, not the next one. Another unfortunate outcome is that these rules and procedures make the organization's behavior quite predictable. This is a great boon from an internal operations management perspective, but it also could give a potential enemy insight into what to expect. That is not a good thing. And the separate hierarchical structures, rules and procedures of the army, air force, and navy, make it really hard to collaborate among them, while in practice the multidimensionality of conflict situations requires close and fast coordination. As in all sectors, the defense forces need to adapt and seek to mirror the open, complex, dynamic, and newly networked nature of the problem situations they need to deal with. The speed of the development in the new networked technologies easily outpaces the ability of these organizations to adapt. Therefore, the question to explore is: How can a core value like reliability be achieved without resorting to planning and control? What other principles could one use as a basis for organizing? For inspiration: What organizations in other fields are known for their reliability? How do they operate, which principles do they use? What methods do they use to make it happen? What kind of actions does this lead to? (A comparison with car manufacturing, where companies seek to create reliability in their products while working with a flexible network of suppliers and partners, turned out to be particularly fruitful.) Ensuing discussions explored the creation of very quick feedback loops, placing decision power as low in the organization as possible, using cases and storytelling to create a common basis of situated knowledge ("in this situation, that was a good action," rather than trying to devise rules that would apply in all situations)—and exploring the completely different type of leadership that is then required.[3]

The implicit choice for one particular principle (here "planning and control") takes center stage in this case study. Principles often remain implicit because they are conflated with the values level. This hides the very important choice of the underlying rationality as we move from values toward action.

The consideration of practices in terms of these four layers also opens up the possibility for practices from different fields or backgrounds to be cross-linked; looking from the value level up, it is inspiring to see how a value can be achieved through different approaches and methods that originate in completely different domains. The cross-linking of practices among disciplines lies at the basis of a special strand of transdisciplinarity, called *creative intelligence*.[4] Practices can be woven together in a rich transdisciplinary practice, irrespective of where they originally came from.

3.2 FRAMES

The notion of frames was brought to prominence by the work of Donald Schön, a pragmatist philosopher who returned to academia after a career in consulting—only to be frustrated by the fact that education at universities seemed to be exclusively focused on filling the students with (academic) knowledge. He could see that this would not serve the students very well; it would not help them to become good practitioners. In his quest to describe what professionals actually do, he studied professional practices across many fields (medicine, architecture, policy, etc.). His understanding of their practices (the "craftsmanship," the "art of being a(n) . . .") led him to a model of professional behavior as a reflective practice (see figure 3.3). In this model, practitioners start by *naming* what is important in a complex problem situation, then *frame* an approach and set out to make *moves*, taking on a course of action. They then *reflect* on the effectiveness of those actions. If the action taken doesn't seem to be leading in the right direction, this is learned from, and the practitioner

NAMING
- what is important? -
▼
FRAMING
- how do I approach this? -
▼
MOVING
- acting, based on the chosen approach -
▼
REFLECTING
- am I going in the right direction? -

Figure 3.3 Schön's model of reflective practice. *Source:* Author.

enters one of three feedback loops: from reflection to moving ("need to try a different action"), to framing ("this approach doesn't work"), or to naming ("apparently, I have missed or ignored something important in the problem situation"). This is a process of active exploration, driven by the framing of proposed actions and learning from their results. In this, Schön distinguishes between reflection-*in*-action on a micro scale—the very quick, almost subconscious, inadvertent adjustments when you are in the flow of doing something—and reflection-*on*-action, the explicit stepping out of the flow of action to consider how you are doing, reflecting with the intent to steer the next action in a different direction. In Schön's model of practice, active exploration and learning are central.

Within this model, a new approach to a problem situation is called a *frame*. By *reframing* a problem situation, we set out to think differently about the matter at hand. We step out of the "normal" way of thinking and shape the intent differently by using our experience and/or imagination to propose a new way forward—thereby exercising our free will. The latter point is important: We seldomly realize that in approaching the world, we are always within a frame. Frames may come from habit, our culture, our professional field, or from a community of practice that we feel part of. The accepted frame is the normal practice. Frames are so universal that they are hard to spot; they only show themselves anew when something is wrong, when the current frame doesn't lead to a desired result anymore (which Schön kindly called a *surprise*). Frames show themselves when they are broken; only then are we forced to look under the hood of normal practice. This means that we only talk about frames in the context of reframing: In a sense, all frames that we will discuss here are actually reframes.

And reframing is not easy to do. You are creating a different approach to a problem situation, effectively pulling the rug out from under yourself.

Case Study: The Counterterrorism Bin

The public provider in Sydney asked the Designing Out Crime Research Center to help decide on a new rubbish bin for use in train stations and on platforms. The problem centered on the perceived threat of terrorism in these places. Terrorists have used bins to leave bombs in crowded, public places before. A study of the available designs revealed a wide range of solutions: from small bins with very narrow openings to all kinds of clever mechanisms that actually make it quite tricky to get rid of your trash—all the way to the extreme case of a heavily armored "bombproof" bin that cannot explode sideways; on detonation, the force is directed upward. (This is extremely expensive, and very impractical; it's not a good idea to have this under an awning—let alone underground.) On reflection, all these designs had the same unresolved issue: basically, if you can put something of the size of a packet of cigarettes or a can in a bin, then you can put a bomb in the bin.

But going back to what is important and reframing the issue led the designers in Sydney in a completely different direction. The real issue, of course, is to assure safety in these crowded public spaces, ensuring that the train can run and life can take its normal course. A bomb threat means that a station has to be evacuated and searched before the all clear can be given. More likely than not, this will result in the whole transport network grinding to a halt, causing hours of disruption. In terms of spreading fear and disturbing public life, this is just what terrorists want.

In the end, the designers created a bin that is transparent at the front. When there is a suspicion that something might be wrong, a first check can be done visually. If any reasonable doubt persists (one wouldn't want to be the person that says "she'll be right" and then—BOOM), an X-ray plate can be slid into the back of the bin, and the image will create 100 percent certainty. These bins were installed all through the stations, and the response time to a potential hazard, which could run into multiple hours, was brought back to under ten minutes. There is no way that the original frame of "creating countermeasures to avoid bombs being placed in bins" could have led to this type of design. But when this frame was replaced by "how to minimize disruption while keeping people safe," the solution was in reach.

Frames are not "true." Any frame is only a proposition, a tool to navigate the problem situation and to help reach progress. If it doesn't work, you have to try something else. This is in line with Schön's background in pragmatist philosophy—in which knowledge is sought in the context of needing it for action, and truth can only be defined as a provisional agreement, holding good as long as it is useful for action. Such "truths" are social constructs, "justified true beliefs,"[5] and therefore always provisional in nature. They can be upended or superseded.

The notion of frames is central to the models in this book. In terms of reasoning patterns, frames play a crucial role in second-order abduction: frames are connections from *value* back to a possible *how*, a pattern of relationships (see figure 3.4).

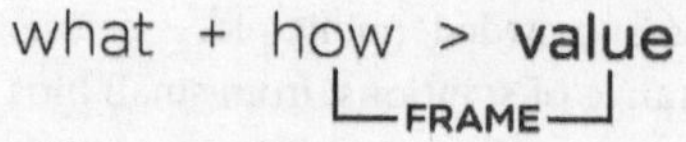

what + how > value
        └─FRAME─┘

Figure 3.4 The position of a frame in second-order abduction.

A frame is the proposition that a certain how will lead to a certain value to be achieved.

> IF we look at the problem situation AS IF it is a . . . (frame statement), THEN . . . (intended value)

In terms of the practices model that was introduced earlier, frames give shape to intent toward action, by bridging the value to be achieved with a principle of how to go about that (see figure 3.5). Frames are quite amorphous; basically, they are every statement that functions as a frame, whether this is done by a metaphor, a single word, or by a story that opens up a whole world of shared experiences among people. After all, framing is an action, an intervention; once a frame is accepted and becomes static, it loses its power and starts to fade.

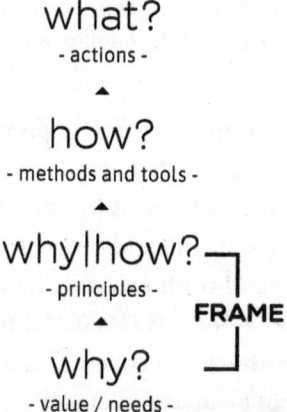

Figure 3.5 The position of a frame in the layers-of-practices model.

But . . . what is a "good" frame?[6] There are many answers:

- Good frames organize perception, thought, and action in a way that is useful to think with. Although frames can sometimes be paraphrased by a simple statement, they can be quite complex conceptual thinking tools.
- Good frames are coherent, providing a stable basis for further thought and action.
- Good frames ideally manage to create a conceptual space that spans and integrates a broad range of issues under consideration and potentially draws in more concepts (and thereby potential value) from outside the original problem arena.
- Good frames are also social entities. For a frame to really work, it has to come "alive" in a problem situation; it has to be inspiring, challenging, and captivating. It should immediately draw forth mental images in people and ideally trigger a quick-fire stream of consciousness of solution ideas.
- Good frames should harmonize the thoughts of the various stakeholders within a problem situation, a common narrative that holds the episodic, integrative knowledge needed to furnish a foundation for ideas.
- The best frames are inspiring and original, new to the problem setting, and thought-provoking and lively, engaging people's imagination so that they readily think along.

3.3 FRAME CREATION PROCESSES

How can we create such good frames?

The process of frame creation is described at length and much more detail in *Frame Innovation*.[7] The explanation here will be limited to a quick run through the main points. The reflections at the end of this chapter will include some more details and further clarifications to address some of the issues that have come up in the ten more years of practice since the *Frame Innovation* book was published.

Before we launch into the *how*, it is probably good to recap *why* the frame creation process was created. Basically, it was to address an issue highlighted by Albert Einstein in this statement that is commonly

ARCHAEOLOGY
How did this problem situation come about?
What has been done to solve this?
▼
PARADOX
What makes this hard?
▼
CONTEXT
What is important to the current stakeholders?
▼
FIELD
Who could be involved, and what is important to them?
▼
THEMES
What underlying themes emerge from this broader field?
▼
FRAMES
In what ways can those themes be addressed/actioned?
▼
FUTURES
What, then, are new and interesting possible outcomes?
▼
TRANSFORMATION
What changes are required to make this happen?
▼
INTEGRATION
What can we learn? What new opportunities arise?

Figure 3.6 The frame creation process model.

attributed to him: "A problem can never be solved using the same thinking that created it." But reaching a new way of thinking about a problem situation is not easy. It is hard to escape the gravitational pull of the current framing.

The question "How does one create a new frame?" can be addressed by studying the practices of creative professionals (in the case of my original research, expert designers). Although all practitioners create frames, this is often a largely implicit process. In the creative professions, the ability to create new frames is very central—so creative professionals have developed more explicit articulations of the practices and process(es) involved, as well as methods and tools to support the practitioner.[8] But how does this creative practice work? The very experienced creative professionals I studied start with the understanding that a problem has its roots in a

FRAME CREATION   39

specific context. To create a new frame, that context needs to be looked at critically, reconsidered, and—perhaps—changed. This is how these experts move beyond the assumptions and simplifications that underlie conventional views of the problem situation (as often expressed in the brief). The creation of new frames can be modeled conveniently as a process of nine steps (see figure 3.6). A process of nine steps may feel a bit long, but there is a clear flow from step to step. Central to the process is the fifth step, where an analysis of the values of the broader field of stakeholders leads to the themes from which new approaches (the frames) can be created (see appendix 4). The first four steps lay the groundwork, while the later steps explore the implications of the potential frames and proposed solution directions. This model, of course, is quite abstract. Let's clarify the flow of actions with an extended example.

Case Study: Of Tunnels and Visions

The A9 highway around Amsterdam is one of the busiest roads in the Netherlands. To improve the accessibility of the city, improve the air quality, and reduce sound levels around one of the bottlenecks of the road, a new twelve-lane land tunnel will be built that can take up to 130,000 cars per day. A park is planned on the roof of the tunnel. The construction work is expected to take about five years, and these works will heavily impact the environment: not only the adjoining residential neighborhoods, the Bijlmer (a multicultural district of 80,000 people from 186 nationalities), and Gaasperdam, but also a large concentration of office buildings on the Zuidas (multinational headquarters), the VU University Medical Centre, and the Ajax Amsterdam Arena further along the ring road. This is a tightrope job for the stakeholder manager, whose task it is to communicate the program to those impacted and to handle complaints. The organizational context in which the stakeholder manager operates is one of hard facts and figures: Building a new road takes place in a world of strict planning and tight control, complex process diagrams, and tough budgets. Communication with external stakeholders is professionally handled through extensive consultation processes, in order to prevent delays (and thus political fuss). Any delay translates in higher costs, reinforcing the simmering public perception that these projects are always running over in time and cost anyway.

André Schaminée (partner and head of social design at the consultancy firm TwynstraGudde, who has a deep knowledge of infrastructural projects) suggested investigating the relationship between the construction works and the Bijlmer area through frame creation. He teamed up with Vera Winthagen (Van Berlo Design / TU Eindhoven) and Tabo Goudswaard (social designer at Studio Goudswaard). Together they facilitated a process to which the Department of Public Works and Water Management (Rijkswaterstaat), the municipality, and the construction company all contributed. The process that unfolded is mapped in figure 3.7.

This was a long process, and much can be learned from it.[9] Here we will concentrate on some highlights that help demonstrate the frame creation approach. After going through the first four steps of the process by mapping the problem situation, its existing context, and the broader field, the researchers spent time in the multicultural Bijlmer and Gaasperdam areas, to glean which underlying themes were important in the lives and minds of the people, the municipality, and the companies there. This was a very rich process, and many fruitful themes were identified, leading to multiple frames and solution directions:

- Within the communities of the Bijlmer, themes that emerged combined a strong feeling of belonging and pride (identity) with a sense of being left behind, of feeling isolated from broader society. People feel unseen and suffer from a negative narrative (a stigma) with little opportunity to correct it. This results in a feeling of not being understood and empowered, of not getting a fair chance to progress in life. There was a very strong desire for the next generation to get more opportunities, to do better. (Note that we have seen this more often as a key driver in people's lives, on a very existential level; they sacrifice a lot to make this happen [see § 6.3]). This driver has to be dealt with very cautiously and realistically: It can be almost too strong—so strong that it is scary. When we deal with these deep drivers, we have to be aware that in engaging on this level, we give people hope; we need to be sure we can deliver, or grudgingly step away if we know we cannot.
- Interviewing the engineers, they expressed a pride in the massive works undertaken and in their own efficiency in delivering them. They were clearly motivated by the feeling of doing great things for society. But there also was a sense of being a vulnerable giant, of being misunderstood. They felt exasperated for always being blamed when things do not go according to plan, leading to overruns in cost and time.

These are very different worlds, but the divide can be bridged: not by coming up with one big solution, but by creating many small ways forward. For example, the researchers discovered that there were many small entrepreneurs in the area, but that a good many of them were only semilegal; one had to be part of the community to even find them. And, of course, being not quite legal, they could not attract investment to grow, so they were limited/stuck within the local ecosystem. Many conversations in the Bijlmer revolved around jobs—on the one hand, many saying that there are hardly any jobs in this economically disadvantaged residential area, but on the other hand, entrepreneurs saying how hard it was to hire people.

This theme led to the development of a new frame that captured the needs of both the people and organizations in the area: What if you could see the building of the tunnel as a new "temporary economy"? What new connections could we

FRAME CREATION

ARCHAEOLOGY
Professional engineering organizations.
- "planning and control" -
▼

PARADOX
Need to maintain a good public image despite the impact
of the works while not delaying them.
▼

CONTEXT
The inner circle of stakeholders: Department of Public Works,
construction companies, local councils.
▼

FIELD
The various groups of people in the Bijlmer,
the commuters, and their families.
▼

THEMES
Identity, self-confidence.
Care for the next generation.
▼

FRAMES
The construction workers as temporary inhabitants,
the construction project as a temporary economy,
the construction site as a dynamic stage set.
▼

FUTURES
Food stalls, childcare, repair services, accommodation,
events, homework support, a BMX track, etc.
▼

TRANSFORMATION
Support bottom-up initiatives from the local community.
- instead of "planning and control" -
▼

INTEGRATION
How to foster the new opportunities that arise for all parties when a big building
project comes to a neighborhood, and how a temporary situation can be used to
experiment with the permanent inhabitation of the space once the works have finished.

Figure 3.7 Reframing the disruption caused by the highway tunnel construction.

make then? Both the municipality and the department reacted enthusiastically. The framing of five years' construction work as a time for experimentation and renewal really struck a chord with the local community. Welcoming the workers as temporary inhabitants of the area and supporting them with small-scale entrepreneurial activity that springs up around the works (e.g., food stalls) is a great way to prototype the facilities that might eventually populate the park that is to cover the tunnel. The building site itself can be seen as a temporary landscape, as it is always in transition; we can imagine that at different stages, this creates opportunities for concerts, mountain biking tracks, and so on. Embracing such ideas was a big shift for the Department of Public Works and Water Management, the municipality, and the construction company, relaxing some of their planning and control paradigm, and allowing them to discover the local community as a source of innovation.

And there is more. The authorities, construction company, and people of the Bijlmer have come together and created a social enterprise (*De Buurbouw*, a wordplay based on the words for *neighbor* and *building*) that organized numerous projects throughout the time of the tunnel construction works. The term *Buurbouw* sets a frame that is purposefully vague; it needs to be completely filled in by the people engaged. It does highlight one particular, crucial relationship, wanting to be a good neighbor. Neighborliness has actually proven to be a very rich source of themes and potential projects: good neighbors look after one other, they manage potential conflict in the sharing of space, they are thoughtful in being quiet when it really matters, and so on. The Buurbouw as a social enterprise set up many projects in this vibe. For instance, a homework assistance program was set up, away from the noise and disturbance of the building works—and completion rates for high school and professional degrees in the area shot up immensely. During the nationwide high school exams, which have to be taken in the original school buildings, the building works were quiet. There were lots of school competitions, projects, and tours on the building site, to give the smaller kids a sense of what was happening, connecting the works into the school curriculum (with the building works as physics experiments on an impressive scale). Some of the unavoidable adverse impact of the building works were ameliorated in close consultation with the neighborhood (e.g., recycling the trees that had to be felled, using the wood to build play equipment, and so on—symbolic gestures, but appreciated). The building works have been finished, and the tunnel is there, yet the Buurbouw social enterprise is a model that shows true vitality and the potential to keep changing, beyond the activities that had been planned in the original framing. In a way, the vagueness of the Buurbouw frame is its strength. By leaving it to people to make sense of what it is, what it should be, it creates an ongoing dialogue and a space for change. In this case, one can see the social enterprise as an outcome, perhaps the key outcome of the whole project.

The frame creation process shown in figure 3.6 is just the skeleton; the practices and methods presented in the coming pages will put some flesh on those bones. They will come alive in the examples and case studies of the next chapters. But first, in the next pages, the steps of the process are separated out and presented in a *method card* format[10] as a support and tool for workshop sessions. On the front of each card, you will find a very brief description of the why and how for that particular step. On the other side, the question that drives the activities of the step is put in the middle, surrounded by subquestions. Around those subquestions are some of the methods, tools, and practices that we have found useful in twenty years of frame creation practice. Please consider this open description as an invitation to add practices, tools, and methods of your own, from your discipline, to the mix. There is a whole landscape that needs to be populated. A PDF of these cards, as well as some background material on the tools and methods referred to in the cards, can be downloaded for free at https://mitpress.mit.edu/9780262553742/deep-change/.

ARCHAEOLOGY
How did this problem come about?
What has been done to solve this?

To
Create a basis of insight and understanding of the current situation—and respect the history.

By
Digging, creating a deep map of the current situation.

Introduction
The apparent problem, as well as earlier attempts to solve it, are investigated in depth. Delve deeply into the world of the problem owner to understand the history of the problem situation. This also provides insight into the role the problem owner has had in creating the problem situation, and it gives a first impression of the dynamics over time.

document analysis
　　　　　　　　　history
　　　　　　language used
　　facts and figures
　　　　　　conversations

structured interviews with the problem holder / problem owner

　　　grounded theory (coding)
　　　　　　　　　　　espoused vision/strategy

　　　hidden rules of the game

　　　　　　　　　　laddering

ARCHAEOLOGY
How did this problem situation come about?
What has been done to solve this?

listing assumptions

　　　listing prevalent metaphors and frames
　　　　　　　　　　conceptual mapping
stakeholder maps

　　　timeline: key moments
　　　　　　creating a rich and deep narrative

seeking feedback for accuracy

　　mirroring
　　　　　　　reflective conversations

PARADOX
What makes this hard?

To
Achieve clarity about the network of tensions.
Build a common understanding, while deferring judgment.
Prioritize key tensions and relationships.

By
Proposing simple statements (oppositions), putting them together as an arena.

Introduction
The lead question is: What makes this hard? Often, there are several issues that are intertwined in a problem situation, but to keep the frame creation process on track, it is important to take some time and clearly identify the core paradoxes or deadlock(s) that keep us from moving forward.

analyze the key concepts used in the current language

formulate the tensions between these

map changes in tensions over time

check for completeness

cover the problem area

PARADOX
What makes this hard?

covering the dynamics

ensuring neutral wording

seeking feedback on these paradox statements from key stakeholders

testing these for recognition

CONTEXT
What is important to the current stakeholders?

To
Understand the embedding of the tensions and paradoxes.

By
Mapping the values of the key partners: What is important to them?

Introduction
An exploration of the practices of the inner circle of key stakeholders that have been involved in the problem situation before and who are clearly going to be necessary in any possible solution. By carefully examining them, we seek out their values and the principles underlying their modus operandi. We need clarity on this, to later deliberately turn away from the core paradoxes and shift the problem situation.

building on the results of the Archaeology,
but focusing the investigation around the paradoxes

identifying the key partners that have been involved before, and will be in the future

what are their espoused values?
what is their "currency" (Bourdieu)?

key practices

structured interviews

laddering

CONTEXT
What is important to the current stakeholders?

studying underlying sector paradigms

for organizations: studying . . .
   . . . underlying sector paradigms,
      "document analysis,
      key theories and methods"
         . . . narratives (episodic knowledge),
            . . . disciplinary matrixes
            . . . the infrastructure of the sector
mapping
   context mapping

creating a table of key parties and values/drivers

FIELD
Who could be involved, and what is important to them?

To
Investigate the potential of the broader network.

By
Casting the net wide, mapping the values of potential stakeholder/partners: Who could be involved, for whatever reason, and what is important to them?

Introduction
Radically widening the context beyond the current stakeholders, covering anybody who might be connected to the problem or the solution at some point in time—actively or passively, by just exuding some influence. In mapping the field of players, we concentrate on their "currency," power, interests, values, and, in particular, the practices and frames they bring that could push the problem in a new direction.

building on the results of the Archaeology,
but putting the paradoxes aside
identifying potential stakeholders . . .
　　. . . that have not been actively involved before
. . . that are inspiring
　　　. . . that move away from the thinking of the current
　　　　stakeholders
　　　　　. . . that upset the current balance of tensions
. . . that bring in new value sets that could be addressed
　　　　　　　. . . that have not had a voice
structured interviews
　　　"laddering"
　　　　　　　what are their espoused values?
what is their "currency"
　　　　　　　　　　　key practices
　　　for individuals: personal lifeworld analysis /
　　　hermeneutic phenomenology

FIELD
Who could be involved, and what is important to them?

　　　for professionals: professional/disciplinary lifeworld analysis

for organizations: studying . . .
　　　　　. . . underlying sector paradigms, "document
　　　　　analysis, key theories and methods"
　　　. . . narratives (episodic knowledge),
　　　　　　　　　　　. . . disciplinary matrixes
　　　　　. . . the infrastructure of the sector
mapping
　　　　　　　　　　document analysis
　　　　　key theories and methods
broader Field map

　　　　table of (potential) key parties and values/drivers

THEMES
What is this about?
What underlying themes emerge from this broader field?

To
Understand the deep human values at play, what this is actually about.

By
Clustering, emergence of underlying human values, and deep conceptual analysis.

Introduction
In theme analysis, we identify and seek to understand the deeper factors that underlie the experiences of the "players" in the wider field. A theme analysis ends with an understanding of the *universals*, a selection of themes that are relevant to the problem situation on the deeper level at which players in the field have much in common. These deep human themes sit in the lifeworld of people.

creating a conceptual map of the
values from Context and Field steps

naming the emerging clusters

lifeworld analysis on these names (hermeneutic
phenomenology)

create nomological networks of the themes:
synonyms
antonyms
associations
intrinsic vs. extrinsic
individual vs. social
past vs. future

THEMES
What is this about?
What underlying themes emerge from this broader field?

theme analysis (see appendix 4):
personal experience
philosophy
art
scientific theories and knowledge
state changes over time

check whether the clusters validly capture the
values that surfaced in the Context and Field steps

check whether the tensions behind the paradoxes are
represented in the relationships between these values

FRAMES
In what ways can the themes be addressed/actioned?

To
Create new value, bypass existing paradoxes.

By
Proposing new approaches to the problem situation.

Introduction
Themes that are shared among many of the players in the field are particularly interesting as they could be the basis for frames that are attractive to a network of partners. Although these inklings can be a strong springboard, the ideation of a new frame is inevitably a creative leap. The frame that results can be formulated as the implication that adopting a certain pattern of relationships (e.g., a metaphor) will lead to valuable outcomes. This implication can be written down as follows: *if the problem situation is approached as if it is . . . , then . . .*

explore approaches that address several
of the themes (in an integrated way)
clustering

association

using prior experience
(lived experience and professional experience)

inspiration and emergence from the theme analysis

seeking analogies in other cultures

looking at practices from other professional fields
that address the same themes (transdisciplinarity)

FRAMES
In what ways can those themes be addressed/actioned?

check that these new approaches
are inclusive of important stakeholders

check that they address the tensions underlying the
paradoxes

check that they step (far enough) away
from the existing frames and practices

prioritize the frames that do address most of the problem
situation in the simplest way (Occam's razor)

FUTURES
What, then, are new and interesting possible outcomes?

To
Explore the desirability and fruitfulness of the proposed frame.

By
Mapping potential solutions going forward, thinking through scenarios.

Introduction
A proposed frame is applied back to the problem situation, to investigate if the frame can potentially lead to fundamentally different but also realistic and viable solutions. This is a *thinking forward* exercise that is part and parcel of second-order abduction. In these playful explorations, we creatively envision how things might work. Experts tend to talk about this process of proposing and trying out frame ideas in terms of *fruitfulness*: a frame and the solution ideas it generates are only as good as the interest and commitment they spark in the parties who are needed to implement them.

generate ideas based on the proposed frame

map the potential solution space

compare with the current solution space
and practices of the stakeholders in the context

check whether the new space is inclusive
of new parties from the "field"

check whether the vitality of the overall system
is increased by adoption of this frame and ideas

FUTURES
What, then, are new and interesting possible outcomes?

create the new narrative

float frame and ideas with key stakeholders
for initial feedback (desirability)

build an expression ([re]presentation) of the new narrative

(potentially using the history / existing narrative
as a jumping-off point: "before and after")

TRANSFORMATION
What changes are required to make this happen?

To
Explore the viability of the new approach (frame).

By
Building the strategic story and sketching a "business plan."

Introduction
This is where the representation of ideas becomes important, as a means to explore their merit in conversations with parties in the field, to weed out frames and ideas that may be great in themselves, but whose implementation will require huge changes in the practices of a stakeholder who has very little to gain. They need to go because they will never happen. The time is not ripe.

analyze the value created by the frame and
ideas for the various stakeholders/field parties
map out ways to get from the current situation (paradoxes) to adoption of the new frame
conversations with stakeholders
workshops
presenting alternatives (including not-acting)
bringing in new parties from the Field
check who has most to gain
check who has a vested interest in the current problem situation continuing—who has most to lose?

explore how these could be persuaded
what is their "currency"?
what are their values, principles, favored methods, etc.?
what could make them change their mind?

TRANSFORMATION
What changes are required to make this happen?

what could be a more attractive story for them, compared with the current one (narrative therapy)
what could be cultural blockers (attitude toward risk and uncertainty, etc.)
create change scenarios for all parties involved
create a matching web of "business models" for/with the key stakeholders

different roles (conductor, curator, convenor, etc.)
value network
Business Model Canvas

design the innovation ecosystem needed to make this happen:
relay race
colors of change
inspiration, intrinsic motivation
futures literacy

INTEGRATION
What can we learn? What new opportunities arise?

To
Develop and grow.

By
Personal and social reflection.

Introduction
The new frames and the developments they initiate are well-integrated into the broader context of the organizations involved (be it the original problem owner or a whole new network of players). New thinking means that new opportunities and connections will arise. On a deeper level, what has been learned in the discovery of the underlying themes can now be integrated into the "field" of the organization as active knowledge.

create a narrative of the process, themes, frames,
ideas, and the new field

double loop learning within and around the organization

triple loop learning across the new network and field

reflecting on the themes, and how the close knowledge
of them can be of value to the organization

reflecting on the frames, and the implication
of this extended repertoire of practices

INTEGRATION
What can we learn? What new opportunities arise?

reflecting on the increasing system vitality
creating complete learning loops
the drive of intrinsic motivation
embedding futures literacy

reflecting on personal development and growth

looking forward
new possibilities to create value

new possibilities to enrich the network of relationships

new and different roles: conductor, curator, convenor, mentor, etc.

new horizons for inspiration

3.4 REFLECTIONS

EXTENDING FRAMES

What's in a frame? In the preceding text, we followed the lead of Donald Schön and described frames as involving the introduction of new ways of seeing (perception), thinking (approach), and doing (action). But that is not all.

By introducing a new way of seeing, thinking, and acting, we are also inevitably creating new relationships or ways of relating among the parties that together make up the problem situation. We have seen that happening in the case of the A9 highway tunnel: Although the ideas and initiatives that came out of the new frames are good, they have a limited lifespan. What endures are the structural changes in the relationships among the community, the ministry of public works, and the construction company.

The introduction of a new frame also creates a new quality in the relation between us and the problem situation. This feeling is important as it guides our intuition in future problem situations. This is how we learn the real art of frame creation over time. The importance of these extensions to the notion of a frame (see figure 3.8) will become apparent in the coming chapters as we move away from seeing frames as one-off

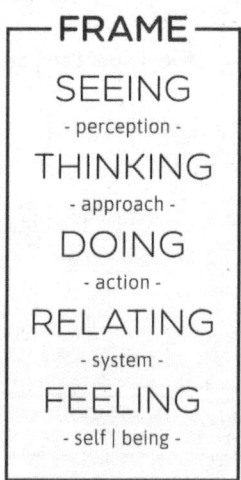

Figure 3.8 Extending the notion of a frame.

interventions on a project level and see them instead as building blocks for structural change and growth.

THE MODEL IS NOT THE PRACTICE

Frame creation is a process of thinking around the problem rather than confronting it head-on. New solutions cannot be found by addressing the problem as given, but by exploring the values and themes in the broad area surrounding the original context. To access these, we need to bypass the assumptions that have led to the original problem formulation and embrace the complexity we find in this broader field. As you have seen, the movement in the frame creation process is one of zooming out, expanding, and concentrating again as new frames come into view. It is the expansion of the problem space that allows new patterns to emerge. Crucially, the transition between a field and themes is helped by purely concentrating on the values of the parties in the broader field and *completely* forgetting about the original problem. This frees up the mind to look for the value that can be created with fresh eyes. Then we need to deepen the themes—the depth and richness of understanding of the themes really determines the quality of the end result of the whole process[11]—and make sure the frames are strong enough to evoke a very clear picture in the minds of all those involved.

These steps in themselves are not frame creation, but they provide a bit of a map of the practices involved and the way the process might run. They outline a method—but then, a method isn't frame creation either. A method is merely a crutch, never to be followed slavishly and to be thrown out when not needed anymore, when experience has led to a growth of personal expertise and fluency.[12] For the expert, the frame creation model is useful through the fact that there is a sense of completeness to it: These bases need to be covered, these things need to be considered. This is what models and methods are for. In contrast to what people tend to think, they don't speed you up but instead make you slower by building in moments of thoughtfulness and reflection.

But as to the unfolding of frame creation over time, well, real frame creation practice is always driven by the content, rather than any preconceived pattern of steps. And the succession of steps is a bit of a mirage:

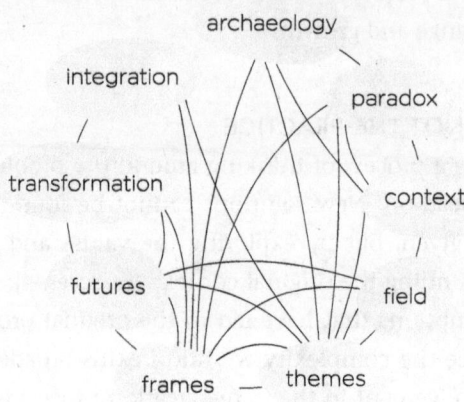

Figure 3.9 The model in a circle to emphasize the nonlinear nature of frame creation practice.

In healthy processes, there are many links that need to be made between all steps, as some of the steps can't be taken without anticipating later ones. We build on what we know, but we are also pulled forward by our expectations, by the possibilities we think they might open up in later steps. Good iterations are a sign that learning is happening. They will become less with the growth of expertise—or, that is to say, they will then become more implicit (moving from explicit reflection-on-action to intuitive, quick reflection-in-action).

But rather than a succession of steps, it is better to represent frame creation in a circle of stepping stones—as in figure 3.9. Over the years, practitioners have created many different versions and various mappings of frame creation to adapt it to their use, and these are certainly worth sharing here as they may be inspiring and helpful. Figure 3.10 shows a version from André Schaminée (the project leader on the highway case study) that helpfully highlights the *arc of abstraction* experienced by participants as they are going through a frame creation process. Others have mapped the frame creation process as a landscape. For teaching frame creation at an art school, the lecturer Madelinde Hageman has developed a playful, all-graphic method to support all the steps; see figure 3.11 for an impression. Waag Society, a foundation that aims to foster experimentation with new technologies, art, and culture, has produced a set

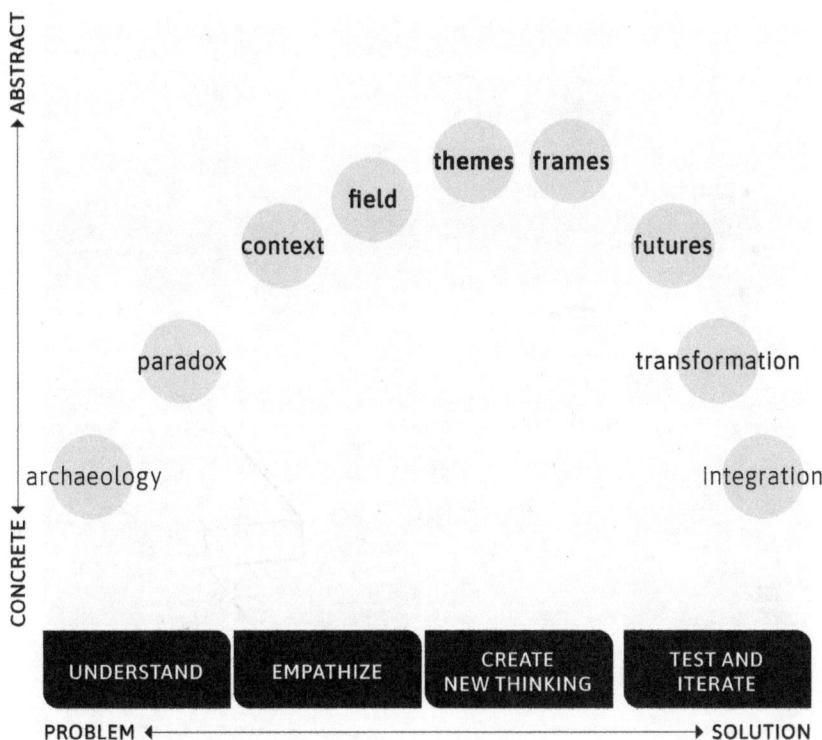

Figure 3.10 The frame creation process as climbing a mountain of abstraction. *Source:* André Schaminée, *Designing With and Within Public Organizations: Building Bridges Between Public Sector Innovators and Designers* (BIS Publishers, 2018), 35—the Sisyphus model.

of workshop materials for using frame creation in the context of social innovation (see figure 3.12).[13] All the cases in the upcoming chapters will serve to illustrate and elucidate these frame creation processes, as they have happened, in all of their diversity. These are based on more than twenty years of frame creation practice, and offer more tricks and tips on the practicalities of running frame creation workshops.

THE ART OF FRAME CREATION

The nine steps don't do justice to frame creation as an overall practice: Although each step in itself is relatively straightforward, it is the combination that creates the transformative change (the "magic"). This can't be

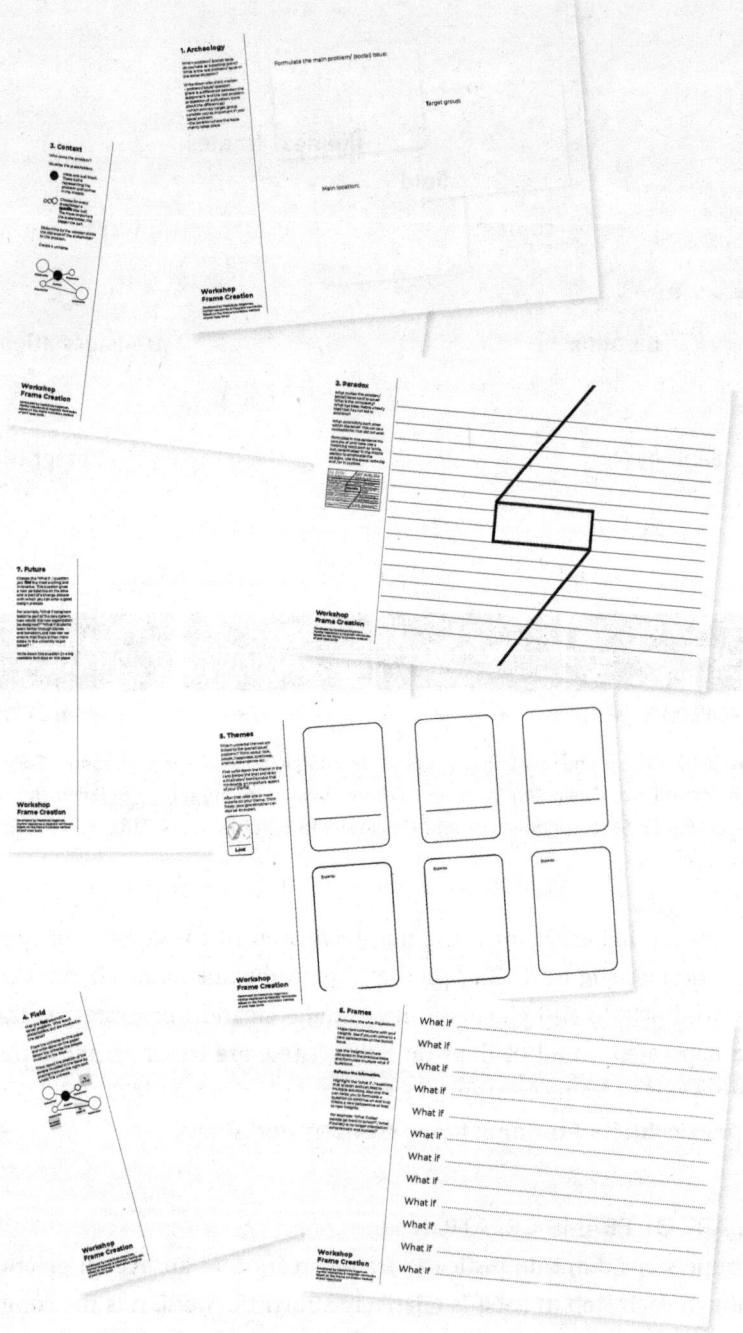

Figure 3.11 Graphic translation of frame creation steps by Madelinde Hageman and Marjolein Vermeulen.

FRAME CREATION

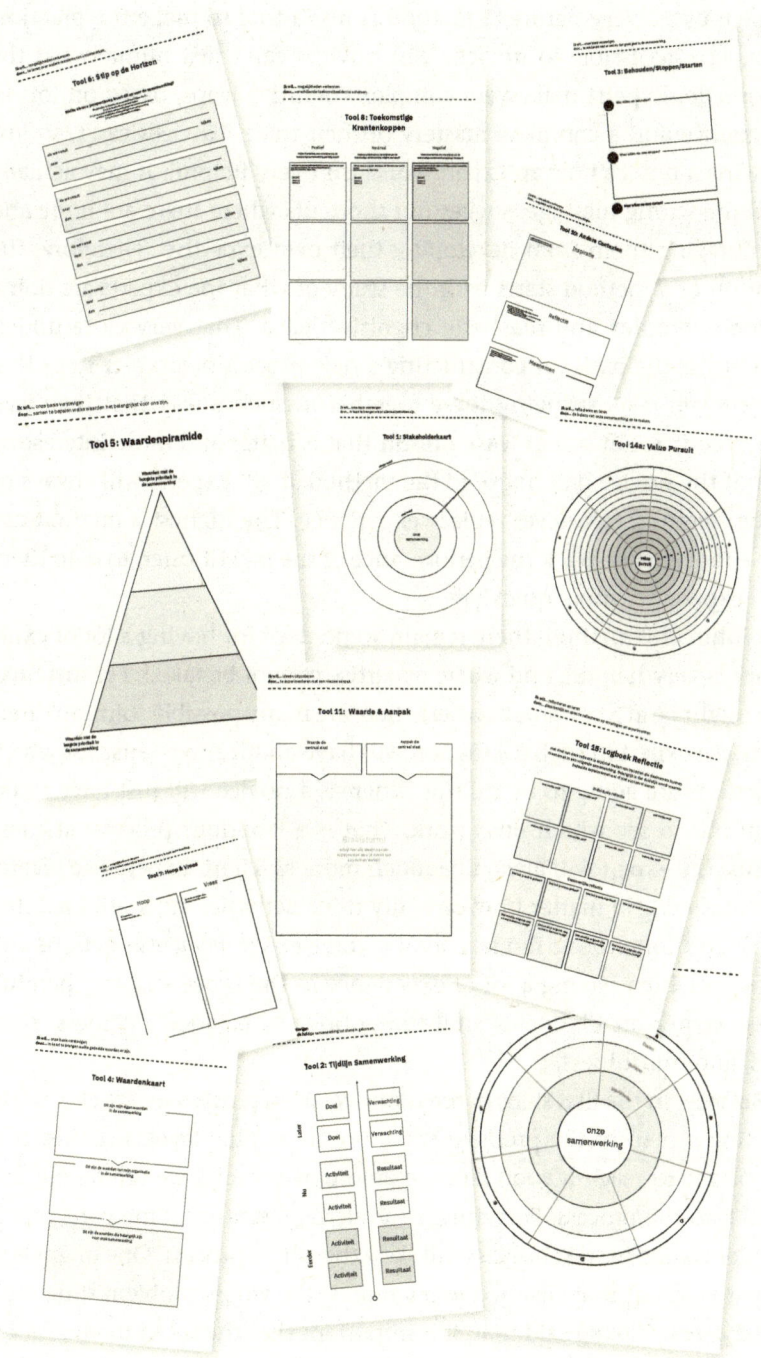

Figure 3.12 Waag Society materials to support a social innovation workshop.

helped; by its very nature, a method is just a tool to make the practices of experts accessible to novices. But novices can't just mimic what the experts do. Experts make very complex cognitive leaps, based on lots of experience and a complete mastery of their trade. Novices can't, so just showing a novice how an expert works isn't very helpful. It may actually send the wrong message, suggesting shortcuts where there are none and discouraging them from developing their own expertise. Therefore, the creation of a method starts with the study of what the experts are doing in their complex and masterful cognitive leaps. That very close understanding is the basis for constructing a new process of simpler steps that novices *can* take, stringing these together in such a way that they lead to a "good" result—or at least a result that is better and more interesting than if the novice had not used the method at all. Experts will always be better; method can never replace experience. The highest a method can strive for is to fast-track the performance of the practitioner, to help them gain experience more quickly.

Within any method, there remain some steps for having a lot of experience is very helpful, and where expertise cannot be faked. For instance, you might be at a crossroads where there are many possible solution directions. An expert in such a situation will have an intuitive sense for which directions are going to be fruitful, whereas a novice will just have to try them out to see which ones work. That is a laborious process; at these points, the expert will always be much more efficient. Experience creates true mastery. No matter how carefully these activities are scaffolded, the frame creation process model contains some *expert moments*—actions and steps for which having a lot of experience in the process is very helpful. These center on high-level strategic notions of balance, edginess, richness, and fruitfulness.

Balance. In the first steps of the frame creation process we are effectively creating a map of the problem situation on a value level. For this, it is important to reach a good balance among the values we are taking forward into the process. Forgetting or underrepresenting some parts of the problem arena or stakeholders will skew the whole process. One might end up with a result that clearly doesn't address the whole problem situation.

Edginess. Having said that, it is important that the set of theme values strays far enough from the current framing of the problem situation to ensure the next steps will lead to new and interesting results. Staying too close often means that later on in the frame creation process, as we are reintroducing the problem arena and the contextual constraints, we will fall back to the current way of thinking.

Richness. In frame creation, it is important to ensure you have several themes that together cover the problem area (several, but not too many, because that gets confusing: around three to five is a good amount). This has to be a rich set of themes, full of contrast, so that a multitude of new frames can emerge between them (about three to ten frames seem to be a good amount). When a frame emerges that addresses several of the themes simultaneously, in an original, simple, and compelling manner, that frame becomes a *dominant concept* worth exploring further.

Fruitfulness. Which directions to pursue depends on the anticipation of where they might lead. This is a difficult call to make for anyone—but again, experience helps the expert to identify similarities to situations they have dealt with before, successfully or unsuccessfully, and choose frames that "open up" (in their terms) the space over ones that are likely to turn into a dead end.

Note that in these paragraphs, we have described the core of frame creation, on a project level. In the coming chapters, we will see how the thinking behind the frame creation approach works out on the level of organizations, sectors, and society—changing the dynamics of the steps and introducing many new factors. Yet this project level is a good place to explore, develop, and explain frame creation as a way of thinking.

4
CREATING CHANGE IN ORGANIZATIONS

We have met the enemy and he is us.
—Walt Kelly, *Pogo*[1]

4.1 PROJECTS DON'T CHANGE THE WORLD

Frame creation processes done well often result in fascinating new solution directions that are literally captivating; the insights and ideas are so clear that they become very hard to ignore. It is almost impossible then to revert the old frame. But the new frame and its solution directions are bound to require deep change in the organizations involved before they can be brought to realization and impact. After all, the organization was originally shaped around the way of thinking that included the old frame. As a first investigation of the barriers to change, we will now look at a case study of a radical reframe and follow its influence and impact in the fifteen years since the original project. This longitudinal case study closely follows the many twists and turns of this story, allowing us to perform a critical postmortem analysis. Then we will develop a model to better understand and support the move from a project-level intervention to strategic impact.

Case Study: Kings Cross: The Initial Reframe and Intervention

In 2009, the Designing Out Crime (DOC) Research Center was approached by the City of Sydney (a local council) to look into the problem of "alcohol-related violence" in Kings Cross, an entertainment district that had a reputation as a significant crime hotspot.

Here is the situation: This particular area with bars and clubs attracts about thirty thousand young people on a typical Friday or Saturday evening. There are problems late at night, including drunkenness, fights, petty theft, drug dealing, and sporadic violence. Over the years, the government has used strong-arm tactics in response to the ongoing stream of incidents in the area: increasing the police presence, requiring clubs to hire security personnel, and placing CCTV cameras everywhere. All this extra security has made for a grim public environment, and the problems have persisted.

Note the compelling logic of this existing framing: In speaking about alcohol-related violence, the presence of alcohol and violence are implied to be related—so if we want to bring the level of violence down, we have to do that by reducing the alcohol intake. But as the DOC researchers found out, the crime was not much linked to alcohol at all. They realized that the issues that were presented to them as law-and-order problems, in a briefing that unquestioningly called for law-and-order solutions, needed a different approach.

The researchers and designers followed a frame creation process and studied the behavior of the revelers in more detail. What emerged were the facts that the people concerned are overwhelmingly youngsters (noncriminals) wanting to have a good time, and that they were becoming increasingly bored and frustrated as the night progressed. Paradoxically, while coming to Kings Cross to have a good time, they were not getting a good experience at all. The designers framed what were originally presented as crime issues differently by studying the themes in the broader problem situation and by proposing a simple analogy: that the Kings Cross issues could be seen *as if* they were dealing with the organizing of a good-sized music festival. This frame encapsulates a new way of seeing the situation and thinking about Kings Cross, and it also highlights new possible avenues for action to explore. The question to ask is, "What would one set out to do, if one were to be organizing a music festival?" Then you can compare the answer with the situation at King Cross. This simple comparison immediately led to new scenarios for action—including the following, just to name a few, out of the many design directions that were sparked by this one frame:

- **Transportation.** When organizing a music festival, it would be important to make sure that people are able to get there and get away. In this entertainment quarter, the peak time of young people coming into the area is about 1 a.m., and the last train leaves at 1:20 a.m. Getting a taxi is expensive, and it can take hours late at night. So once you are in the entertainment quarter, you are basically there until the trains start running again in the early morning. That leads to boredom, frustration, and aggression. Apart from running more trains, the designers proposed as a fallback position a system of temporary signage projected on the pavement, helping the partygoers get to Town Hall Station, where there are buses running throughout the night.
- **Crowd control.** When organizing a music festival, the good atmosphere comes from small attractions that are continuously available. The headline acts on the

big stage don't perform this role; people have to wait for them to begin. As it happens, Kings Cross has a few big clubs that form the main attractions. Young people that have visited a club and spill out on the street might find that the queue for the next one is too long for them and wander along with nothing to do. The designers proposed that this can be minimized by providing an app that tells people how long the waiting time for the next club is before leaving so that they can make an informed decision about when and where to go.

- **Different vibes.** When organizing a music festival, it's important to ensure that there are different types of spaces for people to socialize, drink, dance, and engage with the music, and also quieter spaces to catch your breath and chill out from all of that frenzied activity. In Kings Cross, everything happens on one main street that can get very crowded. People get in each other's way and get on each other's nerves. The designers proposed to clean up the smelly, dark alleyways that lead from the main drag, using projections and street art to create spaces where people can relax.
- **Safety and wayfinding.** When organizing a music festival, it's important to ensure that staff will be around to help people and keep an eye on safety. The designers proposed a system of very visible, young, "Kings Cross guides" in bright T-shirts. These guides could help people find their way through the area and are also approachable when help is needed.
- **Sanitation.** When organizing a music festival, you typically hire lots of portable toilets and put clusters of them around the hotspots. In Kings Cross, there originally were only three public toilets (one of which was at the police station, so nobody would go there). Considering the enormous amounts of beer going through bodies in any night, of course this led to a street urination problem.
- **And more.** This portfolio of ideas was built on over a number of years.[2] By its very nature, the radical reframing of Kings Cross (from a place with alcohol-related violence to a music festival site) is a game changer: It cannot be implemented without having deep repercussions for the key organizations involved. This implies a change agenda for the stakeholders that framed the issue, defined the problem, organized themselves around the response—and thereby, possibly, inadvertently kept the problem in place.

Toward a New Strategy

The City of Sydney quickly picked up on the possible role that it could play within the music festival frame, and recast its organization to become a "conductor" of nightlife in the Kings Cross area. From this much more active, creative position, the city recalibrated its relations with a wide group of stakeholders that could be involved in shaping the future of the Kings Cross experience. It also went much further. The music festival frame has obvious limitations: (1) many elements of the complex Kings Cross environment cannot be captured within this frame (e.g., the experience of local residents); and (2) this frame only applies to Kings Cross, which is only a couple of streets, and merely to a couple of nights per week, mostly in the summer months. For the City of Sydney to become a true conductor of nightlife throughout its local government area, it would need frames or development agendas for all of its different neighborhoods; some are local entertainment oriented, others more tourist focused, and yet others quiet and residential. These would need to be based on evidence as to the current state of the nightlife there, and of course involve the participation of citizens, local businesses, and other societal stakeholders. The City of Sydney commissioned research into the nightlife and consulted with residents and stakeholders about appropriate ambitions and frames for various areas. This resulted in a comprehensive Open Sydney strategy[3] that captures the local ambitions and translates them in hundreds of action points for the short, medium, and longer terms.

Toward a New Organizational Structure
The original 2009 Kings Cross project was done in collaboration with the Safer Sydney unit of the City of Sydney as the commissioning party. In the years after the project, this unit spun out the Nighttime Economy Team. This team takes a much more comprehensive and inclusive view of the meaning, significance, and the value of nightlife. The dollar value of the economic transactions of the city at night became part of a positive bottom line. In 2019, Sydney's nighttime economy was $27 billion per annum.[4] The Nighttime Economy Team set about implementing many of the recommendations of the Kings Cross project. For example, the chill-out zones designed in the context of the music festival frame became "Take Kare Safe Spaces"; the projected Kings Cross guides became "Take Kare Ambassadors"; and portable urinals were implemented, as well as portable dynamic signs and secure taxi ranks. The Take Kare Safe Spaces had an immediate impact, and in the first three years of operation they provided direct support to more than fifty thousand people. In some cases, this support was lifesaving.[5]

Toward Sector-Level Impact
The Kings Cross case study story has been impactful, both in professional practice and in academia. It is seen as an early example of social design, and a successful case of design contributing to public sector innovation.[6] The project has had a direct influence on thinking about nightlife in cities like Vancouver, New York, London, Amsterdam, Berlin, and more, with direct follow-ups in Seoul, Hong Kong, and many other cities. The founding director of the Nighttime Economy Team won a Churchill Fellowship to study best practices around the world. In parallel, the *night mayors* movement emerged to help cities think about the importance and potential of the nightlife in a city. In 2019, this movement had spread to forty cities across the world, supported by a series of Global Cities After Dark conferences, sharing practices and lessons on the creation of a thriving nighttime economy from around the world—and thus recognizing the various roles that the night mayors play in curating nighttime as a space for "trust and identity building."[7] The Kings Cross project is one of the iconic examples that helped establish this new paradigm and community of practice, and Sydney has hosted the Global Cities After Dark conference several times.

Toward a Program for Ongoing Change

Some of the new Kings Cross projects that DOC was involved in built on the original reframe (the music festival); others were much more detailed and specific. For instance, one project focused on the problem of violence: to a certain degree, groups of young men get into fights because they want to fight, as part of their specific group culture in order to establish a hierarchy within and between groups. The reframing here was based on the realization that the key theme behind this behavior is competition, not violence per se. Creating other arenas for competition, like urban sports, helps them achieve these goals by less violent means. As it turns out, they are quite happy to compete in these less harmful ways. In the end, DOC worked on various problem situations in Kings Cross for more than ten years.

Tragedy Strikes

But then, in 2012 and 2014, two young men were killed in separate unprovoked one-punch attacks in Kings Cross. These tragic deaths were front-page news, putting pressure on politicians to clamp down on the "alcohol-related violence" in Kings Cross. In response, the state of New South Wales introduced "lockout laws" (reducing trading hours; preventing people from entering/reentering a pub, café, or restaurant after a certain time; and limiting the service of alcohol). These laws served to make the King Cross area very unattractive as an entertainment district. Restaurants, cafes, nightclubs, pubs, and shops left or went bankrupt. In total, 176 establishments closed as a result of the lockout laws. The introduction of the lockout laws also led to ongoing protest from the community and business owners in the area. A political party (Keep Sydney Open) was created to advocate for their repeal. This sparked an impassioned societal discussion of what being an "international city" actually means, what the role of night entertainment in the life of a city is, and how a society can support young people going through the confusing years in which they are coming of age. The City of Sydney actively facilitated these discussions while advocating for Sydney as a twenty-four-hour city, commissioning research on the state of the nighttime economy to benchmark with other major cities around the world. Seeing this, the New South Wales Government then also commissioned its own research into the matter. A public inquiry attracted more than two hundred submissions,[8] and in the end, the lockout laws were largely repealed in 2019. The New South Wales Government launched its own 24-Hour Economy Strategy in 2020, and in March 2021 the inaugural 24-Hour Economy Commissioner took his post.[9]

Reflection

In many ways, the Kings Cross project initially unfolded as a best-case scenario, achieving strategic impact early on as it was taken up by the City of Sydney—and it was widely published as a success. Yet in the longitudinal analysis, we run up against some limitations in the original approach and intervention. There are several sides to the story: On the one hand, there is the emergence of a compelling frame and the creation of boundary objects that capture people's imagination and lead to success on the project level; on the other hand, it proved difficult to create real and lasting change. In retrospect, there were some weaknesses in the original Kings Cross project: (1) The designers had not fully realized that responsibility for the area was shared between the City of Sydney and several departments in the New South Wales Government. (2) The designers didn't involve the media in the project and hence failed to influence the societal discussion of Kings Cross. When the two tragic deaths happened, that societal discussion naturally restarted where it left off—from the old frame of alcohol-related violence. (3) The most influential voices in this societal discussion were the emergency ward doctors at nearby St Vincent's hospital, who advocated for the lockout laws with all the moral authority that comes with their profession. They also were not involved in the original Kings Cross project.

Reflecting on the case study, it is interesting to compare the different approaches from the City of Sydney and New South Wales Government—with the latter driving a classic strategy development process, ostensibly motivated by "evidence-based" approaches. Although the sad irony of the story is that the lockout laws would not even have prevented the two deaths, as they were both early in the evening and not the result of late-night drinking. So the "evidence" was not even there in the first place. In the years since, the societal discussion has moved on. There is now a much more resilient and robust societal discussion and a better context to really change the situation in Kings Cross for good.

There is much more to be said. We will return to this case study several times in the texts below and in the next chapter, in § 5.2.

4.2 GAME CHANGERS

The Kings Cross case study is special in that the developments are well-documented over a period of fifteen years after the initial project and interventions. Yet we are convinced there is a pattern here: numerous authors have documented how new frames and solution directions encounter friction and have difficulty achieving real and lasting change.[10] New frames have the potential to lead to new practices and spark change in organizations, yet they rarely get to this full strategic impact. Even when they do, chances are the project outcomes remain vulnerable because the context of the organization is still holding on to the old frame; that is, it has failed to shift to a new state in which the new frame is a natural fit.[11] So, if these projects in themselves don't change the world, what should we do to get them to the full impact they deserve? To explore the dynamics of reframing and strategic transformation, we need

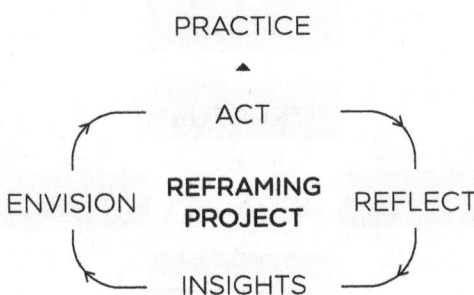

Figure 4.1a The washing machine.

to learn from cases like these and find a way to model them to get to a better, deeper understanding of what is the matter.

For a new frame to change the game, it needs to exert influence beyond the confines of the reframing project. The innovation project is done for a purpose, so it is—often implicitly—surrounded by an organizational learning loop.[12] The activities in the project lead to *experiences* that can be *reflected* upon, leading to *insights* that can trigger the *envisioning of new experiments* (see figure 4.1a). This is what Charles Leadbeater has called the *washing machine*.[13] These activities go round and round in circles, creating great local impact but not necessarily influencing the organization much at all. Innovation projects tend to get stuck in this washing machine, exacerbated by the mistaken assumption that doing projects equals doing innovation (therefore, project money is often the only type of money to be had for innovation). For real change to happen (to escape the washing machine), these projects and their learnings need to impact the practices in the organization(s) involved.

To support these new practices beyond the tactical level requires a change in the strategies of the organization. This in turn influences the processes and structures that make up the organization (see figure 4.1b).

What we see here is a chain of bottom-up impact, where the projects have a learning cycle of post-project reflection that generates insights in order to envisage new project approaches. This continuous learning loop then informs new organizational practices and influences organizational strategy, in turn influencing the organization's structure. Yet the achievement of strategic impact is not a foregone conclusion; innovators find it

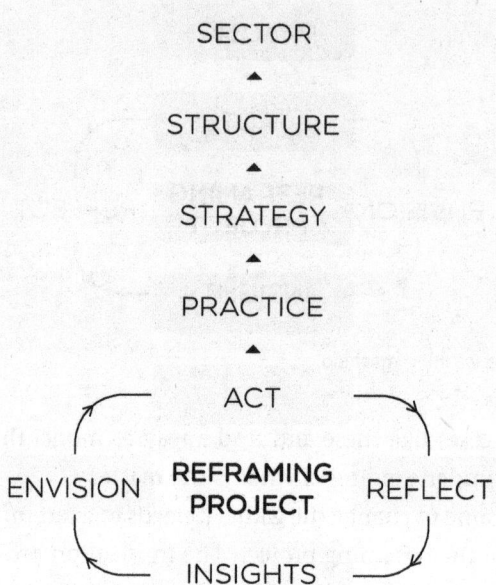

Figure 4.1b The path to change.

difficult to be heard, and they report on this process as an uphill struggle (figure 4.1c).[14]

In the case of Kings Cross, the New South Wales Government reacted to public pressure by reinforcing the old strategies that the DOC project had sought to dislodge. But the practices associated with the new music festival frame, while successful on the ground, were just not part of the strategic discussion when the New South Wales Government reacted to the two incidents at nighttime. The problem is that strategy is normally determined from the top down.[15]

The fact that this is a top-down process creates a blockage in the middle of the mode, between practices and strategy: The project-based bottom-up lessons and practices become stuck. They are kept from strategic impact by the top-down approach to strategy formulation. It is fiendishly hard for them to get a place in the discussion; they come from an unexpected angle. One can be lucky if some of the people involved on the project level are also players on the strategic level, but then *they* struggle to get heard (for particular reasons; see also § 5.1). There is one addition that needs to be made to complete the model: The organization reacts to

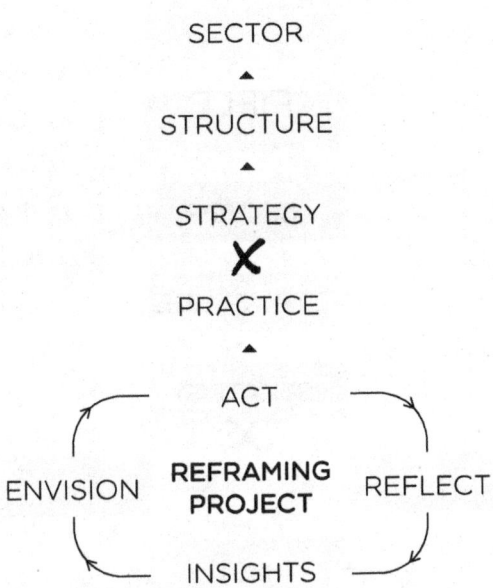

Figure 4.1c The blockage.

what is sees as its relevant context, what Bourdieu would call the *field*,[16] and adapts its structures and strategies accordingly (figure 4.1d). The field consists of the prevalent *paradigm(s)*, the *infrastructure* and *disciplines* that support the business as usual, as well as the *narratives* about its role in the world and relationships with other sectors and the lifeworld of people. It holds the "rules of the game" in place. In this model, organizations actively engage with the field. But let's not assume that organizations are innovative, in and of themselves. Most organizations are not more innovative than they need to be; they are followers, rather than leaders. They do more or less what all the others in their sector do.[17] They will only change when the sector changes.

This struggle for the bottom-up lessons to be heard is not intended, and it should not be there. But it is very much part of the reality of the innovator. This barrier can be bypassed by using the insights that come from the projects to directly influence the field, changing the perception that an organization has of its relevant environment (figure 4.1e). This creates a new dynamic, combining the two movements: as the insights that come from the projects are used to create a new field, the organization

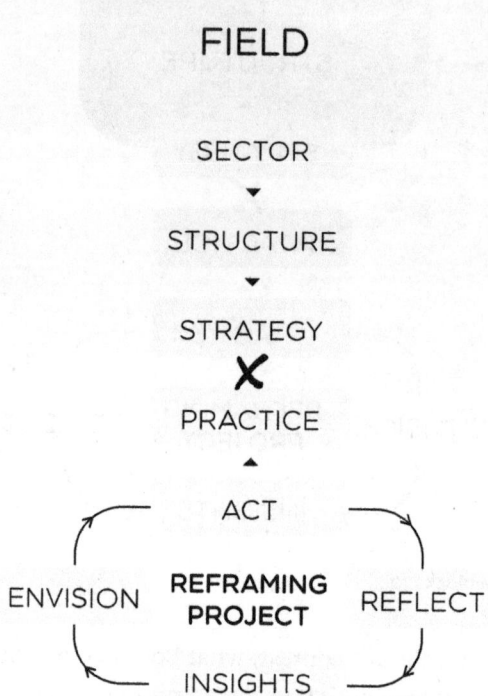

Figure 4.1d The top-down movement, from field to strategy.

adapts to this new field by using its normal top-down adaptive processes, and it meets the bottom-up movement halfway. Organizations are adaptive, striving to mirror the developments in their relevant environments.

As seen in the aftermath of the Kings Cross project, the societal discussion that was sparked by the lockout laws (in figure 4.1e, see the shift in the field—in this case, the societal discussion) has finally created the context for the outcomes of the initial Kings Cross project—and its reframing of the Kings Cross situation as a music festival—to be supported.

With this model, we have a conceptual framework connecting reframing projects with their strategic and organizational impact. We have experimented with the game changers model over the last ten years, through many projects, and in the context of a professional master's degree program (see appendix 6). It has proven to be useful for innovation

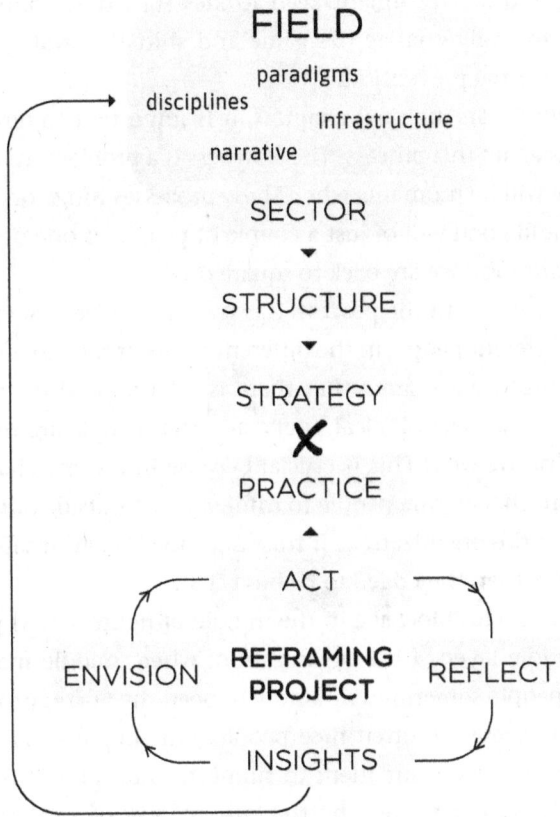

Figure 4.1e The complete game changers model.

practitioners, both as a map of their current situation and as a help in creating new ways forward toward strategic impact.

Here are some first comments arising from that practice:

- Note that this conceptual model, like any model (see § 2.3), is based on a number of abstractions/simplifications. In reality, the processes are not nearly as linear as they are portrayed. The arrows between the layers should go both ways as there is always learning happening across them. The orientation of the arrows in the figure just indicates the main direction of influence in the relationship.
- These processes can be very slow: in the case of Kings Cross, this realignment has eventually occurred, but it has taken ten years, two

tragedies, and a government keen to kick-start the economy after a recession to really change the game and shift the strategic thinking away from crime prevention.
- As you will see in the next chapters, it is important to develop practices to speed up this process. The slowness is a problem in itself. There inevitably will be moments when these processes hinge on the understanding and good will of just a couple of people. If one of these happens to shift jobs, we are back to square one.
- For the continuity in the process, it is good to realize that we are dealing with different people in the different layers of the model. For innovation to flow, we assume that there is a basic level of trust in the organization, a psychological safety, and that people are relating and communicating well. This is crucial because in a game changers process, we are challenging people to think and act outside of the normal practices of the organization. If trust and psychological safety cannot be assumed, then they need to be built first.
- The major process blockage in the middle of figure 4.1c is positioned in the middle layer of the organization, where middle management sits—the people sometimes unkindly dubbed the "permafrost." In our experience, these are often nice people, but they cannot say yes to the new things we want them to support. Their positions and roles are completely determined by the current way of working and the active strategy of the day. This is where the problem-solving machine is hardwired within the organization. They cannot suddenly say yes to something that is completely, fundamentally different from that way of working. A new frame will almost invariably cut across the responsibilities of their roles in different departments. Normally, their authority to act comes from (1) following procedures, (2) a demonstrable efficiency gain, or (3) being well supported in the network.[18] In the case of a radical reframe, (1) and (2) are not on offer. To take part in change, the unwavering and public support of the leadership is all-important.
- In contrast to the position of middle management, there is some freedom of thinking at the bottom of the organization, to improvise in the face of complex real-world problem situations. And at the top of the organization, there is also some space to think differently—although

the freedom to act on those thoughts can be limited by power, political concerns, or the short-termism that comes from having to deliver immediate results (and/or shareholder value).
- You will see in the coming examples that to be effective, timing is of the essence. There needs to be a synchronized motion of top-down and bottom-up processes. For real change to occur, they need to work in concert. This is how we can change the game and achieve meaningful transformation.

This conceptual exploration is still pretty abstract; the examples in the next section will help create a more sophisticated understanding of how this plays out in practice.

4.3 INNOVATION BEYOND THE PROJECT

To sharpen our thinking, we will now look at two case studies that hold a promise of organizational change: one that was initiated top down, the other bottom up. This allows us to check the validity and usefulness of the game changers model. For validity, we are interested in gauging if these case studies can be described and understood in terms of the game changers model (even if it is just helping us understand the misunderstandings). Usefulness is assessed by looking at whether the game changers model can predict and explain how these projects get stuck, and if the model helps us by suggesting new ways forward. These case studies are critical in the sense that they illustrate the dynamics of the process as well as the friction that an innovator can encounter. Despite excellent-quality project work and great local impact, they are both merely qualified successes in terms of strategic influence.

Case Study: Partners in Recovery

Partners in Recovery is a broad coalition of organizations in the health domain. They commissioned the Design Innovation Research Center of the University of Technology Sydney (UTS DIRC) to support them in designing a better systems response for people with a severe and persistent illness.

When people go through an acute episode of a severe mental illness, they often end up being admitted to a mental health unit of a hospital. Sometimes the acute episode can lead to criminal behavior and incarceration. Many different agencies are involved to support people with a severe mental illness when they are in acute need of help, including mental health professionals, ambulance paramedics, police officers, social workers, and nongovernmental organizations (NGOs). Unfortunately, the way the system is currently organized is not always conducive to people being able to provide the appropriate support, in the right place and at the right time. Signs of distress are often detected too late, leading to a crisis situation; then, being forcefully transported to the hospital and staying in an emergency department can be very traumatic experiences for people with a mental illness. There is also an increasing workload for service providers, and there are often conflicts between service providers about responsibilities. In this research project, the researchers of DIRC used the frame creation methodology to tackle this problem. The people experiencing mental health issues (called *consumers* in the language of the sector), their carers, and people across service providers in the sector were asked to contribute to this process through participating in interviews and collective frame creation sessions.[19] The following themes emerged from these sessions, capturing the broad domain in terms of the deep human values at play:

1. **Connection.** Many of the consumers lost friends and connection to family through their mental illness. Connection to peers is needed to be able to share stories and to feel you belong.
2. **Empathy.** Many carers and consumers indicated that they wanted people to understand what it means to have a mental illness.
3. **Empowerment.** Empowerment is a reoccurring theme across both consumers and their carers. Empowerment is necessary to be able to live an independent life, through encouragement, employment, accommodation, and other life skills. Carers know their loved ones better than anyone and would like to be given a voice in decisions.
4. **Peace of mind.** Carers need peace of mind as many indicated high levels of anxiety, particularly in the lead up to a crisis.
5. **Consistency and stability.** Every interviewee expressed the need for consistency and stability. When consumers and carers have to interact with many different service providers on their journey, there is no time to build trust, and they might have to share their stories again and again.
6. **Trust.** Trust is needed to be able to ask someone for help. Although building a trusted relationship requires time, this can be accelerated through personal introductions.
7. **Respect.** The people affected and their careers also indicated that they wanted to be listened to. The level of respect experienced varied a lot.

These themes were the input for frame creation workshop sessions, from which several ideas for new approaches emerged:

- **Support facilitator.** This person engages people with a mental illness with the appropriate services. As mental illness impacts all aspects of people's lives, many different types of services are available for people, making it hard to navigate the

system. The support facilitator can be framed as a combination of a coach and a broker.
- **The individual crisis plan and diary.** It is very difficult for people who provide emergency response to know what an individual person might need. The solution was framed as mapping the journey.
- **A crisis kit and training.** The period leading up to a crisis is very difficult. During this time, carers feel very anxious and worried. The underlying theme of this problem is peace of mind for carers. This can be framed as the need for first aid training.
- **The carer event and forum.** This aims to provide support for carers not just in mental health support skills, but also in how to deal with how the mental illness affects their lives in general. This can be framed in terms of agency and the development of care skills through peers.
- **The coaching team.** This addresses the frustration and sense of futility among many of the service providers. When you know that what you do has a positive effect, you get a sense of achievement, which in turn sustains your drive. When supporting someone with a severe mental illness in a crisis situation, this feedback loop is often broken. The solution was framed as a coaching team; just like a coach of a sports team, this team observes the collective action of the people on the ground. The same underlying frame also led to the next solution.
- **The satellite team.** Many of the crises should have been prevented. A problem with prevention is that the solutions in place to support people in a subacute situation require a consumer to actively engage. The solution is a subacute team or satellite team. The main goal of this team is to provide people with the necessary support within twenty-four hours when they are in a subacute situation (not yet in a crisis).

These are ideas; they all need a lot of work to become compelling proposals and plans. The Partners in Recovery teams decided to first refine the coaching team and the additional solution, the satellite team. Both were presented to stakeholders in co-design sessions. This led to adjustments to the ideas, as well as the addition of a third stream of activity as the need for subacute accommodation surfaced. In a final synthesis session, conclusions were drawn and decisions were made on progressing these solutions further.

In terms of the game changers model, there was a clear top-down commitment from Partners in Recovery for the sector to create change; that was the very reason to create the Partners in Recovery coalition in the first place. The system as it is can't deal with these pressing issues, so there needs to be change. But in creating the coalition, the common problem situation is also a bit in the middle between the various partners, and there might be a lack of clarity about who is going to pick up the solutions that come out of the bottom-up frame creation process. Paradoxically, the initiative started with the assumption that there *is* a system, while the issue might be the lack of connections. In the end, the solutions were not brought much further as a common effort when the coalition came to the end of its funding (unfortunately, the project was sparked toward the end of the Partners in Recovery coalition funding cycle). This doesn't mean that this project was without impact; organizations from the coalition have drawn lessons and adopted more collaborative practices in this space, there is a much better understanding among the organizations, and the people involved report great insights and impact on a personal level. These are significant and durable results. Here are some things we can learn from this:

- In retrospect, the project focus on a problem outside of the system should have been about the system itself. The project ended up with proposals that add elements to a system, making it more complex; a deeper shift could have led to a reduction of complexity.
- For this to happen, the organizations should enter the collaboration with a learning question, implying an up-front willingness to change, rather than the motivation to "solve a problem out there." However, eliciting the learning questions of the key organizations in a problem arena up front takes time and effort, and the freedom to ask these probing questions. This is seldom understood: Especially when a project briefing has already been formulated, there is an understandable eagerness to get to "solutions," and so projects are often formulated with a problem-solving framework in mind ("let's go forward, not backward").
- In addition to the learning questions, it pays to create clarity on the organizational paradoxes that need to be addressed in the various stakeholder organizations. Insight into the paradoxes helps guide the process so the frames and solutions can be more precise in addressing them. In this case, the paradoxes run deep and touch upon the paradigms that underpin the whole care sector. For instance, in giving voice to consumers and carers, the project clashes with the classical medical paradigm, in which a patient is seen as a passive subject and in which there seems to be an assumption that in order to care for a patient, the medical professionals need to control them first.[20] These are deeply rooted professional attitudes, reinforced within the medical system and education. They are shifting, but slowly (though the very fact that the coalition was set up is a good sign in itself).

Case Study: The Waterwolf in Gouda

The Waterwolf program was initiated and led by Professor Dick Rijken with colleagues and students from The Hague University of Applied Sciences, as part of a larger vision to fundamentally shift the way the cultural sector operates within the networked society:

Culture plays a central role in our digital networked society. In networks, the players are interdependent and connected. Everybody has to connect and shape their own identity in connection with others. Personal expression becomes really crucial and many new forms of connection emerge (see social media). By expressing ourselves, we show the world who we are. And this happens in dialogue, in which we are seeking value and meaning—reflecting and learning together. This creates a new role and position for culture in the networked society: where the "cultural sector" used to be the central place in society for the creation of meaning, expression and reflection, this is now an integral part of our day to day lives as citizens, professionals, patients, carers, friends etc. . . . This creates huge opportunities for the cultural sector in the networked society. The challenge is for the cultural sector to shed some of its thinking that kept it away from engaging with society (the "white box" of the museum, the "dark box" of the theatre—in which the viewer is a passive audience), and open out into the world.[21]

The Waterwolf program[22] is set up as a series of experiments in which cultural institutions are engaging with society in this new, intimate way. The setting for the exploration of this bigger agenda is the small Dutch city of Gouda (a beautiful old medieval town, famous for cheese and waffles—a wonderful day trip for tourists.). Gouda is situated between much bigger cities, and due to its excellent rail and road connections, it has become a commuter town, which has led to social issues (a whole section of the population leaving for the day every weekday). It is also one of the lowest-lying cities in the Netherlands, several meters below sea level. Gouda is a complete city, a mini-universe of a scale that allows for direct contact and quick action. The idea behind the Waterwolf program was to co-design a new field, locally, to show what can be done. The partners in the coalition were the Regional Archives, the Gouda Library, and the city's museum (which later dropped out), supported by the city and two cultural funding bodies. Out of seven years of activities, we will briefly highlight two projects that illustrate the nature, breadth, depth, and dynamics of the engagement.

Case 1: Regional Archive: We Care

Gouda is a picture-perfect medieval city, yet it is also a living city; it should not be a museum. Protecting the heritage in such a dynamic environment starts with people's understanding of its value and meaning. The current burghers of Gouda should feel connected and care for the city as a common heritage. Knowledge of this heritage is held in the Regional Archives. But how can that knowledge be activated for the city now and in the future? On the back of that, what role can the archives play in the life of people? An enthusiastic coalition was built with a local DIY retailer, an architectural firm, and the archives to help people take care of their old houses in the proper way. This led to many great interactions and inspired the citizens to look anew at what they have. In a sense, house ownership is reframed as stewardship: You are taking care of the house for future generations. There have been many owners before you, and there will be many after you; you are passing the baton of taking care of your house and can take pride in doing this well, in the greater scheme of things. This connects the individual not just to history, but also to community in a new and meaningful way. This changes the way of being a citizen, an inhabitant—a deep cultural impact way beyond the DIY challenges of home maintenance—and it reframes the role of the council, moving away from enforcing the restrictions placed on changes to official listed monuments and toward the deeper motivation of care.

Case 2: Library: Learning Together

The classic library, in its existing form, is a place to borrow books for study and pleasure. Within society, the library is a public building that functions as a holder of knowledge and wisdom. This form is under threat: As the internet is making information freely and easily accessible to anyone, libraries have seen their attendance drop. This has inevitably also undermined the library's public function as a hub in the community. In this project, the library was deframed and then reinvented from a new perspective. To go beyond the thinking in current forms, the deframing started from the position that the library is not about the books, and that a library may not be about lending. The underlying themes that came up in the frame creation process are expression, reflection, and sharing. In a reframe, we can reconsider the library to be built around these values, as a place to facilitate *Bildung* and citizenship. The library then becomes a place for learning together—a role that it can embody within the community in many different ways, through actions like debates, lectures, courses, quiet study places for the public, and collaborations with other cultural institutions (interestingly, this is close to the original concept of a public library as a place for the "elevation of the masses"). The proposed shift is not easy, of course: The library is such an ancient institution, and the professions that are associated with it (i.e., the librarian) are well-established. A radical reinvention like this would be hard for people that have chosen a career as a librarian because they like the existing form; they just love books (personally, I very much sympathize with that). But for those whose intrinsic motivation is all about public engagement, this will feel like a logical and meaningful next step in the development of their profession.

Over the seven years of the Waterwolf program, there were many more projects touching on societal domains. For instance, the Green Glasses project looked at the city from a nature perspective. With Wellant College (a vocational training college), an inventory was made of the green spaces in the city, and multiple programs were developed (with local garden centers) to engage the citizens in creating healthy green environments. In this case, just bringing together existing organizations around the shared value and meaning was enough to spark a lively collaboration. The potential must have been there all along. Later, we will discuss a case study that brings this engagement to yet a deeper layer (see § 6.5). What all of these projects have in common is the shared, local inspiration found in the people of these organizations. Unlocking their powerful intrinsic motivation (see figure 5.2) creates the robustness of these initiatives, which all go beyond the normal call of duty. Yet organizationally, these radical reframes are still hard, for several reasons: (1) As discussed for the library, not everybody will come along on the journey. (2) Right when the Waterwolf projects came about, cultural organizations were put under pressure from the government of the day, facing substantial budget cuts. In principle, this pressure could spark a rethink. But in an environment of shrinking finances, a fundamental questioning of one's own assumptions is very hard. (3) Then there is the capability question: People are educated as professionals to operate in a stable world, not to deal with such fundamental changes; how they see them then really depends on their personality. Fundamental changes like this cannot be separated from the development of "new mastery" and capability building (see § 6.2). (4) The "theory of change" (see § 5.2) behind the Waterwolf initiative was very much based on learning. When initiatives became stuck, it was mostly due to organizations and situations in which learning is not the dominant style for creating change. (5) In times of pressure, organizations tend to become defensive, and the appetite for outreach and change is limited.

In terms of the game changers model, the Waterwolf project was inspired on a field redesign, and through its reframing projects, it endeavored to create new practices for the cultural sector. The results, though quite convincing, were not picked up and progressed by the national funding bodies that originally sponsored the Waterwolf project, beyond applauding the local impact and supporting the dissemination of the outcomes. In retrospect, that might be difficult for these funding bodies as they get caught in the paradox of representing and supporting the cultural sector as-is (through advocacy—fighting with other budget priorities), while also wanting to support new developments and stimulate the development of the disciplines into the future. In this case, the balancing act veered toward holding the existing paradigm in place. The cultural institutions are part of the system and easily feel threatened when the existing forms of cultural expression are being questioned. It is easier if you can just add new elements to a system, without changing what is there—but that is not what Waterwolf set out to do. This is about a fundamental rethink of the role of culture and cultural institutions in society—a point we will return to in § 6.5.

What can we learn from these cases? What does it take to create deep and lasting change? There are a couple of key points here that will give us insights, elements, and criteria to take forward into the coming chapters:

- First, it is important to get the systems border right; in all of these cases, the system to be addressed was broader than originally imagined. In the case of Kings Cross, who would have thought that the doctors in St Vincent's hospital would exert such an influence on the public discussion in the media? This is easier said than done: In times of transition, the system border will be fluid, and it might need to be adapted time and time again as the system moves.
- Taking a different starting point does pay, even just as a thought experiment, and then creating new forms from that perspective allows a fresh approach to the practices in an organization or sector. The carer perspective in the Partners in Recovery example galvanized fresh thinking across all parties.
- It is crucial to understand the tensions and paradoxes of all stakeholders involved and to make sure there are new insights and shifts for

everybody. Concentrating on the formulation of learning questions for all parties involved, before the project starts, makes this explicit and anchors the project outcomes.
- Alarm bells should go off when project outcomes are seen as additive; there is a real danger that in creating superficial patches, we are making an existing system more complex, rather than rethinking it more deeply. The perspective should be that the projected new situation should not add extra work.
- Innovation is a relay race. An initiative must travel from first spark to realization through the organization and/or network. The trajectory that it should travel from person to person, from department to department, determines who needs to be involved in the project (this is the nature of a relay race; if the baton is dropped, anywhere along the way, there is no result for anybody). This is evident in the Waterwolf project: It's important to involve, inspire, and create new value for everybody on the critical path, from beginning to end.
- According to the game changers model, we need to ensure that the bottom-up and top-down movements are synchronized. They need to meet halfway; if one arrives before the other, it might lead to trouble. (Consider this quote from a senior civil servant: "I like to be surprised, but don't take me by surprise."[23])
- All of this is about people, their personal motivation, drive, and courage to step out of their normal role, their normal way of thinking and working. Trust, inspiration, and courage are key. In the end, the Waterwolf program stalled when the remarkable, visionary director of the Gouda museum that had held the space for this deep change left for a different position.
- Every meaningful transformation is accompanied by an implicit or explicit form of capability building; new practices require a shift in mastery. In these cases, we saw that the City of Sydney was very capable of taking on the challenge of the Kings Cross change, but some other organizations, perhaps not so much. They may honestly *want* to change the game, but then it turns out they can't. Appendix 3 sets an agenda for the change that is needed in public sector organizations. Appendix 6 outlines a curriculum I developed to address this need.

In several of these examples, we have seen that achieving change in practices on an organizational level is hard when we do not address the different way of thinking needed on a field level too. It could be that an organizational change more or less presupposes a paradigm shift; an outlook on sector-wide change makes this easier. Looking from a project perspective (the bottom of the model), spending time creating a new field narrative to feed the top-down development may look like a waste of time. Yet from these cases, you get the sense that we need to carefully develop this narrative to achieve the change. We will take this up in the next chapter, on paradigmatic shifts and sector-wide change, and then extend the scope of our practice to societal change in chapters 6 and 7. These deep change processes are easier on a bigger scale, because to achieve progress, they need that type of backing from the reframed field.

4.4 NEXT CHALLENGES

To clarify the steps and practices of the game changers model, we will keep applying the model as a lens to study the upcoming cases in the next chapters. This helps in mapping these very complex trajectories, and a rich case study basis can allow us to see new patterns emerge. A typology of these open, complex, dynamic, and networked problem situations could be of great help to the practitioner that needs to navigate this landscape.

From these two last cases, we can identify what amounts to a *change paradox*: Even organizations that are acutely aware that their current approaches, strategies, and structures are not suitable for dealing with the open, complex, dynamic, and networked problems they are facing remain problem-solving machines that are very set in their ways. They may want to change, and frame creation projects may show them a clear way forward toward new practices, but they still resist. For the change agent, this may mean resorting to workarounds to do what is good for the organization, what needs to be done, despite the organization's best efforts to shoot this down.

Perhaps we are making a fundamental mistake here by concentrating on organizations. Perhaps the issues that arise from trying to create change in organizations do not originate within these organizations at all, and therefore cannot be resolved at this level. Perhaps, like Don Quixote, we have been tilting at windmills.

You will see in the next chapters that creating deep change requires an approach that goes beyond these organization-level problems, as they are symptoms of deeper issues. After all, an organization's behavior is anchored in the field it finds itself in (the narrative, the practices of the disciplines that make up its DNA), and in creating deep change we will need to engage on that level.

We will be exploring this in the next two chapters. In chapter 7, we will then go on to devise *how* to organize around deep change. We have already seen glimpses of that way forward in these cases.

5

PARADIGMS

I don't believe in the value of argumentation. I can talk to people that disagree with me, but I will only convince them if they were convinced all along.
—French philosopher Michel Onfray, interviewed by Geert Groot[1]

5.1 CREATING THE NEW NORMAL

The model in the last chapter helps with understanding some of the stuckness that we can feel in organizations, and it proposes a way to create a new dynamic between the layers of the organization. But the real source of the stuckness doesn't lie within the organization itself; that is just where it shows up. The root of the problems lies in the patterns of thinking in the field, which the organizations use to establish what is "normal" and "good" in the sector, and in the disciplines and infrastructures that hold current practices together.

If we want to create a "new normal," we need to address the "old normal" that is held in these sectors and disciplines. Their underlying patterns of seeing, thinking, and doing is what we call a *paradigm*.

The term *paradigm* (literally, *exemplar*, an example that is deemed worth following) is borrowed from the history of science—in particular, the work of Thomas Kuhn. He describes progress in science not as a steady growth of knowledge, but in terms of periods of "normal science" and times of "revolution." In periods of normal science, academics steadily build knowledge within—and add knowledge to—the existing theoretical framework, the field. But after a while, more and more anomalies appear, which cannot really be understood through this existing paradigm; they can only be catered for by creating "exceptions." In the long run, this will undermine the paradigm's coherence and render it complex and unwieldy. This creates space for other theories to emerge that are superior in the sense that they can include these anomalies quite elegantly within a coherent new framework of thinking. These are times of revolution, when the way of seeing the world and thinking about it shifts. The standard example is Newtonian physics, which served scientists and academics well for centuries, until succeeded by Einstein's special theory of relativity. The key word here is *succeeded*—not replaced. For most real-world applications, if we stay well away from light speed, Newtonian physics still works just fine. Now, Kuhn was a historian of science, and he describes this alternation between periods of normal science and revolutions almost as a naturally occurring process. The question before us here in this chapter is how to do this deliberately, how to *create* deep paradigmatic change when we need it.

The first clues on how to do this can be found in the later work of Kuhn himself. The preceding narrative is as plausible as it is superficial. Kuhn went on to study these shifts in thinking in much more detail, unveiling a much more subtle process.[2]

First of all, Kuhn stresses the incommensurability of the old and new paradigms. They belong to different worlds as it were. A new paradigm might well pick up on other elements of the situation than the old one (in Schön's terms, naming different things as important), and the definition of what is considered "good" is also very different in the new paradigm. This makes it hard to talk about the new paradigm as an "improvement" on the old one; after all, an improvement supposes that their qualities could be compared. But they cannot be compared; they are incommensurable. This creates huge problems if we want to convince people to shift their thinking from the old normal to a new paradigm. As Charles Darwin wrote, at the very end of *The Origin of Species*: "Although I am fully convinced of the truth of the views given in this volume . . . I by no means expect to convince experienced naturalists whose minds are stocked with a multitude of facts all viewed, during a long course of years, from a point of view opposite to mine. . . . But I look with confidence to the future—to young and rising naturalists, who will be able to view both sides of the question with impartiality."[3] This sentiment is echoed and amplified by the physicist Max Planck: "A new scientific truth does not triumph by convincing its opponents and making them see the light, but rather because its opponents eventually die, and a new generation grows up that is familiar with it."[4] But in our current predicament, change happening at the pace of one funeral at a time is way too slow. So the question becomes: How can we convince people that the new paradigm is somehow "better" and worth adopting? Kuhn is not convinced that this can be done at all; after all, there is no way to reason logically from one paradigm to the other. Their logics by definition don't match; there can be no bridge or fluent transition between the two. Convincing people based on practical arguments doesn't work either, because, the problem is, the new paradigm is not better. *The new paradigm is worse than the old one.*

This makes sense: the old paradigm is very detailed and coherent, well entrenched in people's practices and disciplines. A lot has been invested in this paradigm, and people have built whole careers based on these known truths and established (normal) practices. The proposed new paradigm, on the other hand, is most likely still very sketchy and may look odd. It may address some issues that were jarring in the old paradigm— but those irritants may well have been patched up to everybody's satisfaction, or they may have been accepted as "facts of life," not worth serious engagement. The fledgling new paradigm, by its very sketchiness, is bound to bring up many questions that had already been dealt with to everybody's satisfaction in the old way of thinking. And it brings up new questions, too:[5]

The early versions of most new paradigms are crude . . . usually the opponents of a new paradigm can legitimately claim that even in the area of crisis it is little superior to its traditional rival. Of course, it handles some problems better, has disclosed some new regularities. But the older paradigm can presumably be articulated to meet these challenges as it has met others before. . . . In short, if a new candidate for paradigm had to be judged from the start by hard-headed people who examined only relative problem-solving ability, the sciences would experience very few major revolutions. . . . But paradigm debates are not really about relative problem-solving ability, though for good reasons they are often couched in those terms . . . a decision between alternate ways of practicing science . . . must be based less on past achievement than on future promise.

Kuhn originally used the term *disciplinary matrix* for the concept he later called a *paradigm*. The former term would serve us better here, highlighting how an approach and manner of thinking becomes completely embedded in people's professional lifeworlds and communities of practice. Kuhn then goes on to argue that the transfer of allegiance from paradigm to paradigm is not based on logical reasoning, but is a conversion experience, a leap of faith taking place beyond the realm of logic. Yet there is hope:[6]

Most of them (proponents of the old paradigm) can be reached one way or another by persuasion rather than proof . . . individual scientists embrace a new paradigm for all sorts of reasons and usually several at once . . . [and] some of these reasons lie outside the sphere of science entirely . . . fortunately, there is also another sort of consideration that can lead scientists to reject an old paradigm in favor of a new. These are the arguments, rarely made entirely explicit, that appeal to the individual's sense of the appropriate or the aesthetic—a new theory is said to be "neater," "more suitable," or "simpler" than the old . . . the importance of aesthetic considerations can sometimes be decisive. Though they often attract only a few scientists to a new theory, it is upon those few that its ultimate triumph may depend. If they had not quickly taken it up for highly individual reasons, the new candidate for paradigm might never have been sufficiently developed to attract the allegiance of the scientific community as a whole.

For an illustration of such a conversion, we return to the controversy around Copernicus's new paradigm in astronomy (see § 2.4). The old paradigm ("the planets and sun revolve around the earth") was quite good in explaining and predicting the movement of the stars, but it did not work so well for the movement of the planets. As Kuhn noted: "The term planet is derived from a Greek word meaning, 'wanderer' and it was employed . . . to distinguish between those celestial bodies that moved or 'wandered' among the stars from those who relative positions were fixed." These planets seemingly had a much more complex behavior than the stars, going "retrograde" and traveling at different speeds. Copernicus's theory positing that the earth and other planets move around the sun resolved some of these issues, but it went against the current paradigm—and against the orthodoxy of the church. He published it with much trepidation, just before his death, and it was not met with much enthusiasm—until, that is, Johannes Kepler, the great astronomer of his time, got behind it. The question is: Why did Kepler do this? It turns out he was driven by a spiritual reason: In his mystic theology, the physical world mirrors the spiritual world. The universe itself is an image of God, with the sun corresponding to the Father. Therefore, he was convinced that the planets should revolve around the sun, rather than around the earth. For Kuhn, this is as good a reason as any to switch allegiance to a new paradigm.

One cannot reason from one paradigm to the other—which is a worry, because it means that in these all-important discussions, argumentation really does not work.

5.2 CHANGING PARADIGMS AND PRACTICES

In the middle of a paradigm shift, there is a moment without structure, where the old thinking is left behind and the new thinking cannot quite be reached. Then we find ourselves suspended between logics, in the middle of the leap of faith. In the coming paragraphs, you will see what is needed in this moment and how the deep change we envisage can be brought to others—in such a way that they can pick up the new practices and act upon them.

How can we do this? Paradigmatic shifts are usually sparked by big questions, and people then tend to look for big answers too (the knee-jerk reaction from a problem-solving perspective). But paradigms are so multifaceted and play out on so many different layers—they are expressed in narratives, as practices, as the infrastructure of a sector, even the shape of a physical environment—that the big question does not have one big answer, but many small ones. To get a sense of the dynamics, let's introduce an extended case study and then use six short reflections (see § 5.3) to delve more deeply into the practices and mechanisms at play.

Case Study: Teaching and Learning

There is an age-old discussion among different paradigms that lie at the basis of education. On one side of the discussion, the "teaching" side, education is framed as the transfer of knowledge, as "what you should know." This way of seeing leads us to a particular way of thinking about education, and an impressive, well-established action repertoire of useful practices. Education is talked about in terms of teaching predetermined subject matter, held in a structured curriculum to ensure completeness of the knowledge transfer. Quality of the knowledge transfer is tested by examinations in which students are compared on their ability to reproduce knowledge. Students are encouraged to do well by being in competition with one another in this well-defined playing field. They are trained for a set exam and will enter a profession that is predefined.

On the other side of the discussion, the "learning" side, education is framed as conveying "how you can get to knowledge." This way of seeing leads to thinking about education in terms of exploration and growth, often using the metaphor of a journey to structure the actions that scaffold experiential learning. Active curiosity is stimulated. The hierarchical distance between teacher and learner is minimized, as it gets in the way of open discussion and reflection. The learning journey is different for different learners; the fact that they are hard to compare means that quality is largely measured in terms of levels of reflection. Learning is seen as both an individual and a group process.

In terms of Schön's model (see § 3.2), these are both frames that are plausible and right, in a self-referencing way. Each contains its own notion of quality, so the (often heated) discussions between them are always fundamentally inconclusive.

But the practices they result in can be put to the test through acting upon them in a concrete situation. Traversing the territory between these two paradigms is very much part of the innovation at a secondary school in Sydney. Christina Luzi, a passionate educator, describes how the tension between these paradigms leads to a number of paradoxes in the running of a school:[7]

> Schools are places for students to learn,
> **YET**
> their voices are often neglected in their design and implementation.
>
> Schools are no longer fit for purpose
> **YET**
> we keep reinventing the same rigid curriculum and expect something to change.
>
> Students thrive when they feel connected to their school and peers
> **YET**
> this time is not mandated in the curriculum.
>
> We want our education system to change and evolve
> **BUT**
> all our time is spent on short-term fixes to our current problems.
>
> We know future change starts with the students who are in schools now
> **YET**
> we don't trust or empower their voices.

We want education to change
> **YET**

we train teachers the same and make it too hard for other professionals to transition into education.

This formidable list of paradoxes describes the tensions that hold the current system in place and make it hard to innovate. But they can also be seen as creative spaces, jumping-off points to propose reframes of the practices that make up the school. In the last few years, Luzi and her great set of colleagues have been experimenting with interventions that show how these new practices can work. To name just three:

- **Student agency.** To highlight to the students the power and value of their voice, lots of practices throughout college life need to shift. For instance, the hierarchical structure of the school was evident in the way the Student Leadership Team was selected. In the past, being a member of this team this had been a role limited to the most academic students. They were tapped on the shoulder by staff, required to write a letter addressed to the principal, and asked to deliver a speech to the student body. Upon examining this process, it highlighted the many hidden rules at play holding the old system in place. Student leaders represent the student body, yet they had to have their worth assessed by adults. The preselection meant only some students were able to apply, and hence the Student Leadership Team really did not represent the entire student body at all. Until . . . the experiment started with an open nomination process, after which prospective student leaders were asked to pitch ways to build connectedness and community in the college. They then collaborated with the other applicants to host an event for their peers. The student body was able to see an individual's leadership in action and were able to participate in an event conceived by the students, for the students. They then created an advertising campaign, leading to a 500 percent increase in applications for student leadership. The students are given the autonomy to create initiatives and make decisions that align with the school vision. This shift also saw pupils go from just voicing their opinions to feeling they have the agency to do something about it. As Luzi notes: "We ask our students to not come to us with just a problem, but rather a solution and we will support them to make it happen . . . Our students are empowered to develop their own initiatives, and if it doesn't work out, it's an opportunity for a lesson to be learned." The frequency of student-led initiatives continues to increase, highlighting the health of the innovation ecosystem.
- **Space for learning.** The school library was not used very much. Students used a variety of creative tools, including imagining the library as a character, creating narratives around their sensory reactions to sounds, smells, and textures in the space, to diagnose what made the environment difficult for them to use

as a space for learning and collaboration. Students held ideation sessions with architects and created mood boards with visions of the color palette, layout, and furniture. What emerged was a harmonious space that met the needs of the stakeholders.
- **Challenges.** Schools have maintained the same hierarchical leadership structures for ever. But what if schools were seen as learning organizations in their own right? What different roles and structures would emerge? This set the school on a path to learn from innovative organizations and reimagine the ways of working, thinking, and being to ensure that as a community, they are pioneers of change. People (staff, students, the broader community) were asked to help define "challenge spaces" in the school, to pitch an area of the school they would like to explore and improve in order to ensure this community is at the frontier of education (as the vision says). The pitches led to eleven experiments taking place across this learning community.

The COVID-era lockdowns created an unsought opportunity to question the dominance of the teaching paradigm, radically reshuffling the playing field in education. Suddenly the school had to reframe itself, from "being a school" very much defined by its infrastructure (the buildings) to supporting parents' homeschooling their kids for extended periods of time. This could only be done through very strong community engagement and support. As the lockdowns dragged on, it was clear that this is not just about the kids; it is about an "authentic partnership"[8] to further whole-of-community learning and being uplifted together. This gave a profound new meaning to the role of the school as a linking pin in the local community. The school became a key agent of community support and social change in its own right.

The results of these reframes and the experiments (moves) that flowed from them are presented through a podcast series. This opens them up for reflection and evaluation—from the perspectives of both paradigms. This is important because, in the end, a real paradigmatic shift in education will require structural change, while the structures in the sector are still very much set by the teaching-oriented disciplinary matrix. So next, Luzi seeks to create space for change by decluttering the syllabus and rethinking approaches to the measuring criteria that evaluate student success. Through this approach, she's optimistic that the education system can keep up with the demands of modern society and raise a new generation of "confident, emotionally intelligent and socially responsible leaders."

This case illustrates the sheer variety of approaches and initiatives needed to traverse the terrain between two paradigms—and the excitement of taking this on as a creative challenge, creating new practices that provide the evidence for systems change.

5.3 WHAT DOES IT TAKE? ELEMENTS OF CHANGE

As chapter 1 discussed, the structure of this book is a bit of a journey in which we take the thinking and practices that were developed through the research on frame creation from their original habitat on a project level (in chapter 3), to organizational change (in chapter 4), to sector-wide change (here in chapter 5), and to societal change (in chapter 6). Of course, this cannot be a straight "application" of the original body of work; each of these levels come with its own unique challenges. In this section, we will describe some of the challenges and the elements of change on this level as we have found them over the years of our practice, and introduce some helpful models and methods for the reader to ponder. In doing so, we have avoided the temptation to create an overarching model of everything; on each level, you can find yourself in many, very diverse problem situations, and there is no way to second-guess what will be most important or helpful to you. Therefore, in this section, the landscape of sector-level change will be sketched through drawing some loose lines. It is for the active reader to pick up on what is relevant and inspiring for them. If one of the points doesn't resonate, it probably isn't relevant for now; feel free to skip it. This is a smorgasbord of insights, models, methods, and tools: Please pick and choose among them!

CHANGING YOUR MIND

When we advocate a shift in paradigm, we are basically asking people to change their mind on a very fundamental level. It is good to pause here and, before we start attempting to change somebody else's mind, ask ourselves this question first (as the aircraft safety card says, "put your own mask on first before helping others"):

"*When* in my life have I actually changed my mind?"

On the whole, people find it surprisingly hard to come up with more than a couple of instances. Changing your mind probably doesn't happen very often. Next, we can start unpacking this moment, asking some follow-up questions:

"What was this about?"
"What was the situation/moment?"
"What preceded this moment?"
"What came after?"
"Was there a specific trigger?"
And so on.

These are important questions: If we want to create deep innovation, we will need to deeply understand this. This *is* the key process of innovation and change. Yet we tend to pass it over, hardly think about it, presuming that giving strong arguments in favor of our view will do the trick and sway others to our position.[9] We argue constantly, in the belief that argumentation actually works to convince the other on a deep level. (But do we really believe this? The French philosopher Onfray would disagree; see this chapter's epigraph.) In discussions, people may give in—maybe because they are overpowered, or maybe because on reflection they decide that they do not care that much either way. But if they do care, if they are committed, how could they really be swayed?

Being Wrong

In my own experience, one moment when I had to change my mind came when we were setting up a new degree program for a design department at a university of technology. We had spent many months developing a curriculum that was pretty solid; we were ready to start teaching a course based on well-formulated intended learning outcomes, covering the knowledge and skills the students needed to pick up. Those were woven into lectures and studio projects, safeguarded by best practice assessment methods, all benchmarked against other schools we were comparing ourselves with. Then at the last moment, a new director of education was brought in who changed the model completely: only problem-based learning, no lectures, no marks (but workplans and reviews instead). I disagreed with this and was completely convinced it wouldn't work. But I was not in a position to push my opinion through, so the curriculum started on this new footing. *And it worked*. In my world, it should *not* have worked, but it did. Students launched straight into it and thrived. This was real, and I could not deny it. Although I was glad for them, I also had to deal with my own confusion and rearrange just about all my thinking about what education is, how learning works, and what students can achieve when you challenge them in the right way.

PARADIGMS

It is worthwhile to spend some time reflecting on your own on what Kuhn called *conversion experiences*. These conversion experiences may also be quite revealing in explaining how you intuitively try to influence others and which mind-changing strategies you tend to intuitively use because they sit well with your own life experience and character. This can make us pause and think about what *they* might need as a trigger to change position.

LEARNING STRUCTURES

Going back to the game changers model, this is one of the big frustrations for people who want to create top-down change in organizations. Their theory of change is built on the assumption that when they change the structures, processes, and strategies of the organization, and explain this well to all of their employees, then the staff members' practices will also shift (see figure 5.1). But these practices don't shift, for many reasons. The big cross in the middle of the game changers model works both ways; in the last chapter, we saw how it can deeply frustrate the bottom-up innovators, yet the top-down visionaries can't get past it either.

Figure 5.1 Top-down failing to change practice.

The Team of Teams

A radically different approach is proposed by General Stanley McCrystal.[10] He was leading the US troops in Iraq at the time when the Al-Qaeda terrorist organization arose, and it turned out that his troops were desperately vulnerable to attack. In the end, he realized that the classic divisions between the US Army, Navy, Air Force, and Intelligence Community made them all vulnerable, and that the hierarchical structure of the military machine led to decision-making that was always too late when up against an enemy that was locally organized, quick, and nimble (basically, working as a network of freelancers). He experimented with peer-to-peer communication that bypassed the organizational hierarchy and delegating decision-making down to the operational teams themselves. Still, the response was sometimes too slow—especially when, despite his best efforts, the decision about intervention was sent up the chain of command, all the way to his desk. In the end, he realized that he didn't only need these teams to be multidisciplinary, but that they should work together organically as a "team of teams." When dealing with an enemy organization that had an open, complex, dynamic, and networked structure, he had to find a way to recreate his military organization to become open, complex, dynamic, and networked itself.

INTRINSIC MOTIVATION

In his work on paradigmatic shifts, Kuhn mentions a *back door*, as it were, via which people can be swayed to adopt a new paradigm by appealing to a different, deeper motivation. For our purposes, this back door is probably the front door: If reasoning only gets us so far, what else can we do to support people to make this leap of faith? Both in academia and in the commercial world, there has been lots of research into the deep, intrinsic motivations that actually drive people's behavior. A book from Diller, Shedroff, and Rhea lists many positive drivers.[11] The following list includes just the top fifteen entries (in alphabetical order) from a longer list that was based on an extensive survey of people from around the world. Read this list slowly; register which of these fifteen resonate most with you. These deep inner motivations are important as they sit in the lifeworlds of people and naturally cross boundaries between disciplines and modes of thinking. They can help scale the walls people create around their senses of quality and identity as professionals (see § 6.4). We can *feel* these intrinsic drivers, and we can appeal to them.

ACCOMPLISHMENT
A sense of satisfaction that can result from productivity, focus, talent, or status.

BEAUTY
The appreciation of qualities that give pleasure to the senses or spirit.

COMMUNITY
A sense of unity with others around us and a general connection with other human beings.

CREATION
The sense of having produced something new and original, and in doing so, to have made a lasting contribution.

DUTY
The willing application of oneself to a responsibility.

ENLIGHTENMENT
Clear understanding through logic or inspiration.

FREEDOM
The sense of living without unwanted constraints.

HARMONY
The balanced and pleasing relationship of parts to a whole, whether in nature, society, or an individual.

JUSTICE
The assurance of equitable and unbiased treatment.

ONENESS
A sense of unity with everything around us.

REDEMPTION
Atonement or deliverance from past failure or decline.

SECURITY
The freedom from worry about loss.

TRUTH
A commitment to honesty and integrity.

VALIDATION
The recognition of oneself as a valued individual worthy of respect.

WONDER
Awe in the presence of a creation beyond one's understanding.

The Beauty of Work

The clustering of high schools into a bigger umbrella organization was leading to staff issues. Inevitably, the need to coordinate the education of thousands of students across multiple locations throughout the city led to a layered organization, with formal systems, checks, and balances. People become teachers because they are motivated to help kids learn (life) skills. But it can be an intense job, and it can be hard: the schedule is quite relentless, the salary isn't that high, career opportunities are very limited, and the social status of the teacher has eroded over time. In the thick of it, it is sometimes it is difficult to remember the original spark. This is a self-reinforcing mechanism: a teacher can spiral down on the way to burning out, or they might defend themselves from harm by disassociating (e.g., by becoming bureaucratic or cynical). To address these vicious circles, it is important to find a way to periodically reaccess the original positive drivers. In the high school under study, sessions were started around the question: "What is a beautiful day at work?" This brings *beauty* as a driver into the mix, and beauty is a very important hidden driver in our lives: Many of the decisions we make in our lives, the choices we make, directly or indirectly, are driven by a sense of beauty. These sessions were very valuable: By just going back to the experience, people can start to articulate what makes a beautiful day at work for them and see what could be changed to make those more likely to happen. It also makes people realize that not every day can be beautiful. But there should be enough beautiful days in the mix to recharge the batteries and feel inspired again. Nurturing this beauty is a gentle approach to self-care and care for others. The fact that it actually matters to the organization whether you have a beautiful day at work is also a positive and motivating point in itself.

Thinking back to my own portfolio of innovation projects, it is the ones that had a real closeness to the positive drivers of the participants that were the most stable, went the furthest, and had the most impact. This makes sense: The fact that they were really personally important to people in their own lifeworlds gave these projects an inherent strength and stability that other projects didn't have. The more of these positive drivers that can be built into an initiative, the better. This is one more reason to take the time to get to know people well, to learn what makes them tick. This could involve understanding people a bit better than they might understand themselves. Looking at people and relationships through this lens of deep intrinsic motivation opens up a much deeper level of understanding of what is actually happening for them, and this empowers us to act compassionately.

Beyond Optimism and Pessimism

After a lecture on the UN Sustainable Development Goals, and the difficulty of effecting systems change on a world scale, a student asked whether I considered myself an optimist or a pessimist. I realized that for me, neither position is very important. My family comes from the Bible belt in Zeeland, in the south of Holland. The driver that I was brought up with from an early age is *duty*. I have to do the best I can. From this perspective, optimism and pessimism both get in the way.

COLORS OF CHANGE

The next step in strategically shaping our interventions is understanding the dynamics of change itself. For this, we need to turn to the field of change management. Up to this point, we have more or less equated change with learning. The literature on theories of change shows that this is only partly true. To capture the dynamics (or lack thereof) of organizational change, Vermaak and de Caluwé have created a metamodel of change paradigms that sheds light on the challenges/forces at play when working with organizational structures and the various cultures around change that live there.[12] In the context of this book, we cannot do justice to the extensive body of literature on change management, or to this *colors of change* model.[13] This model came from practice, and there are many case studies that cover its application in various domains. It has also been extended beyond the core version we present here. To just skim the surface, we briefly explain what the various colors of change stand for.

De Caluwé and Vermaak take pains to stress that all these colors are valid and useful; one might posit that for an organization to be resilient, it probably would need elements of all of these. Each of these different colors of change comes with tools and strategies, and the authors place them within a general innovation framework that expresses their dynamic interrelationships over time. The attractiveness of this model lies in its comprehensiveness, and in the fact that it seamlessly works

YELLOW-PRINT CHANGE
Yellow-print thinking assumes that something only changes when key players are backing it and that little will happen if key players oppose it. In this view, enabling change require getting the powers that be behind it, whether their power is based on formal positions (e.g., board members) or informal influence (e.g., opinion leaders).

BLUE-PRINT CHANGE
In blue-print thinking, rationally—not power—matters most. The assumption is that change happens only when you first analyze what the problem is, suggest the best possible solution, and implement it according to plan. Change is thus deemed a linear endeavor: you think first before you act. The process is expert driven: the activities are executed by those who have the necessary know-how and experience.

RED-PRINT CHANGE
In red-print thinking the emphasis is not on power or rationality but on motivation. The key assumption is that change is not about policies and plans but about behavior, and that people change their behavior only when they are stimulated to do so. In its simplest form this comes down to barter: the organization hands out rewards and offers support in exchange for personnel taking on tasks and responsibilities and trying their best. It can also go beyond that by taking an interest in people's wellbeing and creating an inspiring working environment.

GREEN-PRINT CHANGE
In green-print thinking everything is about learning. Changing and learning are deemed inextricably linked: they are thought to mean almost the same. From a green point of view, however, motivational (red) strategies only work when people are already sufficiently aware and capable to do something differently. The only way forward from a green point of view is then to dig deeper: to discover one's limits and expand and deepen the way we see and act in the world. The process is characterized by setting up learning situations, preferably collective ones as these allow people to give and receive feedback as well to experiment with more effective ways of acting.

WHITE-PRINT CHANGE
White-print thinking can be regarded as a reaction to the previous colors, in the sense that these still tend to view change as a planned affair, albeit to a different extent. In contrast, white-print change agents view change as constant and taking place of its own accord. The key assumption is that people can make the most difference when they understand and catalyze a change that is about to happen. In white-print thinking, change agents do not create evolution, but they do support transitions or stand in their way. They embrace complexity as an enriching view of the world that allows one to see what the time is ripe for. They see self-organizing and dialogical processes as an effective way to deal with that complexity and they take an active part in their emergence. The outcome of such change is unpredictable.

across different scales: from macro—using these colors to characterize the dominant change strategy of a sector, organization, or unit—all the way to micro—providing insight, tools, and advice that can be used in workshops and one-on-one conversations. This is exactly what we need as deep change plays out on all levels simultaneously. Most of the models that are brought together in this book have this same Russian doll (a babushka, or matryoshka) quality.

We have found that the colors of change model is particularly useful in analyzing conversations. We sometimes send people on a "birdwatching tour" in their own organization, just observing meetings with this framework in mind. That is an amazingly insightful thing to be doing. Many misunderstandings and half-understandings can easily be led back to the fact that change means very different things to different people, and they show their perspective through the way they talk about change.

On reflection, the model also helps reflect on the role that creative practices can play for achieving change on and across these levels: They are not neutral but are closely aligned with the colors red (motivational), green (learning), and white (motion). This is exactly why design thinking and creative practice are so attractive to some people in hierarchical command-and-control organizations: Designerly approaches then hold the promise of moving away from the often dominant yellow (power) and blue (planning and control) styles of thinking, and they broaden the repertoire of practices for achieving change. The yellow and blue styles can be seen to represent a problem-solving paradigm, yet creative practices' concentration on learning comes with its own set of assumptions about the capability of the organization to support learning as a change strategy.[14] This is where such an approach to strategic change becomes quite vulnerable. When we take all five of these change strategies to be omnipresent in most organizations, then it is precisely the ones that people do not engage with that become blockers.

When Colors Clash

You have seen this in the Kings Cross example: The intervention from the New South Wales state government wielding its power (yellow) through the lockout laws (blue) is what held back the progress in the area for many years. It was only when the societal discussion moved away from polarization and toward a learning dialogue (green) that the results of the design intervention could become embedded in new ways of working and new strategies for the New South Wales Government. Only then could the intervention achieve a lasting strategic impact. Using the colors of change to reflect on the changes General McChrystal was seeking to execute, they clearly show a move away from yellow (power, hierarchy) and blue (planning, problem-solving), toward more of the red (empowering people), green (in learning cycles), and even white (embracing complexity and opportunity). In this book, you will see that this is a general movement. After all, we are dealing with open, complex, dynamic, and networked problems, and they do not sit well with the assumptions behind the yellow and blue approaches that all too often dominate organizations across many sectors.

The colors of change model is very much a living body of work. More colors have been added to the original five presented here, and many case studies have been published in which the colors have been applied, alone and in combination. We will further illustrate the dynamics of the colors of change in the coming case studies and in appendix 7. It is good to remind ourselves that these colors of change have deep roots: They touch the very logic that people use to reason with. In table 5.1, the thoughtful consultant and author André Schaminée compares different thinking styles that people use in change conversations. This is a telling comparison, showing the enormous potential for misunderstanding each other across these divides (for instance, a design thinker might table an inspiring example as evidence of the merit of a new direction, whereas the others wouldn't even recognize it as such; in their worlds, only rational explanation or evidence of support count).

EXCHANGING PRACTICES

These days, innovation often happens between disciplines, rather than within. The people that are valued and successful then are the ones that have deep knowledge of several professional fields and manage to combine them in new and interesting ways.

Table 5.1 A comparison of styles of thinking

	Cognitive: Knowledge and truth	Negotiation: Power	Design thinking: Learning
Source	Logic	Ideology	Emergence
Approach	Thinking (rationality)	Wanting (morality)	Feeling (empathy)
Core value	Objectivity	Intersubjectivity	Subjectivity
Basis for judgment	Evaluation	Argumentation	Aesthetics
Starting point	Definition of the problem	Conflict	Engagement
Relationship to subject	Distance	Influence	Taking part
Basis for authority	Explanation	Connection	Inspiration
Result	Knowledge	Agreement	New meaning and value

Source: André Schaminée, *Designing With and Within Public Organizations: Building Bridges Between Public Sector Innovators and Designers* (BIS Publishers, 2018), 61.

Replicating the Music Experience

A classic example can be found in the life and work of Amar G. Bose (1929–2013). As a young electrical engineering student at the Massachusetts Institute of Technology, he was so disappointed in the quality of the high-end sound system he bought (the sound quality was great, but it still didn't convey the feeling of being at a concert performance) that he went to the physics department and set out on a research path in acoustics. That led him to the realization that 80 percent of the sound you hear in a concert hall is actually indirect, reflected off the walls and ceiling (and fellow listeners). His acoustics research, in which he sought to model this principle, sparked both a radically new paradigm for acoustics and the development of sound systems to replicate this effect. He founded the highly successful company that bears his name.

How can we innovate between disciplines? On reflection, there are basically three different patterns of combining practices from different fields (see figure 5.2).

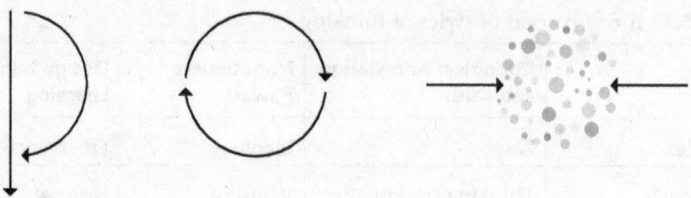

Figure 5.2 The three modes of relating between disciplines.

(1) One field is dominant, and the other is used to help. (2) The fields are combined in a learning loop, and the practitioner(s) alternate between them, like in multidisciplinary teams (this is known under various names, like *concurrent engineering, team science*, etc.). In such combined processes, difficulties might arise through interface issues, especially the communication across the languages of various disciplines. Often, this requires people that can act as translators, bridge-builders between the disciplines. Key to these modes of combining practices is that the disciplinary fields themselves don't have to change. True transdisciplinarity comes about when (3) practices from various fields are combined. This combination of (partial) practices from different fields can lead to the emergence of completely new practices and perhaps, in due course, new disciplines.

Interface to Interaction

One case in which a new discipline emerged from the combining of practices from various disciplines is the advent of interaction design in the late 1980s to early 1990s. At that moment in time, computers were moving closer to consumers ("home computers"), helped by a new generation of graphic interfaces. The internet was possible, and one could think about it, but it was as yet unformed. These exciting developments were spawning a new breed of specialist "interface designers," growing out of the graphic design discipline. This early work in interface design tended to be functionally oriented, geared toward supporting fairly simple on-screen interactions (buttons on screens). In addition, there was more fundamental thinking about the architecture behind the interface (e.g., the desktop metaphor). Visionary thinkers/designers Bill Verplank and Bill Moggridge, working from Xerox PARC and IDEO, realized that this was not going to be enough in the future: The complex interactions *themselves* needed to be designed before the interfaces could be created to support that interaction. This is a huge conceptual leap, putting the interaction at center stage as a new object of design. But how was this going to work? How does one design something as invisible as an interaction? What knowledge needs to be drawn together to do this well? What is *quality* in interaction? How can this be taught? (And to whom should this be taught?) One of the first places where the challenge of creating a curriculum for interaction design was picked up was at the Utrecht School of the Arts in the Netherlands, in a close collaboration with Center for Knowledge Technology at Utrecht University. Designers, researchers in cognitive artificial intelligence, methodologists, artists, futurologists, and visionaries came together in a conceptually strong team under the leadership of Dick Rijken[15] and basically spawned a new discipline.

As the problems of the world have become transdisciplinary—they don't hold to the disciplinary silos anymore—the response to them will need to become transdisciplinary too. This creates a transdisciplinary space, the freedom to branch out and learn from many disciplines that might have principles, methods, and actions that could be adopted into or adapted for the problem arena. In this, we are not so much interested in "mixing disciplines" (after all, they have defined themselves as separate) but in making sure there is a free flow of practices between them. This works because every discipline will have practices for observation, creating newness, judging quality, dealing with complexity, and so on. If we can make these practices concrete and clear enough, they can travel between these disciplines, breaking down the disciplinary boundaries.[16]

Exchanging Disciplinary Practices

To illustrate this, at some point in the development of this transdisciplinary educational program (see appendix 6), a staff member with a background in design came to discuss the exchange of practices with people from the faculty of law. The law representatives were interested in some practices from design: They framed their question by explaining that currently, law is almost always "too late"; that is, when a new technical development emerges, the law profession only starts focusing on its issues once the first case is brought before the court. These court cases tend to take a long time (because there is no clear precedent), they tend to be expensive, and in this way the judicial system inadvertently holds up innovation. Yet creative disciplines have sophisticated practices for looking ahead (scenario methods, technology roadmaps, forecasting/backcasting, etc.). The law people took these practices on board as they created a "future law center."

Conversely, the design representative sought to learn how the law field deals with precedent: Court cases are kept and archived as situated knowledge, so that when the need arises, the earlier judgment can be retrieved, and the old context in which it arose can be compared with the current one before the court. A subtle language game has been built up to accompany this interpretation step. This is in marked contrast to the field of design, which has no systematic way of dealing with memory at all: When designing for a current challenge, one might be trying to use an earlier design instance for inspiration, but there is no way for the designer to identify the most appropriate earlier design and access the contextual information needed to understand it. Thus the field of design has a lot to learn from law—not by adopting its practices (it would be hard to build up a repository of precedents), but by adapting them to fit within the field on a methods level, or perhaps on the level of principles: looking at creative practice not from a perspective of the cult of newness, but as always building on earlier work—agreeing with the philosopher Julia Kristeva, when she says that all writing is quoting.[17]

The paradigm that sits behind a discipline gives it a coherence that creates an identity for a community of practitioners. This identity is anchored and reinforced in education, where the next generation is schooled to be much like previous ones. Disciplines hold on to a specific definition of quality, of what is good. This is expressed in many ways—from professional codes of conduct to the valuing of best practices. In one of the case studies in the next chapter (§ 6.2), you will see how this can play out quite dramatically: Farmers that transition from a large-scale (industrial) farming method to becoming more eco-friendly reported being ostracized in their community ("nobody wants to sit at my table at the farmer's association meeting; my kids don't get playdates in the village anymore"). They are seen as "traitors" to the prevalent farming practices and a threat to the definition of mastery and the pride associated with that. We tend to see disciplines as stable entities, almost as things in themselves. Yet history shows us that they change all the time through a steady evolution that is perhaps imperceptible to the practitioner (although ask a practitioner to look back at their first-year textbooks from when they started their study; it is bizarre how old-fashioned they are). As shown in the interaction design example, if the circumstances so demand, disciplines can also experience conceptual shifts and go through bursts of very quick change.

Death of the Architect

Take architecture, for example. In the Europe of the Middle Ages, there were no architects; buildings were created by master masons. These artisans were organized in secretive guilds that held the technical knowledge of how to build a sound structure. Buildings were effectively designed, measured out, and made on the spot without drawings; the compass and square were five-foot-long master mason's tools to measure out the building on site. Then, in Renaissance Italy, some young professionals calling themselves *architects* started to make drawings of building designs, using mini versions of the compass and square. This revolutionized the process of the design of a building, allowing for more discussion. Understandably, the clients were drawn to this new way of working, and the master masons were effectively sidelined (eventually, they ritualized their secret knowledge and became the society of Freemasons, still using the compass and square in their emblem). Meanwhile, architects worked directly with influential clients, creating buildings that were the prime expressions of power in their time. They became very powerful in their own right. Fast-forward a couple hundred years to the present day, and for most architects, most of that power and influence has evaporated (with some noted exceptions). These days, one of the ways we create our built environment is through property developers, who hire a project manager to manage the building process, including the contract with the architect. Or buildings are commissioned under a design and build contract, in which case a construction company hires a project leader who hires an architect. The architect doesn't have any direct contact with the client anymore, and the role of the architect is diminished to that of the "creative" in the overall building process. What this brings home is that a profession consists of the *role* its practitioners take in a larger process, and from that comes the *position* they hold relative to other professionals. This position has to be based on a *uniqueness*, either knowledge or a set of core skills that others do not have. The strength of this position pivots around the profession's *power base*, which is very much determined by the ability to influence decision-making. Especially within these large projects, many disciplines have to come together and work together (where in some phases, one discipline may have the initiative, and others be more passively involved). At the same time, these disciplines are in fierce competition with one another and have no qualms about elbowing others out of the way. As mentioned, the architect's influence has eroded over time; only being there as the creative in the larger process of building is very shaky as a business model. Architects are seeking to regain influence in many ways; Frank Gehry Architects, for instance, known for the design of organic, wavy buildings, has developed its own software (Catia, based on aeronautical software), which gives the firm a leading role in detailing the construction and construction process. This extends the span of control over large swathes of the building project.

Looking at the incredible richness of practices in all the sectors and disciplines at our disposal, you get the sense that we probably have everything we need to address the big challenges of our time. We have all the practices we need, but not in the right places. We have to become more fluid in exchanging practices, becoming truly transdisciplinary (see appendix 6).

BRINGING OTHERS ALONG

The reason to focus on changing minds here is that when we reframe, we need to get others to come along—in a way that is active in their minds, not passive: We want them to adopt new practices as their own and act upon them. Just explaining a new practice is not enough because only understanding a new practice is not enough for action. How can we help people to really absorb a practice as their own so that they are able to work with(in) it?

Frame Communication

An example of how this can be done comes from a study at Stanford University of the collaboration patterns used by professional design teams.[18] Teams would be invited into a studio to work on a challenge under the watchful eye of multiple cameras. One of the best, most experienced teams worked like a very well-oiled machine: smooth collaboration, almost unspoken division of tasks, great at anticipating what the others were going to do, and so on. They were speaking in very short sentences and needed only the hint of a hint to understand the others and where the team was heading. Over the years, they clearly had developed their own team shorthand. But then, halfway through the concept design phase, one of the members had an idea for how to "see" the challenge and create a new way forward—a frame. In the transcript, you can suddenly see him going from monosyllables to half a page of very vague sentences, full of detours and unfinished suggestions. He was clearly leading his teammates along, not mentioning the frame explicitly but letting his teammates get to the frame idea themselves, encouraging them in the right direction and reaffirming their thoughts when it started to dawn on them: "Good idea," "Oh yes, do you think so?" What he is *not* doing is trying to convince them of his bright idea. That would have been pointless.

In psychology, this technique is called *priming*: gradually activating what needs to be "top of mind" as a context for a new message to land and be considered meaningful. This may feel indirect and vague, but it isn't; it is a necessary, subtle rewiring of the brain. If we don't do this, nothing will change in practice. This is in stark contrast with *rhetoric*, the art of persuasion by reasoning. Unfortunately, rhetoric has a bad name as it gets associated with the art of overpowering people by tricks (using fallacies, straw man arguments, etc.[19]). Rhetoric then is more about "winning the discussion," and it won't do anything to achieve the active adoption of a different way of thinking. The more subtle forms of rhetoric aim for true persuasion through informed and respectful discussion.[20] Yet they often seem to assume that people can be swayed by an appeal to rationality and will change their practices based on a new understanding that comes from a rigorous discussion.[21] You will see later (in chapter 8) that the deep paradigmatic shifts we are focusing on here require an emphasis on *dialogue* rather than discussion.[22]

5.4 CASE: SECTOR TRANSFORMATION

When we first introduced the game changers process (§ 4.1), it was portrayed as starting from the bottom up, with a reframe that is simply too big for the current paradigm, too different, so that it forces an organization to go deeper and find ways to deal with the more fundamental shifts needed to put it into practice. You have also seen that top-down change in organizations happens in reaction to a change in the field, the organization's perceived environment. This is where the paradigm sits in the form of the dominant narratives (including paradigmatic examples), the "normal" practices of the key disciplines in a sector, and the infrastructure that was built to support the current modus operandi. These two movements, bottom up and top down, are each complex enough on their own. Combining them in the deliberate creation of sector transformation requires outstanding strategic leadership.

Designing Out Crime and the Criminal Justice System

In Australia, the New South Wales government's Department of Justice, the city police, and the attorney general established the Designing Out Crime (DOC) Research Center together with the University of Technology Sydney (operational 2008–2022).

The center's remit was to use design practices to revolutionize how we achieve safety and security in society. Prevalent problem-solving strategies in the area of safety and security are focused on the creation of countermeasures, through erecting defenses (putting up fences), introducing CCTV camera systems, and using strong-arm tactics to force people's behavior away from unwanted, illegal, or otherwise unfortunate patterns. These principles generally make sense, but as is often the case with conventional problem-solving, they suffer from the twin sins of oversimplification and overgeneralization. Central to the DOC approach is the pledge to avoid the creation of countermeasures to crime, as these countermeasures create a climate of weariness and fear that destroys the social fabric of our public spaces and our society. In its projects, DOC carefully avoids this pitfall, seeing crime as a symptom of things that go wrong in society and taking aim at "upstream" causes. This requires a reframing, right from the start. The initial briefs or questions formulated by the project partners are often a direct result of their earlier problem-solving attempts, and these questions are almost always aimed at symptoms, rather than core problems. Reframing these questions very broadly is the key to achieving innovative solutions.

The DOC body of work was supported by the assistant attorney general at the time, Brendan Thomas, as part of his mission to reform the criminal justice system—working closely with people throughout the organization and providing top-down support. The DOC projects not only created new approaches to problems in society ("out there") but also, internally, served as exemplars of what is possible when issues are reframed.[23]

Intensive Learning Centers: Learning Inside the Box

Prisons in New South Wales are home to some of the community's most disadvantaged people. Often these people have experienced great trauma in early life, which in turn exacerbates their disadvantage by interrupting their education. Poor educational outcomes then limit opportunities for entering the workforce and having stable living arrangements. All these *criminogenic* factors add up to a relatively small number of adult males who are responsible for a disproportionate level crime in New South Wales.[24]

In attempting to break this cycle of crime, the New South Wales Department of Justice has a number of programs aimed at reducing these risk factors. One such program is the Intensive Learning Centers program within Corrective Services ("prisons"). Corrective Services New South Wales engaged the DOC team to design an education space for prisoners with poor literacy and numeracy. The broader program had been in operation for several years, but the prisons that housed the participating prisoners did not have purpose-built educational facilities. In this environment, the program was struggling, and graduation rates were very low.

The designers worked with prisoners, educators, and prison staff in a co-design approach, which identified that the key value to be achieved through the program was "connection." The ability to reconnect with community was the central motivation for prisoners to engage in the literacy and numeracy program. Contemporary correctional practices were at risk of losing sight of this,[25] and therefore were at risk of unwittingly designing out key opportunities for rehabilitation. Although the involvement of the DOC staff initially focused on designing the Intensive Learning Center as a physical space, they found opportunities to design at a systems level, designing interventions along the whole prisoner journey. The Intensive Learning Center was then seen as the beginning of a rehabilitation journey, a pathway to develop literacy skills, trade skills, qualifications, and work experience that would help prisoners' transition back into the community, creating a journey that would make it much less likely to end with reoffending. This single project turned into a multiyear program that is a collaborative journey of discovery and co-creation among designers, inmates, the prison authorities, and many other parties in society. The first Intensive Learning Center was built and installed within a prison. An architectural evaluation found that participants, educators and security staff all found it to be a positive space for learning,[26] and participants were achieving far greater results in the program than participants in other locations. The program is having broader impact within NSW Corrective Services beyond the initial Intensive Learning Center project. The approach has been applied to the design and construction processes of residential housing, including furniture manufacturing within Corrective Services,[27] and other parts of the justice system: The approach has been considered as evidence in two Royal Commissions and has been adopted by the Red Cross as part of its international design guide for prisons.[28]

Supporting Victims of Crime
Criminal justice systems have evolved over centuries and are inherently offender focused. This focus on offenders is understandable, but it can be detrimental to victims of crime, who can feel like they are forgotten. With a transformation agenda, the New South Wales Department of Justice commissioned DOC to work with them to reimagine the criminal justice system from the perspective of victims.

Over a series of months, the design team developed a workshop that convened representatives from various parts of the criminal justice system, as well as victims' advocacy groups.[29] A simple and elegant reframing emerged from this process, which gave the design team a platform to develop a suite of interventions. The reframe was simply this: Instead of looking at it as a *criminal justice system*, what if we look at it as a *justice system*? Interventions to improve the experience at court, the development of new restorative justice options, immediate help to support recovery, and capability building within the sector were among the approaches that emerged from the work. This body of work provided the department with a change agenda that was gradually implemented in the following years.

The approach to structurally shifting the criminal justice system was two-pronged: The first entry point to change was the effect of the criminal justice system in the lifeworlds of people. The criminal justice system is set up as a system of opposing forces: police, judiciary, and attorney general (the prosecutors). This is done on purpose, as balanced judgement and justice is sought through dialectic;

the confrontations among these forces create checks and balances. But this results in a very harrowing, confusing, and stressful journey for both the accused and the victims of crime—which in itself causes its own injustices. The department was seeking to find ways to connect the dots around the experiences of people and to create better service delivery overall. Second, there is an urgent need to bring down levels of reoffending by people released from prison. Again, the issue was refocused from prison as a punishment regime (with security as the overriding concern) to looking at the prison journey, ensuring that people have a different life to go to so that they do not fall back into their old lives upon release. This led to projects like the Intensive Learning Centers (discussed earlier) and the use of techniques like narrative therapy[30] to help people change their life stories.

In all, the DOC project portfolio has grown to hundreds of interventions, big and small. They have helped convene a broad array of stakeholders. Many of the project results have been implemented, creating real-life impact and showing everybody involved how the field of criminal justice can be shifted toward practices that better serve society. Over the years of reframing projects, the attention of the DOC center has shifted from more or less reactive approaches (after all, even going upstream to root causes of crime is still a reaction to crime, not true prevention), to a focus on creating communities that are robust in the face of their challenges (see § 6.5). The problems of crime are societal problems, they cannot be dealt with exclusively by the criminal justice system. The focus on building a core inner strength in our communities requires the involvement of a new network of organizations from right across society, and new strategies to be co-developed with all of them (see § 7.2).

In a recent interview,[31] Brendan Thomas provided insights into the strategies and shifts that occurred internally at the Department of Justice. The quotes that follow have been sorted according to the colors of change to give an idea of the different theories of change used and the lessons that can be learned. The starting point for this change, the existing criminal justice system organizations, is extremely yellow (formal/positional power and hierarchy) and blue (planning and control, and evidence based to the point at which only strategies that can be measured can be rolled out). To shift this, Thomas subtly combines change strategies.

Yellow and red. Thomas describes the use of power to support people on the front line to achieve change:

I've really come to learn what matters is the power of top creating authorizing environment . . . the people who deliver, the frontline staff who were delivering service or the frontline staff that have to manage change. I think often in management we disregard that and we think about powerful people and middle managers and it is certainly important thing, but if those people on the frontline don't understand it (and) can't have any control over it, feel like something is being done to them (it) almost never works." . . . I think anyone in a leadership position that wants to get people motivated must really focus on that. . . . I want to achieve in my role, but also then empowering others to have the ability to achieving their goals is fundamentally important. And so I'd really see myself as setting a strategic direction that works but making sure that the environment in which we're trying to achieve that direction is properly set. . . . I need to make sure people probably kept up to date with what's going on to know that we're actually achieving what we want to do.

Blue and white. Thomas is fairly skeptical of the dominant planning and control paradigm to deliver good outcomes, while at the same time responding to the dynamics of the day (say, rising crime statistics in an area) in a way that serves the overall goal of creating a justice system that better serves society:

They (prisoners) be coming out the other end and the reoffending is really high, might be coming back in and costing system so much more. . . . Imagine assistance what sorts that out completely. The outcome (would) be a reduction in risks of driving someone into the criminal justice system in the first place. But how do you measure that?" . . . You start with the best planning, the best scoping, the best intention there's a whole bunch of things that happen that you never anticipated are going to happen. There's a whole bunch of things you plan for the never eventuate and there's a whole bunch of things that just turn up out of the blue, that you need to deal with. Or something that you make, that (you realize it is) just plain wrong . . . you create a really strong authorizing environment (to) allow for failure . . . and we expect things to change and we expect that some things are not going to work and that's OK. We constantly iterate.

Green. Experiment and learn:

We've been testing a whole bunch of different service methods and last year we did 8 trials, provide the same service in eight different ways. I've got the guys who are involved in those eight pilots together . . . really understanding what we have learned from that, and how we can apply that. Again being really focused on what you're trying to change—and if something is not working to achieve that, shut it down. Be open and upfront, we know not everything is going to go right.

5.5 REFLECTION

SIMULTANEOUS CHESS

In this chapter, we considered the workings of paradigmatic change, from "changing minds" on a personal level to sector transformation. In covering so much territory, the chapter cannot provide more than a quick run-through of many different perspectives, models, and practices. This list is by no means complete. We have selected only some aspects or models of change that the practitioners we have worked with over the last ten years have found most useful; there are many more, enough for a book in itself. Which ones are going to be most useful to the practitioner really depends on the situation he/she is seeking to address. This comes with a warning, though: Although we may choose a preferred model, approach, or practice for setting the change in motion, we cannot choose the perspective of others in the situation. This is a bit like a chess grandmaster walking from chessboard to chessboard, playing simultaneous chess against multiple opponents. But in contrast to simultaneous chess, every action, every pawn we move on one board, shifts a pawn on all of the other chessboards too. For example, with the best of intentions, we might start creating a learning environment to help people understand possible new practices (a red and green intervention). But somebody in the organization might read that as a deliberate move to undermine their position (yellow), and they will resist. So every move we make on the chessboard of learning also shifts the pawn on the chessboard of power, even if we don't want it to. This is true across all approaches.

ORGANIZATIONS AND THE FIELD

The challenges that we encounter in the world often surface in the context of organizations—for example, the failure of organizational problem-solving, or the difficulty of achieving organizational change. But to properly address these challenges, we need to look at where their thinking comes from and where their practices originate. Deep change on an organizational level requires a redefinition of the surrounding field, the narrative in the sector and core disciplines involved. Changing the field narrative of a sector is not a single intervention: It requires reinvention on many different levels. These include changing the "core disciplines" that carry the way things are done in a certain sector. In his book *Swimming with Sharks*, the anthropologist and journalist Luyendijk[32] gives a close and pretty shocking insider portrait of the amoral world of investment banking in the wake of the 2008 Global Financial Crisis. He concludes that nothing much has changed since then and that the near meltdown of the global financial system could just happen again. Through interviews and reflection, he shows how the professional mores (the "normal") of investment banking hold the sector in place. For real change to occur, this whole system needs to shift—in this case, probably through the pressure of top-down regulation. The impetus for systems change can also be sparked by bottom-up development, as a result from the shifting of professional practices or the introduction of new technologies. For example, going back to defense: The core discipline in the field of the air force is that of the pilot. The pilots are the heroes of the organization, and everything revolves around their training, battle-readiness, and so on. They are also the cultural center of the organization and the picture-perfect drawcard for getting young people interested in joining. Yet drones and other unmanned, remote-controlled craft will be taking over their tasks in the near future. This has huge repercussions for what the air force of the future can be and how it sees itself. The narrative will shift.

CHANGE SITS IN THE MIDDLE

Bottom-up and top-down interventions need to be synchronized, and their impact needs to be based on a close understanding of the middle layers of the organizations involved. As noted, the middle layers are where the new practices have to take root and where transformation actually happens. Labs and other innovation playgrounds have a role in exploring ideas and possible futures,[33] but their separation from the organization creates a barrier to impact this middle core of the organization. The same is true for the top-down approach: Just being visionary and setting the agenda for change is never going to be enough to really change practices. In the end, change needs to live and grow from within the core of the organization. (This requires special care when working with consultants; a purely transactional relationship does not lead to this type of deep, meaningful transformation.[34])

THIS IS ABOUT THE NORMAL, NOT ABOUT INNOVATION

The ability to question one's own practices, one's own "normal," and to pick up, adapt, and adopt practices from other fields is what we call *creative intelligence*. We will need to become transdisciplinary, as the issues we are facing don't keep to single disciplines anymore (if they ever did). One can't help but be inspired by the richness of practices we have at our disposal. Practices, tools, and methods from the creative disciplines are particularly useful for this purpose as they address the open, complex, dynamic, and networked challenges in an open way. This point was also made by Nobel Prize in Economics laureate Henri Mintzberg, in commenting on the developments in this field of management.[35] He laments that business schools are focused on analytical research, and in analytical research, you only find out what worked in the past. In a rapidly changing world, this is hardly a good predictor for the future. [He remarks that you can drive your car at high speeds while only looking in the rear-view mirror, but you have to hope that the road is straight.] These days, the road is never straight. Mintzberg proposes that what business schools should be doing instead is *design research*, by which he means research that is inherently forward-looking because it aims to be curative, aims to make the world better. He names the medical sector as a prime example. This analogy is interesting as there are many different kinds of medical research and medical knowledge, ranging from fundamental research and very specialized knowledge in medical faculties to the very practical and hands-on expertise of your local doctor. The academic hospital is a place where practice and theory come together, where hands-on patient care, thoughtful reflective practice, and applied and fundamental research come together under one roof—and where they can learn from one another. A sector-based approach to deep change like the DOC center pieces together a similar infrastructure. You will see in chapter 7 that in a sense, every sector needs its own "academic hospitals."

6

SOCIETY IN TRANSITION

The good news is, we don't have to get into endless discussions about this.
   We have no choice.
—Bert Mulder (1952–2020)[1]

6.1 TRANSITIONS

The one thing we know for sure is that things are not going to be like they were. We are going to go through enormous transitions in the coming years. Overwhelming changes are coming to how we deal with resources like energy and water and how we approach care, mobility, education, and prosperity. Each of these transitions is monumental in itself—and they are going to happen simultaneously, in parallel. Conventionally, technological and economic development thinking would lead these kinds of change processes, and people's lives and society would be left to deal with the (often dire) consequences. But is vital to get the social dimension right. If we are not careful, the same people as always will be left behind in these separate transitions. For example, it is good to save on your electricity bill by putting solar panels on your roof, but what if it is not your roof? Other fossil-fuel based ways of heating your house are going to become more expensive, and when it gets more and more expensive to be poor, this creates a very deep rift in society. Inclusivity is not a luxury; it is centrally important to avoid resentment and conflict. The shocking images of a city society in free fall after the big car manufactures left Detroit are fresh in many people's minds (and this has happened time and time again[2]). The challenges before us are so radical, systemic, and deep that these ecological, economic, societal, and individual developments need to be considered in parallel—and societal transformation should inform and guide the technical and economic change, rather than the other way around.

The shaping of transitions is the great challenge of our time.

UNDERSTANDING TRANSITIONS

But what is a transition? In the words of the Dutch Research Institute for Transitions (DRIFT), a leading authority on sustainability-driven transitions: *"A transition is defined as a process of fundamental and irreversible change in a society's culture, (institutional) structures and practices . . .* characterized by the emergence of new structures, cultures and practices. . . . Examples of (possible) transitions are: from coal energy supply to gas energy supply, from a linear to a circular economy, or a transition from bureaucratic health care to human-centered care."[3] The dynamics of transitions are often characterized in what has become known as the X-curve model (see figure 6.1). The old regime seeks to optimize its current modus operandi. Changes in the environment will start to destabilize this deceptive equilibrium. In times of destabilization of the old regime, new ways of working also emerge, which then become the harbingers of a new regime. At a threshold moment, the old regime will start to unravel and move to being phased out. The new regime will take over and start its own process of institutionalization and stabilizing, becoming the old regime of the

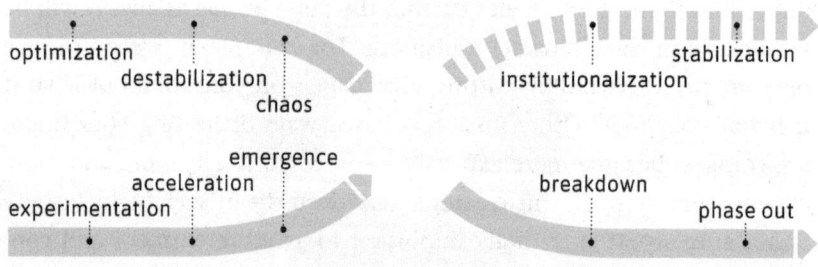

Figure 6.1 The X-curve model of transitions. *Source:* Based on Derk Loorbach, "Transition Management for Sustainable Development: A Prescriptive, Complexity-Based Governance Framework," *Governance* 23, no. 1 (2010): 161–183.

future (see also § 2.2). The field of transition management uses complexity theory, social theories, and insights from the field of governance to understand the dynamics of such processes.[4] This brief introduction will cover only one model, which is just a small sample of the rich transition management literature—and the practices it leads to.[5]

A key question is why we need to talk about this at all: Why don't transitions just happen, when the need to transition is abundantly clear? Why do institutions and organizations full of clever professionals not just move with the times? What makes this hard? Which structures and practices get in the way? To start with the latter, transition management discerns two main types of challenges: blockers within the existing system, and the difficulty of organizing around the common good.

THE CHALLENGE OF REGIME CHANGE

The current way of working, or *regime*, has an inherent coherence and stability as it combines deeply rooted cultural aspects (images/values/paradigm), structures (institutional/economical /physical), and practices (routine/rules/behavior) in an integrated whole. It undoubtedly has been successfully doing so, possibly for many years. Changing the regime means disturbing all of these certainties for an unknown future.

THE CHALLENGE OF DISCIPLINARY STABILITY

Within organizations, professionals use practices that are part of their disciplines; in Kuhn's terms, they operate from the disciplinary matrix. These disciplines have been around, they have arisen and developed within a certain era and environment, and hence they come with their own (historical) baggage.[6] This includes assumptions hidden behind a guise of normality that have therefore become hard to question. Questioning them would also mean questioning the definition of quality that is implied in the disciplinary matrix. Then people can feel attacked and become very defensive ("Am I not doing my work right?"), ferociously protecting their current practice against interference (see the case study in the next section). In the last chapter, you saw that disciplines do develop and go through deep changes over time, but this is often a gradual process that is imperceptible to daily practitioners. To them, disciplines create a false sense of stability and security and thus become a blocker to change.

THE CHALLENGE OF CAPABILITY

But what if there is a will to change, but a lack of capability to change? Transition science lists four ways in which we can lead ourselves astray and limit our organizations' capability for real change:[7]

1. **The implementation-illusion.** We rationally discuss the issues and make plans, in the illusion that somebody will actually implement them—and nothing happens, while the discussion is stuck in abstractions and analysis.
2. **The responsibility gap.** Risk aversion leads to a modus operandi in which only small steps are possible. The responsibility is spread very thinly in the organization, so nobody is centrally responsible for a big ambition (the "empty cockpit"[8]).
3. **The innovation funnel.** Innovation is attractive: always focusing on creating something new, often using shiny new technology, while being blind to the innovations that are already happening—and blind to the fact that in creating the new practices, there is a disturbance of the status quo (What will have to be stopped?).
4. **A lack of imagination.** People are not always able to imagine that things will be very different in the future. The fallback assumption is that tomorrow will be much like today, and any change will be gradual. Research has shown that because in our daily lives we are mostly dealing with changes that are linear in nature, people have difficulty picturing exponential growth and imagining sudden "tipping point" shifts.

THE CHALLENGE OF MISDIAGNOSIS

Another way in which organizations might get off on the wrong foot is through misdiagnosis of a problem situation: underestimating what is at play and therefore starting out with the wrong methods and practices. There is a fundamental difference between the practices, methods, and tools needed for optimization, transformation, and transitions.[9] An example will help explain the difference between these three levels of change. In transport, the change to electric cars is an *optimization* (making the existing mode of transport "better").[10] A move to self-driving vehicles revolutionizes their use, and the role of transport in our lives. This a *transformation*, making transport really "different" (e.g., there is no reason for self-driving cars to park near your home, or to be individually owned; and not having to drive means that the time spent in transit is opened up for other activities. Also, by driving closer to one another, self-driving cars take up much less space, reducing the footprint of transport infrastructure). But then, this becomes a true *transition* when we combine the new opportunities sparked by self-driving cars with transformations in other societal domains to radically change the way we plan and build our cities: For instance, what opportunities does the opening up of space that used to be dedicated to transport infrastructure bring for renewable energy, biodiversity, and agriculture within the city landscape?

THE CHALLENGE OF OWNERSHIP

A key feature of a transition is a lack of ownership: There is no single stakeholder that is dominant in such a complex problem space (in the preceding example, "Who owns a city?"). Transitions are therefore, almost by definition, nobody's problem. They easily fall between the cracks of our organizations and are not furthered because there is no centralized locus and sense of responsibility.

What doesn't help is that transition challenges are often phrased in quite abstract terms and involve long timelines, removing them far from our normal action repertoire. Hence they cannot be approached directly: We need to muster the meaningful transformations that we *can* create (on the level of sectors and societal domains, where we do have agency) and bring these together in an innovation ecosystem to achieve transitions (see § 7.4).

6.2 SYSTEM IN CRISIS

This is not a distant future that we need to start thinking about; great changes are already underway. Crises are happening that cannot be patched within the current systems. As you will see shortly, they may have been exacerbated by earlier patching. It is not by accident that the next case study comes from the Netherlands; in such a small, densely populated country, problems tend to come to the fore earlier than in other places (nothing can be hidden for very long). As far as transitions go, the Netherlands serves as the proverbial canary in the coal mine. The crisis we will be discussing is one that almost every country will have to deal with, sooner or later, but that already surfaced in the Netherlands in 2019. To explore and explain the nature of transitions in practice, let's turn to the case study of the nitrogen crisis.

Case Study: The Nitrogen Crisis

In the late 2010s, the Dutch government was involved in a lengthy court battle about nitrogen pollution. The Netherlands is a signatory to the Paris Climate Agreement, and the lawyers from an activist NGO took the state to court over failing to protect designated nature reserves (designated as such under the European Habitat Guidelines) from nitrogen pollution. Nitrogen oxide emissions mostly come from transport, building works, and agriculture (about 45 percent). The problem is that nitrogen acts as a powerful fertilizer, dramatically altering the soil and thereby also the flora and fauna in these nature reserves—which, the lawyers argued, is not allowed. In the end, the protracted legal process came before the country's high court, and in March 2019 the court ruled in favor of the NGO, rendering the government in breach of the law. This ruling came into force immediately, and had huge repercussions all through society: (1) To reduce the emissions from transport, the Dutch government reduced the maximum speed on the highways from 130 to 100 km/h. (2) About eighteen thousand ongoing building works (which happened to be close to the nature reserves) were ruled in breach of regulations, so all of their earlier permissions were voided. They had to be stopped, immediately. (3) The ruling impacted agriculture more than any other sector; many farms would now have to radically change their practices to cut their nitrogen emissions. Farmers were up in arms and marched to The Hague to protest in front of the Dutch parliament—and they came on thousands of tractors, effectively blocking traffic in the whole country for days, week after week.[11]

The Dutch ministry that was at the center of this crisis, the Department of Agriculture, Nature, and Food Safety (LNV), enlisted André Schaminée and his team from the consultancy TwynstraGudde to look into this matter. Their approach to both understanding the problem situation and creating proposals for ways forward was largely based on the frame creation methodology.[12] They started out by doing about sixty interviews with various stakeholders from across the problem arena. This led to the identification of four main paradoxes: (1) It is a zero-sum game; (2) it is not clear who we are listening to; (3) the farmers are the victim of government policy failures; and (4) the value models and value discussion are not sufficient. (There were more paradoxes, but these four cover the problem arena well enough for the purposes of this book.) Let's look at these in more detail.

1. It Is a Zero-Sum Game

The discussion is stuck in an either-or-pattern (a piece of land is either nature or agriculture); there is only conflict, and no room for dialogue. This lack of a basis for dialogue is exacerbated by the fact that nature and agriculture both have their own value and meaning, but they are of very different kinds. For instance, one of the solutions that could result in short-term improvement of the situation would be to reduce livestock by buying out *peak emitters*, farms that are positioned very close to nature areas. But that calls into question the deep values underlying the very successful intense farming paradigm that has been advocated for and valued in the Netherlands since the Second World War. And on the level of the lifeworld of the farmer, this would probably be the end of a family tradition of generations (in a densely populated country, there is very little opportunity to relocate a farm). Another possible solution lies in transitioning to a new type of nature-inclusive agriculture. This is a valid—but slower—way to reduce nitrogen emissions. In the lifeworld of the farmer, this is not a small step either; adopting such a different paradigm requires new practices and a reconsidering of deeply held values (what it is to be a "good" farmer). It is much easier for both parties to stick to their positions and not move.

2. It Is Not Clear Who We Are Listening To

There is a suggestion that the farmers are united, as they have organized themselves in cooperatives. But it is not clear whether these cooperatives have the same interests as the individual farmers. Some of these organizations represent the farmer in government committees. But do they represent "the farmer"? The farmers who grow fruit and vegetables are not affected by the court ruling; the nitrogen emissions come from high-intensity cattle farms. It is clear that there is tension there: The standpoints of the farmer associations are not always consistent across these discussions. At the moment, this leads to extreme standpoints and political posturing by these associations to reassure their members that they are fighting the good fight. Yet the crisis at hand will only be resolved when all parties are ready to offer considerable compromises. This is not going to be easy: The more combative arm of the farmers movement is financially supported by the industries that have vested interests in the continuation of the current system, like feedstock companies. Who, then, are we listening to? And what is true? In the public debate, the farmer's movement appeals to the cultural significance of farming: Picture small, thatched farm buildings tucked away in a beautiful landscape with hedges and languid streams, the spire of the village church just visible in the distance. Yet the reality of high-yield industrial farming is very, very different (if the bucolic smallholder agricultural landscape still existed, there would be no problem). The farmer's slogan of "no farmers, no food" also sounds a bit hollow because the vast majority of the food produced in the Netherlands is exported.

3. The Farmers Are the Victims of Government Policy Failures

Although the farmers blame "the Greens" for the nitrogen crisis (despite the Green Party never having been in government), the more farmer-friendly political parties whose policies over the years have actually led to this crisis are not widely questioned. The sector complains about going from crisis to crisis, but there is very little appetite to look forward, to the next problems that are going to come to the agricultural sector (drought, water management, nitrate pollution). Some parties—like feedstock companies and, to a degree, supermarkets—see no incentive for change. These same parties also act as consultants to the farmers, and the narratives they push are reinforced by the professional media in the agricultural sector. Farmers that could be willing to reduce their livestock feel they are not heard—and based on earlier experience, they feel uncertain and threatened by the inconsistent nature of government policies over the years. Trust in government is low across the board.

4. The Value Models and Value Discussion Are Not Sufficient

A change in agricultural practices is the only viable option, but there is no clear path of action for the farmer; economically, this could only work if there is a structurally higher price level for high-quality food. The nitrogen problem is framed as a Dutch issue, while food prices are often determined on a European and global level. Because there is no economic value to nature, the only thing that is counted in economic terms is a loss of value to farming, not what everybody would gain from biodiversity in a more natural landscape.

These four paradoxes on the relationship between nature and agriculture have been exacerbated by the lack of connection between the layers of the problem arena (spanning the world of policy, the systems world, the lifeworld of citizens, and the ecosphere; see figure 6.2). These layers all have their own scale, dynamics, timelines, history, and way of addressing the future. They all have their own vicious cycles and learning cycles. But they are mostly disconnected, as worlds to themselves. For

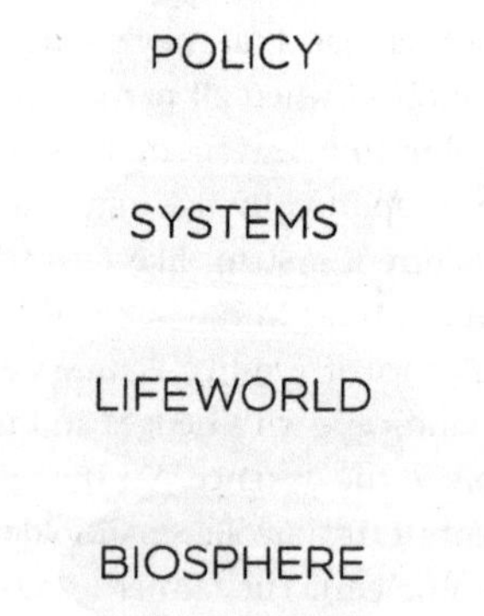

POLICY

SYSTEMS

LIFEWORLD

BIOSPHERE

Figure 6.2 Layers of the problem arena.

example, the timeline for substantially changing the biosphere (having plants change the soil, preparing for the natural succession to other vegetation) takes about fifty to seventy years. In the lifeworld of the farmers, generations are important (handing over the farm to the next generation), so the relevant timeline is twenty to thirty years. In the world of systems and organizations, the horizon is often not more than two to five years, and often substantially less. And in the world of policy, there have been continuous changes in the rules of the game as the government is struggling to influence the sector. This disconnect between timelines plays out in real life in many different ways. For example, one of the farmers interviewed had invested heavily in a technical fix: air cleaners that filter the nitrogen oxide from the air that is emitted from the stables. The hefty investment meant that he needed new bank loans, which can basically only be serviced by increasing the number of livestock. But then, in 2027, a new regulation will come into play that forces the improvement of the surface water quality in the country. This will most likely mean that livestock will need to be kept well away from the waterways (by about three meters). This can only be achieved by keeping less livestock. We can theorize about systems, paradoxes, and the nature of first-order and second-order effects, but what we are looking at here in the lifeworld of this farmer is financial ruin. Society in general doesn't seem to know or understand the situation—which is difficult, as the general societal discussion is the place in the end where a balance between these sets of values for nature and agriculture needs to be reached. The future dimension is also absent in the discussion: From a larger and long-term perspective, farming is adversely affected by a crisis in the realm of nature (the changes in biodiversity and the depletion of the soil). We need to create a new way forward in which all parties can look to the future with a degree of optimism.

Underlying themes that emerged in the frame creation sessions centered around notions of mastery (relationship with the world), identity (relationship with your self and your peers), and vitality (relationship with the future). These led to a very rich collection of possible frames. To illustrate their character and breadth, we will pick out a few frames and the possible interventions they lead to:

1. To tackle the first paradox head-on, we could propose that the different parties team up. A way forward could be to create "fields of freedom," pieces of land that are given in shared stewardship to farmers and nature conservationists to run together, in complete freedom, so long as it is productive and has nature value. In doing so, they will have to sit together and learn from one another, creating new mastery in their professional fields. There will also be practices and knowledge that neither one has and that will need to be sourced from somewhere else in society. This is crucial: In the long run, the field will only change once the education of farmers and biologists also moves toward this new, hybrid sense of mastery.
2. To take on the second paradox, and the deep mistrust between the different parties, we can envision a transparent landscape. The mistrust is so deep that people are disputing the facts of the situation—for example, the data provided by the

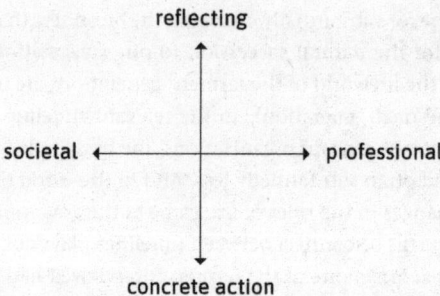

Figure 6.3 The axes of the learning cycle.

independent research institutions that measure the nitrogen in the air and in the soil. To get around this, the proposal is to measure together and know together. Later on in the project, this led to the idea of creating school projects. If your own kids are measuring the state of the landscape, are you going to disagree?

3. The third paradox is difficult: All the people in the whole sector feel that they are wronged, scapegoated, and have to pay for what is basically a much broader societal issue. The frame that "you are now here" aims to open up the problem by literally opening up the farms and landscape to a much broader public through events, festivals, and so on. These should not just concentrate on showing off the qualities of the current system but also should show some of the dilemmas that farmers are facing. If we want people to understand us, we might need to let them come close to our uncertainties and show authentic vulnerability.

4. The fourth paradox led to the frame "How are we doing?" The discussion about value is largely negative: For example, when farmers move toward more eco-friendly production methods, they are compensated for a loss rather than encouraged, valued, and rewarded. To reverse this, we need to create new language and new narratives about what is important.

5. Overall, the paradoxes were held in place and fed by the fierceness of the discussion—hence the frame of moving from debate to conversation. What interventions can be imagined that would help the various parties to become critical friends to one another?

Note that these frames are ways to approach the problem area; they are not separate projects or experiments. The trick (art) is to position these frames along the learning cycle, combined via simple, powerful experiments on the local area level. This means that we need to create a structure for an ongoing change process rather than a single activity (a project or a pilot). There is no simple silver bullet solution; striving for one is fruitless and will actually distract from the work that really needs to be done. In this program, the team structured its activities in a learning cycle (see figure 6.3) that is designed around two axes: thinking (reflecting) versus doing (concrete action), and professional versus societal conversations. Along the learning

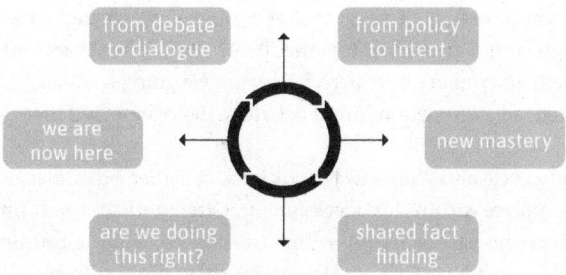

Figure 6.4 Activities along the learning cycle.

cycle, the designers developed six distinct activities that need to be realized in the program (figure 6.4). They have been conceived to address the exact spots where a more linear process would have stalled: In the current situation, policy doesn't correspond to its intent; the stakeholders can just further their own interests because they are isolated from one another; there is no consensus on the facts; there is a lack of clarity on the (long-term) effects of policy changes; and society at large is not involved in resolving what is really a societal problem.

How could this work? Let's take the fields of freedom as an example and follow through the scenario that then unfolds.

New nature can be a threat for local farmers if we keep thinking in terms of a zero-sum game (the very concept of a nature reserve reinforces this thinking). But it could also be an opportunity: Could we conceive of a way to create nature value and be productive in growing food? The challenge then becomes to co-create this new type of stewardship in a way that includes farmers, naturalists, policymakers, and indeed society at large. This requires a joint definition of the new practices and new mastery needed to collaborate across these domains—all the way from agreeing on a way to measure the results in the field to creating new business models for farmers and checking whether the policy is capable of creating the space needed for experiments that bring it closer to realizing the original intent. Sharing experiences and insights will lead to better questions, which spark new experiments, and so on. Because this is an experiment, potentially disturbing variables are muted: These could be the regulatory framework or the market forces of return on investment, for example. Once the experiment is underway and new possibilities emerge, these variables will be brought back into the discussion. The key is that there is an unconditional trust in the craftsmanship and mastery of the participants, and that the field of freedom is used *only* for experiments that cannot be done anywhere else. What does this look like in terms of the learning cycle? Partners from agriculture and nature conservation are selected and make a first rough plan / approach. From the conductor role, the learning cycle is then mapped to create an overview of the way this initiative touches the other frames. What kind of knowledge and skills are we going to need? How are we going to measure the effects (shared fact finding)? How are we going to articulate the various kinds of value that are going to be created here (How are we doing?)? Which stories are woven together here? How do we attract other people to care about the field (you are now here)? How are we going to discuss the value that could be created, and with whom (from debate to dialogue)? And then we are back at the beginning.

The learning cycle also allows us to look back at earlier experiments, value them, and give them a place within this development. Often, earlier project initiatives have concentrated on one part (activity) in the learning cycle, but a learning cycle only works when all steps are performed. Or perhaps these projects have concentrated on one of the four layers of the problem field, limiting their impact because the others have not been addressed / taken along on the journey. In the end, to move forward, you have to mirror the problem area completely: all the layers, the breadth, the intricacies that come from the fact that the problem arena straddles the lifeworlds of the farmers and the world of organizations and systems. The discussion should be expanded by opening up the learning cycle to involve more of society. The learning cycle allows us to easily draw other parties from society into the problem arena at various (and sometimes surprising) points; for example, education can come in not only to support experiments (through student work), but also for the long-term impact of curriculum change (new mastery) in the professions that are at play in the problem arena. On the path of this learning cycle, other parties can be drawn in. The LNV is not even the problem owner: Society is. The ministry is merely the problem *holder*. To really resolve the issues at hand requires a much broader transdisciplinary collaboration. The arts can contribute to experimentation, expression, and dialogue; the museum sector can contribute knowledge on earlier agricultural use of the landscape and expertise on storytelling; and so on. This is a broad societal problem situation, and to shift, it needs a broad societal involvement.

The central theme of this learning cycle is *vitality* (see figure 6.5) The notion of vitality came up as an underlying concept in many of the conversations with different stakeholders, expressed in various ways, such as a concern about the long-term

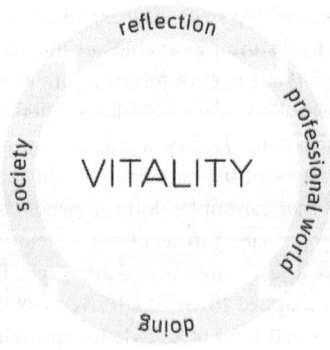

Figure 6.5 Creating vitality.

quality of life in a region or the types of jobs that could support the community in the future.

This underlying theme helped spark new conversations among the parties involved: The fact that everybody means something slightly different by *vitality* is actually helpful (once you get beyond the misunderstandings), offering a good space to compare what is important and what we anticipate the future to be if we do not act now. Note that this only works on a regional level; if we want people to engage, they can only do so from the social space they have (see § 7.2) and feel connected to. The local focus is not a copout or an avoidance of the big issues; on the contrary, smaller-scale (regional) success is sorely needed to feed into the broader, nationwide public discussion. That public discussion tends to be quite abstract and fact free, and it easily gets locked into opinions and ideological posturing. Showing what can be done in a concrete situation is the only way to break the deadlock.

This common learning cycle requires structural support, an innovation infrastructure. Thus we have moved away from starting a project to "fix" the nitrogen crisis and toward laying the foundations for an innovation infrastructure. This infrastructure in itself is the key outcome of the whole program: It can be harnessed to approach current challenge (nitrogen), but it is needed to deal with upcoming issues like (1) drought in the east of the country, (2) salination of the soil in the west of the country, (3) the long-term viability of low-lying areas, (4) and the surface water quality crisis that is going to hit in 2027, just to name four of the main crises that are going to become reality in the foreseeable future. All of these crises are eminently predictable; for some of them, we even know *when* they are going to hit. And it is always going to be the exact same parties that will have to come together to deal with each of these crises. So spending all resources on the first crisis that hits is not a good strategy: The challenge is to develop a robust infrastructure that can deal with all of these as they arise. In the next chapter we will develop a model for such an infrastructure: the studio (§ 7.1).

6.3 WHAT DOES IT TAKE? ELEMENTS OF CHANGE

In this book, we take the thinking and practices that were originally developed through the research on frame creation from a project level on a journey to organizational change (chapter 4), sector-wide change (in chapter 5), and now on to societal change. As in § 5.3, we will here describe some of the key new and different challenges that come up when using this thinking and these practices on this level of societal change and introduce some helpful models and methods for you to ponder. These are again presented as loose points, standing in for a much larger landscape with many more elements that we have yet to explore further. Please focus on what is really relevant and inspiring for you, and feel free to skip other parts for now. Think of it as like a tapas menu: Eating all of it in one sitting is probably not a good idea.

THE X-CURVE REVISITED

The X-curve (see § 6.1) more or less follows Kuhn's original model of a paradigmatic shift: One paradigm demises, a new one rises. Kuhn himself later qualified this by explaining how the new paradigm does not have to be a complete replacement and warning that this change is a fraught process (requiring a leap of faith) as the new paradigm might not be better initially. It is good to realize that the paradigm shifts he talks about take place within the abstraction world of science and the safe halls of academia. This is bound to be much messier in real life:

1. The X-curve seems to suggest that a transition is a *one-off* change.
2. The X-curve seems to suggest that there is no contact or *dynamic between* the developments in the existing regime and the new experiments.
3. The X-curve model concentrates on *a single transition*, whereas we have seen that in practice, the interaction between transitions contributes to their complexity. In the case of the Nitrogen crisis, the plight of the farmers is exacerbated by the fact that there is a housing shortage, which leads to a building boom that makes land more expensive. And more land will need to be reserved for both water capture and alternative energy generation. All of this puts pressure on the farmers' business models.
4. You could wonder whether the small "new regime" initiatives will ever *scale* up to replace the old regime system. This is especially true for bottom-up initiatives, which are often successful because they are small; for example, a common neighborhood food garden, where people share, learn, and grow food together, cannot just be scaled up to the size of the food system of a whole city that needs to feed millions.

But these initiatives are valid examples how the relationship between food and the city could be different. Much can be learned from them as expressions of the values that people are seeking to realize through them. They also help us to step away from the systems-world thinking of organizations and reestablish a close link to the lifeworlds of people. At best, these upcoming initiatives might be seen as prototypes that in and of themselves do not scale up. They are more or less handcrafted by the committed initiators, not products that everybody can use. What does it take to turn such a metaphorical Rolls Royce project into a small, reasonably priced car that gets you there in most circumstances?

5. Then there is the issue of *timescales*. In the short term, we have the practices of problem-solving and design to "turn undesirable situations into better ones."[13] In the long term, we can talk about the transformations that are going to be needed (zero-carbon economy, nature-positive cities, etc.). But the midterm is the real challenge, the battleground: How do we get from one to the other? Both ways of thinking (short term and long term) are not going to be enough. To transition from one to the other, we may need a combination—or, as you will see, something completely different.

6. The assumption that there is *one dominant paradigm* in a sector, and that we are moving to a new state that again will have a singular dominant paradigm in the field, is worth investigating. We will return to this point in chapter 8.

Every model is an abstraction, a simplification. There are some obvious limitations to the idealized story that is captured in the X-curve model. We will now introduce more elements of the complex situation that we have encountered in practice to enrich the picture and put flesh on the bones: What does it take to create an infrastructure for change?

SOCIETAL MIDFIELD: THE MISSING MIDDLE

Who is (or who should be) the driver(s) of such a systems change process? Transitions can severely suffer from a lack of clear ownership, falling between the cracks of different institutions and organizations. If nobody feels enough responsibility to get to action, then there is lots

Figure 6.6 The societal midfield.

of talk, but nothing happens. Or the lack of ownership can lead to parties just contributing to these discussions from their own narrow perspectives, rather than reaching out and taking a more comprehensive view of matters. Something is missing. Societal shifts require a "societal midfield" between the domains of the government, public sector, private enterprise, and the citizen[14] (see figure 6.6). Strategic projects connecting the practices of these four societal domains in this societal midfield will lead to the deep insights needed to create more open, dynamic, and networked "new world" practices between them, to tackle the really big societal challenges.

This model offers a useful lens to situate the case studies. The DOC projects, for instance, were mostly focused on establishing a link between the citizen and the public sector. This did leave projects quite vulnerable to government intervention and to the media that feeds the public discussions in the societal midfield. For instance, the Kings Cross project was kept largely under the radar to protect the public sector stakeholders. But in the end, when the government stepped in, the old framing of alcohol-related violence dominated the public discussion. In later projects, media partners were involved from the start—not so much as a media outlet but as a stakeholder that could help think through and contribute to the common good, just like the others. In general, we can conceive of projects that connect two or three of these domains, but often there is a worrying gap in the middle, where a lot of the issues are so much everybody's problem ("common good") that they become nobody's problem in particular. Workshops that end in statements like "this is very important, somebody should really do this" have failed. The four societal domains need to engage in constructive dialogues with each other and change the way they operate. All four domains need to learn from one another in order to move to the middle: (1) Citizens need to organize themselves, (2) governments need to engage with less formal processes and rules to further experimentation with new approaches, (3) the public sector needs to open up its knowledge and its professionals and make those available to the other three, and (4) private enterprises need to engage with these developments, not only through providing tools and infrastructures, but also through accepting a more responsible role in society (see § 6.5).

In the last decade, there have been great shifts in the way we deal with the common good (at least in the West).[15] The common good was traditionally seen as an overall responsibility of the government, with a public sector taking on the role to support and serve society. Recently, this system has been eroded. The drive from governments to lower taxes and the perception of public sector organizations as inefficient and bureaucratic have created a money stream from the government to the private sector (privatization of public services, public-private partnerships). The idea is that market forces should lead to efficiency gains in the public domain. But the privatization of public services skews the delivery of services and leaves gaps, with the private sector parties cherry-picking the parts of the public services it knows it can make a profit on, leaving the other parts to the public sector (all the "bad risks"). As a result, profit was privatized, while the risk and cost were still in the public domain. This has had all kinds of unintended consequences—like imposing extra burdens on people by giving choice in areas of life where people just need support (e.g., personal health budgets, where assumptions about people's ability to choose have thwarted attempts to create a real marketplace). This has led to the marginalization of the common good (the "tragedy of the commons"[16]). Governments all over the world have also realized this and have sought to empower citizens to take care of the common good (under the banner of a participation society). But the citizens lack skills, oversight, and resources and end up going to the public sector for help. However, the public sector itself is in trouble: It is perceived to be relatively low in status, relatively low in pay, and with limited career prospects, yet public servants are still expected to deal with all the really difficult issues that occur in society.[17]

CREATING LEARNING INFRASTRUCTURE

In a lot of the case studies responding to open, complex, dynamic, and networked problem situations, the outcome is not a one-off solution, but an infrastructure made and shaped to support a learning loop.[18] This ties in well with the issue of the timescales mentioned earlier in this section: In transitions, we to need to bridge the glaring gap between immediate, short-term interventions and the long-term goals that can be abstract and vague (and therefore not very actionable). This gap can only be filled with an adaptive infrastructure, with experimenting and learning at its core. The key is to ensure that this infrastructure is complete: If one step in a learning cycle is forgotten or not supported, nothing is learned. These infrastructures drive systemic and societal change.

Case Study: Taking Charge of Future Challenges

"Transport" is a government department that is responsible for all the physical infrastructure of roads, waterways, and the various forms of public transport, from trains and buses to ferries. These various domains have come together in one organization, creating an opportunity for fresh and integrative thinking across the various component parts. In 2021, the department launched its 2056 strategy, thinking ahead thirty-five years into the future of transport. That timeline is important: We know that our society is facing huge transitions in these coming years. All of these deep changes in these sectors directly impact the domain of Transport. Not just passively: By creating connections, Transport is an important factor that actively shapes these changes. After all, what is possible, easy, or difficult in, say, the domain of care really depends on the ability of people to connect and meet. We saw this play out in the COVID lockdowns, when people with office jobs shifted to remote work. The fact that fewer people were going into work called into question one of the major assumptions that had guided the design of the road system. This used to be made for commuters and designed to deal with peak-hour traffic capacity for people going into the central business district. This design needs a good rethink as not only do people now travel less into the city, but the balance of their various reasons for living somewhere is shifting. If proximity to work is less of an issue, the other values weigh in more heavily: quality of life, being close to family, liking a community, the quality of local schools, and so forth all gain in importance.

This resulted in a complete reversal of the pre-2020 problem of regions emptying out: Now they are overflowing. Regional centers with good-quality public facilities (schools, hospitals, cultural institutions) now see property prices rising. The locals are becoming worried about the younger generations being priced out of the market and that they will not be able to stay close. That in turn could impact which work options they see for themselves. The tensions in one situation start to shift, creating new situations with a new set of tensions. These developments can only be understood by having a close understanding of how the various transitions from all of these domains come together in the lifeworlds of people. To achieve this understanding means working with the pioneers across other sectors, to move from "reading the future" in terms of its risk and uncertainty to "leading the future" through active contact and experimentation. A broad array of industry and public sector stakeholders and invited experts need to come together in an infrastructure that supports common learning.

This infrastructure should do one more thing for us: in picking up the challenges of societal transformations and multiple transitions in parallel, we enter the area of hypercomplexity. In hypercomplexity, the assumptions that come with working within one system are not valid anymore; the problem field sits across several systems and is fundamentally layered, and often these layers are not properly connected. As you saw in the nitrogen crisis case study, chances are good that systems change is doomed because there *is* no overall system in the sense of a clear and coherent arena for intervention. A system is built of connections and feedback loops—but in the agricultural arena, there just seem to be a lot of very different players going in different directions, doing what they think is right or what serves their best interest.

MULTIDIMENSIONAL REASONING

Let's take one more step back and consider what kind of reasoning we need to shape transitions and how we can navigate such hypercomplexity. This will give us a better idea of the kind of infrastructure we need for creating deep change. To deepen the understanding of problem situations and the appropriate reasoning patterns we might use to respond to them, we can revisit the logic model from § 2.4. That model, though it helped distinguish between deduction, induction, and abduction (first and second order), was incredibly abstract. This abstraction was useful to understand the misunderstandings that will occur when these fundamentally different thinking styles come into contact with one another. But if we start adding elements of the real-world situations we are dealing with here into the model, it might also give us a logical basis that guides

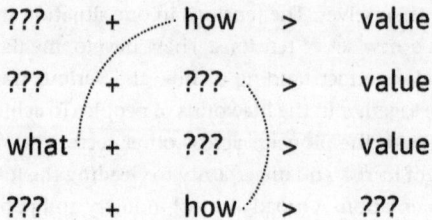

Figure 6.7 Parallel lines of thought.

us to an appropriate response. We will do so step by step. First, when we look at a complex problem situation, there is not one line of reasoning we are trying to get right, but several in parallel (see figure 6.7).

These might also be connected in various ways: Let's say that there is an overlap in values, or maybe a clash between them. There might be possibilities to address several values with the same how or what (the dominant concept). Potentially, there may be a *what* that is already in the situation that cannot safely be ignored—such as an earlier solution that has been invested in heavily and is seen as value at risk. There could be real benefit to reusing that—but how? The cross-connections between these lines of reasoning create a very complex web of interdependencies. This explosion of variables is also a saving grace: The complexity means that new patterns, a new sense of order, can emerge. This is where we have to trust our brains. Our minds are incredible pattern seekers. Just examine the complexity, and let the patterns show up.

But this is not all. These parallel lines of reasoning sit in a context, which before we have called the *problem situation*. That problem situation sits with an organization (the problem owner, or rather, the problem holder), which in turn takes its cue from a sector and responds to what is sees as its relevant field—interpreting the current situation and anticipating what might be happening in the future (see figure 6.8). These layers are likely to reflect the frames and values that are active in the problem situation, as well as many others that could become relevant as problematic factors or as elements of a way forward.

The actor also is missing from this picture: *Somebody* is reasoning. They come to this problem situation with their experience, their expertise, their professional lifeworld (their disciplinary matrix, paradigms), and also their personal and professional lifeworlds, the insights and

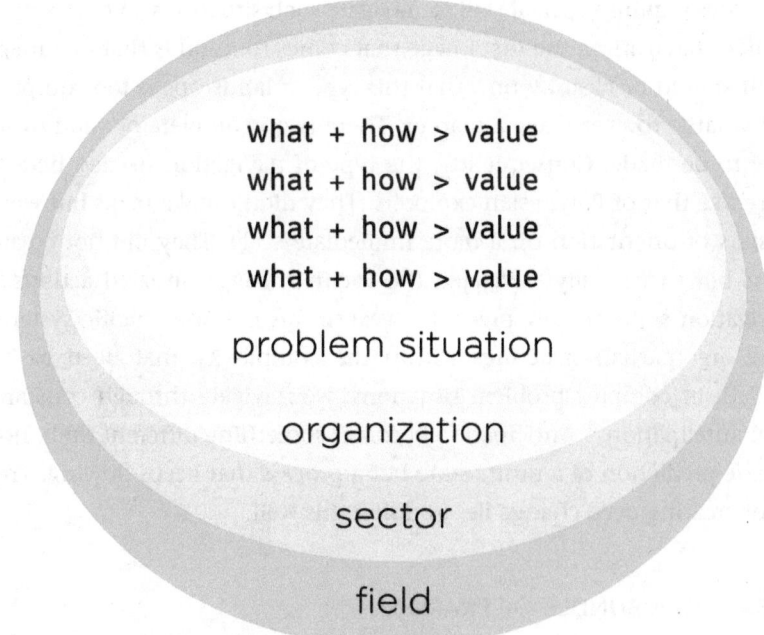

Figure 6.8 Multidimensional reasoning in context.

approaches they bring from their life experiences. All these elements and layers together hold a richness that creates patterns in the problem situation and also opens opportunities for new patterns to emerge. There are connections across the levels, cross-links from properties of the actor to elements in the context, and so on—a myriad of patterns full of opportunities and paradoxes, dead ends, vicious circles. This confusing richness creates the space for change, as you will see in the case studies that follow.

If only the world existed in the single lines of reasoning from § 2.4—but that is not how it works. In reality, we can't choose to only deal with one line of reasoning or dimension for very long; We have to engage with the whole complex system, and become fluent in the art of multidimensional reasoning. In doing this, we are not beyond reasoning, we are not resorting to what people sometimes call *trial and error*—we are experimenting and learning, because that is the only appropriate response to an open, complex, dynamic, and networked problem situation.

It does require a special skill to navigate such situations. When people think of navigation, the first image that comes to mind is that of a map. But it should be clear by now that this type of landscape is too complex and volatile to ever make a map of. There is no complete or valid overview to be made. Consequently, the type of navigation needed here is more like that of Polynesian explorers: They didn't make maps but were masters of orientation on a more immediate scale. They did not create plans but successfully navigated the Pacific through situated actions.[19] Navigation skills are key precisely because this is not a chaotic system: there are (partial) structures within the complexity that need to be heeded. In complex problem situations, we navigate through constant local anticipation.[20] Anticipation becomes something different then, not a static prediction of a future state but a process that keeps flowing. The art of creating deep change lies in doing this well.

CREATING A BUNDLE OF FRAMES

When introducing frame creation as a practice in chapter 3, we highlighted the importance of having multiple frames as these represent (new) ways of acting on the underlying themes. To decide on a way forward, we then looked for frames that serve several themes at once—that is, that overlap. The emergence of a dominant frame that captures many of the themes is an important moment in the creative process.

This scenario plays out when we are dealing with a one-off project. In the complex situations discussed in this chapter, on the other hand, it is important to not settle on a frame but to build up a repertoire of various diverse overlapping frames—a bundle of frames—and hold them lightly to mirror the dynamics of the problem situation as it develops. These frames represent different ways of thinking about the problem situation. They do not align; it is important to hold on to the tensions between them to keep the thinking alive and active. We need these multiple viewpoints for several reasons: (1) Any intervention will create a new system state, a new problem situation that sparks new questions. (2) The problem situation is dynamic; some stakeholders might become more important, or their influence might wane, events can change the balance in the situation, new possibilities might emerge, and so on. (3) On the surface, on an action level, everything can change very rapidly. The underlying themes are much more stable; they shift very slowly (if at all). Frames are important because they are more dynamic than themes, but also durable.

We have already seen this dynamic at work in the case studies in the last chapters. In response to the complexity of these problem situations, the proponents did not just create several interventions based on one single frame, as in the original Kings Cross case study (the music festival frame). They created multiple frames from which to approach the problem situation, turning from projects to broader programs that develop and change over time (e.g., the Waterwolf program in Gouda has run for seven years, and Partners in Recovery had a six-year stint). We will return to the dynamics of such programs in § 6.5 as we look at agents of change. In § 7.1, we will see that the rich knowledge of themes and frames is the core intellectual capital of a creative agency, and it is core to the ability of a studio to build new practices. In problem-solving we are looking for a solution and closure, but in this thinking we are looking for the opposite: for ways to keep our options open and fluid. The bundle of frames that are ready to go makes us nimble and quick in response to the changing situation.

FOCUSING ON LIFEWORLDS AND SOCIAL SPACE

What do you navigate by in complex societal issues? You navigate by the values that the system should achieve—and we have mentioned before that in the end, value only exists (is experienced and realized) in the lifeworlds of people. So in creating value, we need to intimately know what the lifeworlds of people we are working for are like. The themes, as we have used them in frame creation, are ways to make sense of the lifeworlds. They are the "knots in the webs of our experiences"[21] and often represent tensions between values. Van Manen gives the example of the experience of parenthood and how it changes over time as a child grows up: as the young person becomes independent, there is an experience of fulfilment but also one of loss. Our lifeworlds are complex places that are full of these tensions. Good art, such as novels and movies, expresses these all-too-human tensions in deep ways that touch the core of our humanity. Striving for an important value inevitably will be at the detriment of other values: This shows if something *is* a real value; if we are not ready to sacrifice anything for it, then it cannot be important. Extending this sacrifice to benefit others goes to the core of what makes a society. We have learned in societal projects, such as in a neighborhood, that it's important to go there and always ask two questions of the people we meet. The first question is: What do you need or want? In answering, everybody sounds like an egoistic idiot—but then, we asked them what they themselves wanted. Therefore, it is very important to ask a second question: What would be good for the neighborhood or street? The difference between these two answers shows how much people are ready to sacrifice for the other, how much they hold back on their own interests for the common good. This is the social space, and it shows their true compassion and humanity. At times, these answers can be noble, beautiful, and heart-warming (as an aside, the social space tends to be bigger in neighborhoods that are having a rough time than in the very rich parts of the city). Social space is about sacrifice, not about self-interest. The Burning Man festival has picked this up and amplified it to an extreme: at the core, the whole event is purely about the social space that people can create together (see the Burning Man rules in appendix 5).

In creating change that impacts people's lifeworlds, it is often assumed that either people are economic beings that need to work to their own interests and that the dialectic between these beings will create a just and equitable society for all, or that people are nice[22] and that a social space is just there. What we have found is that just like the lifeworld, the social space itself is something that needs to be understood, and often worked on, in order for a change to land. In the Newcastle case study (§ 7.5), you will see that creating a social space is a major element of the change program. In shaping the change itself, we need to create interventions that are in tune with the lifeworlds of the professionals involved. Dick Rijken expressed this well.[23] The following box presents some of his ideas.

Professional Lifeworlds

There is a tendency to contrast the notion of the lifeworld against that of the system world, with an underlying suggestion of "lifeworld good, system world bad": Customers, citizens, or patients are often seen as "victims" of cold, technocratic systems that don't really care about them. The reality is not that simple. Systems don't exist without people who order them, design them, and work within them. All systems express values—explicitly (because they were designed to express them) or implicitly (when they just happen to favor certain values over others). This is a daily reality for professionals who work in these systems. They are part of those systems and have different kinds of agency within them. And they are also people with their own values and emotions. Their professional practices—what it is that they do on a daily basis—are important events in their lifeworlds. Understanding the lifeworlds of professionals is just as important as understanding those of patients, customers, or citizens. Many professionals genuinely care about their jobs and find meaning in them. They want to make a difference in the lifeworlds of real people. Many workers in health care or in education see their work as their calling and expect their jobs to be a source of meaning or purpose in their lives. When the reality of their professional practice does not allow them to experience personal values like caring for others or inspiring young people on a daily basis, they feel alienated in their professional lives. Making systems more meaningful often requires a stronger connection between the values of people who work inside them and those of the outside world. We want a car mechanic to truly care about our car, teachers to truly care about our children, doctors to truly care about our health, and all of them to feel that they act on those passions on a daily basis. If an organization has a hard time finding employees, then they are advised to rethink the alignment of the values expressed in the lifeworlds on the job of their professionals with the personal values of those professionals. Don't expect a care worker or a teacher to find meaning in spending hours and hours to satisfy organizational values like accountability or efficiency. For many people, professional life is not a roleplaying game where they act out a role in a script that was written by others.

In retrospect, the deeper source of conflict in the nitrogen case study lies in the fact that the personal and professional lifeworlds of the farmers have not been heard, understood, and respected within the broader system. Sometimes just listening, sitting at their kitchen table with no set time limit or agenda, was in itself the beginning of healing. There was anger, frustration, even tears. And there was generosity: the ways forward that could be created on a regional level (around the notion of the "vitality of the region") were based on people's ability to see the region as their social space and to sacrifice some of their self-interest for the common good. The lifeworld is what really matters. Things can be done in the lifeworld, on a human-to-human level, that are much more powerful than what any organization can achieve. Consider the example in the following box.

Human Goodness in Action

Some years ago, DOC was approached by the local council that is responsible for an area of Sydney that includes the Gap—a spectacular cliff near the entrance to Sydney Harbor that unfortunately has a reputation in the city as the place where people go to commit suicide. The problem that the council presented was basically that Don Ritchie was getting too old to walk his dog at twilight. Don Ritchie lived in one of the last houses next to the nature reserve that includes the Gap. He used to walk his dog at twilight and would approach people who were looking distressed, asking them, "Why don't you come in for a cup of tea?" Over the years, he chatted with hundreds of people at his kitchen table and saved many lives (the estimate is about 450). Now that Don was getting on in years, what should the authorities do? They realized that putting an emergency phone at the spot was probably not going to do the trick: too deliberate, too institutional, too obvious, too authoritarian, and, despite good intentions, also too inhumane. The fact is that Don's kind deeds, emanating from basic human goodness, cannot be organized at all without losing their essential power. Human goodness and generosity are incredibly powerful forces in our lives.[24]

All the real quality of the projects presented in this book comes not from the cleverness of the methods used or the funky visualizations. Real quality comes from the fact that somewhere along the way, somebody involved in the project (a local council member, a social worker, a student—whoever) was personally inspired to bring his or her own force to bear on the problem.

CREATING SYSTEM VITALITY

What do we strive for as we are trying to transition and (re)organize ourselves into new systems that are fit for the future? In the end, we need to create systems that have vitality: the ability to survive and thrive on an ongoing basis, to keep learning and changing with the changing circumstances. For organizations, this kind of flexibility rests in the quality of the relationships within and around the organization—in particular, the amount of trust; systems of distrust are transactional, inflexible. The nature of the qualities that make up the vitality of an organization differ over specific situations. They could, for instance, include the capacity to call on a bigger system when in need of inspiration or to weather a crisis, as the creative industries do, banding together in *creative precincts* (a creative industries company that is located far from its peers has less vitality than a company that sits in this kind of support network). In their book *The Rainforest*,[25] Horowitt and Hwang describe Silicon Valley along the same lines: They see the success of the valley spring from richness and a (quite inefficient) variety of players, in particular from the people they characterize as "weeds" (connectors, sometimes opportunistically so). Vitality, as in systems vitality, helps capture a dynamic to strive for, in a way that the more popular term *resilience* doesn't. Although resilience is important, it is often used in a limited sense as the ability of a current system to bounce back from disruption. That will in the end not serve us when the challenge is bigger than the current system can handle, when we are talking about systems change. Vitality captures what we want to achieve much better than resilience does. At the same time, it is a word for something that is quite invisible; intuitively, we can grasp whether a certain intervention increases or decreases the system vitality. But it is hard to put that into words; vitality is as elusive as it is useful. This is because vitality is a deeply human notion: We *know* whether or not a situation, an organism, or an organization has vitality. You may remember that earlier in this chapter, vitality surfaced as the central underlying theme in the nitrogen crisis case study. One of the directors of the Ministry of Agriculture, Nature, and Food Safety later complained to the project leader: "I just can't look at a proposed policy now, or take a decision without thinking how it will impact the vitality of the system." *Precisely.* Once we look at the world through this lens, the concept of vitality is everywhere, as an undercurrent in so much of our history and culture. More on this later.

6.5 AGENTS OF CHANGE

Now we will take a look at four very different and original agents of change, as further inspiration for the model of the studio that will be introduced in the next chapter.

Case Study: Thriving Communities Australia

This systemic change agent arose from what seems to be an unexpected organization: Yarra Valley Water, Victoria's largest water retailer. It operated as all such utility companies do: If people don't pay their bills, they are sent a reminder, and then another one. It then escalates with debt collection activities and potential water restrictions for the customer. However, the water company realized that the water bill is the last one you don't pay. Water is vital to life. If you can't pay for water, you must be defaulting on lots of other bills too and be in real trouble. This set the company on the path of thinking from the perspective of the lifeworlds of the people and communities it was servicing and linking that to its own behavior in the systems world.

Here's an example from the company:

Yarra Valley Water invited a panel of "citizens" from the community to tell their stories to senior leaders of the executive team. One particular story came from a mother whose child was sick. The mother had owed $200 in overdue water bills. On this day, she sat in front of the executive team and told them her story of how she had rung up to explain that she didn't have the $200 to pay. However, she did have $20 which she could pay immediately. The mother asked if she could pay the $20 now and finish paying the remaining debt in small instalments over the coming three months. The answer that had come back was "no." The staff member reiterated that the amount that she owed was $200 and she would have to pay the full amount. She was offered a two-week extension to pay the full amount otherwise there would be debt collection and her water could be restricted. When speaking with the Yarra Valley Water executive team, the mother recalled that at the time she was barely affording the medication needed for her sick child, and was often going without food so her other children could eat. Her immediate thoughts were, "How am I going to pay? I don't have the money. How will I survive and support my sick child?" The mother was then asked by the executive team, "What would have made a difference?" She replied that if her offer of $20 had been accepted, she would have kept paying whatever she could until she'd paid the full amount. Instead, Yarra Valley Water got nothing.

Through the process of listening to community citizens, Yarra Valley Water realized that it had a really important role to play in owning its responsibility to individuals and created an industry-leading customer support program. It also realized that the lifeworld problem was bigger than just the water company, and it organized a "vulnerability roundtable" with other utility companies (electricity, gas), banks, insurance companies, and communication companies (telcos), along with community sector and government organizations, focused on how people experiencing hardship can be supported. The company made sure that there were people with lived experience of these situations in the meeting, telling their stories. Others were as shocked as the water company executives had been. The vulnerability roundtable led to the founding of Thriving Communities Australia (TCA), a not-for-profit organization that enables collaboration across multiple sectors, including business, academia, government, NGOs, and people with lived experience of vulnerability. The goal was to see everybody have fair access to essential services they need to thrive. TCA seeks to understand the often complex influencing factors of vulnerability, aiming to reduce the barriers to access and embed sustainable and effective change in the practices of partner organizations. It creates a movement of organizations working collaboratively within and across sectors to provide holistic support, that reduces the need and trauma of people to retell their stories The challenge is not to "fix" people but rather to unite and shape a system that works better for the people that need it most.

The central modus operandi of TCA is brokering: setting up projects that connect the partner organizations with the people, seeking to (1) connect—build deeper connections and networks for collaboration and platforms for collective learning and action; (2) build capability—build a collective understanding of vulnerability and increase the collective capability to better support people; and (3) change—establish platforms and initiatives for place-based and national collaboration for impact. This is applied across four focus areas, corresponding with four key risk factors of vulnerability: (a) family violence, economic abuse, and institutional abuse; (b) health and accessibility; (c) unexpected life events; and (d) cost of living. Tackling vulnerability and hardship in the community is not an easy job, and it is not the responsibility of a single organization to do so. Collaboration on projects is vital to support people experiencing vulnerability. The TCA team is bringing the corporations they work with a keen sense of moral obligation and inspiration for how things can be done differently, with much better results for everyone. These companies are so big and important that they are part of the vital infrastructure of people's lives, and this comes with a societal and human responsibility. This can only be done by bridging the gap between the lifeworld of people experiencing vulnerability and the systems world—in which the real lifeworld is always right, and sending a bailiff to collect money that people don't have is very, very wrong.

In the next example, you will see that the Care Republic avoids the systems world altogether.

Case Study: Care Republic (Zorgvrijstaat)

Their motto: "Care is human, never transactional. Never exclude anyone. Never claim anything." The Zorgvrijstaat (Care Republic) is a local initiative in the Dutch city of Rotterdam that got out of hand—in a positive way. It helps communities by assisting locals to organize care for one another, shaping empowerment and ownership. The Care Republic creates community through fostering relationships centered on the deep human theme of care. It contributes to existing networks and initiatives in the area, strengthening what is already there locally, close to the people; it has turned away from the systems world (e.g., by not becoming a care organization in its own right). The role/position of the Care Republic is very much that of a convening space: It creates magnets for activity and ensures that those initiatives are connected in a network. This contributes to a very strong and quite comprehensive informal care system for a whole neighborhood.

With the name Care Republic, the initiative positions itself as a part of the counterculture (a pirate ship). Yet it has grown beyond repairing gaps in a system to become something in its own right: There is a pride and a unique identity. The Care Republic is a nonorganization that holds together organically, as an ecosystem of activities rather than a formal entity (shared intent and principles, rather than rules and roles). It is also very much grounded in the local Rotterdam can-do attitude: bottom up, realistic, and aimed at actions, not words. It works solely through influencing and steers away from positional power and from transactional relationships. This can only work through staying true to the people's intrinsic motivation and when there is a very fluid sense of the role and identity of the Care Republic itself. Sometimes it takes the initiative to start an activity, sometimes it is a collaborator, sometimes it plays an advocacy role, and sometimes it is just a cheerleader. What is clear and consistent across all the activities is the grounding in the local context. Care Republic knows it is part of a chaotic stream of social initiatives and activities; sometimes it is hard to distinguish who did what, but Care Republic will never claim anything as its own. At the same time, a caring society is not something that just arises. The creation of a caring society is a design question, one that can be approached on many different levels and in many different ways, by many different people.

A snapshot of some of the initiatives in the Care Republic landscape:

It will work. It offers walking frame repair drop-in hours and small home improvements that help people live independently.

We are not alone. Neighbor help: Strengthening the role the neighborhood can play a role in responding to (care) questions. Some lessons of neighbor help: (1) It is helpful in itself to know you can share your worries and concerns. (2) Recognition creates a bond; you know how it is and can feel the dilemmas. (3) The more concrete the question, the better you can respond. (4) Sometimes you have to take the lead in a situation and create some rest and space. (5) Sometimes you just need someone to listen—and this is what professionals can't offer. (6) It's good to bring together the need and response, like in a dating network. (7) Join the help team and experience what it is like before asking questions. (8) Respond to questions closely. (9) Helping others makes us happy. (10) Where possible, make visible . . .

Club money worries. It has created a network in which poverty and debts can be discussed and in which people can find tools to move forward.

Come in and let's talk about it. There is a network of informal and formal conversations to just get the difficult subjects on the table and call out difficulties and injustices. This has also then led to a map of the informal and formal parties that people can go to for advice on all kinds of matters.

Have a seat. A coalition of community groups makes healthy, affordable meals for as many people as possible, with school lunches and a network of meals for the locals. Join us for a meal. The meeting and connection are central, open, and affordable for all locals, and it's healthy and regular (weekly).

Kindred spirits. It invites people to connect around questions and challenges, providing mental support to each other. This community for self-management and recovery has become the heart of Zorgvrijstaat.

Start-up coffee. Have a Monday morning coffee to share your plans and challenges for the week.

A house for the neighborhood. Huize Middelland: There is a network of spaces where people can come with questions around well-being and that host activities (with twelve other organizations).

Although some activities, like the DIY "it will work" initiative, have a stable financial backing, the Care Republic has kept itself outside of the care system. It has always started from the informal system and sought to create relationships that strengthen existing activities. It then explores what else is needed that can be developed, and from this standpoint it has shaped its interactions with the organizations in the systems world. The key working principle of Care Republic is creating connections between formal and informal communities and organizations (connecting the lifeworld and the system world, but always starting and ending in the lifeworld). In its experience, staying away from managerialism, hierarchy, and power thinking is hard work. When division of tasks and a degree of coordination is needed, power could easily slip in. But the lack of structure can be a well-guarded asset. What Care Republic is, generally, is quite unclear to outsiders; there is no recognizable form or formalized structure (it is not a foundation or a charity). This means that it normally takes interested people quite a while to become active (joining the Friday general meetings is just about the only way to get a sense of what is going on). One can only describe Care Republic through its intent, its activities, and the relationships it creates. This raises a question of scale: Could this only work in a reasonably small initiative? Answer 1: This is already quite sizeable. Answer 2: There is bound to be a limit; this all works from a basis of shared intent, personal involvement, closeness, and empathy. Answer 3: Would this need to grow or be stable at all? Through its impact, a little bit despite itself, Care Republic has also become a model that has influenced policy, advocating for the vital importance of community care.

Case Study: Bioto

The growth and growing density of cities is a threat to biodiversity worldwide. How can we create a city as a biosphere, an ecosystem of people, plants, and animals—a thriving ecosystem that can be a source of biodiversity, and even a source of food? This a rethink of what a city is. Municipalities are developing (top-down) plans for execution and monitoring of the greening of the city, but often there is not much enthusiasm or support from citizens. Yet of the outdoor spaces in a city, about 60 percent are privately owned. If we add balconies and roofs, there is a lot to gain in making these less barren and turning them into a fertile environment for people, plants, bees and other insects, the neigborhood, the city, society, and so on. If we really want to make a difference in biodiversity and climate adaptation, getting the people on board is absolutely crucial. A great opportunity presents itself in Oud Mathenesse, a typical late nineteenth-century neighborhood in the city of Rotterdam; in the coming years, all its drains will have to be renewed, and the whole area needs to be raised by adding soil. This creates pretty much a blank slate as far as the public spaces and private gardens are concerned. Bioto used a mobile tea stall to get into contact with the people of the neighborhood, creating with them an "energy and opportunity map" that pinpoints areas where there is local commitment and a good chance to create a biodiverse environment. The people are actively involved in the design process. The human scale is key: Bioto's sensor technology (a "plant listener") and database provide the know-how to create clever combinations of plants that help each other grow, attract insects, and provide protection against pests. Crucially, the collective data from these sensors can be used to inform local and citywide policy development, creating feedback loops that track the impact of all interventions, big and small (e.g., on microclimates) as a contribution to climate adaptation. The technical learning loop of the sensors and database of observations needs to be in sync with people coming together in the social learning loop; the overall city biosphere can only thrive when these are in balance.

As a network organization, the positioning of Bioto is a bit ambiguous. It holds the same promise as Care Republic of articulating a crucial link between people and institutions, but whereas Care Republic takes sides and bases itself in the lifeworld, Bioto needs to straddle both sides. Early projects have concentrated on a mix of institutional and lifeworld parties—for instance, working with child care centers and schools to create natural playgrounds. This opens an avenue for further change: A lot of the social network in a neighborhood centers on schools. For a healthy living climate in the city, we ultimately need all the parties in the societal midfield to get involved. The challenge for Bioto in the midterm is to ensure that the current short-term experiments and bottom-up projects lead to change in the thinking (the field) and, for instance, to policy changes that create the context for the bigger shift. The long-term perspective is a true transition to a natural and productive city.

There is an attractive long-term vision of green cities: Great visualizations abound of cityscapes dominated by spectacularly tropical-looking high-rise buildings. On an institutional level, this narrative is generally accepted, but it needs detailing and a *how*, which is where Bioto positions itself. The challenge for Bioto as a change agent is to navigate the multidimensional problem space, balancing technology development, community outreach, and institutional development. This all needs to come together at the same moment to make this work, across the different layers of the problem arena. In terms of colors of change, Bioto as an initiative has no positional power in this system of forces, so the immediate change strategy has to be white: When there is alignment in one area, it must move quickly, and then move on to the next. Over time, these projects strategically build into the small-big connection, the public-private connection. Bioto is typically the kind of elegant initiative that connects parts of a problem area that are normally separate. It also finds itself in a space between established funding sources, sometimes resorting to small conventional projects to keep afloat (but doing them in a different way, as far as is possible within the constraints of the project). It is clear that there is great value in the concept, but Bioto might have to wait for the big game to shift—and make sure that it is ready to pounce.

Case Study: Arts 2030 (Kunsten 2030)

System vitality depends not only on the quality of the nodes of the network but also on the infrastructure to support relationships. A quick illustration can be found in the work that designer/entrepreneur Jeroen van Erp did as part of his role on the board of the Dutch artists association and advocacy group Kunsten 92. He instigated a "critical friend" review of the arts sector and an exploration of how the sector could operate differently under the banner Arts 2030 (Kunsten 2030). The first challenge he started the series of workshops with was this: "If God in heaven had a cultural sector, would it look like the one we have now?"—a rhetorical question, to which the obvious and inevitable answer is "no." But this does open the space for thinking about what such a sector would look like. And if our current situation doesn't match this image, why don't we change it? His second intervention asked the group to step back from talking about this sector in isolation (which it does incessantly, and it is very good at going around in circles), in order to consider the overall value of the sector as it contributes to general well-being in society. How can we redesign the current arts infrastructure to be more fit for this purpose? The third and most crucial intervention to move away from the current system and its well-entrenched positions was to ignore the "nodes" in the system and concentrate solely on the relationships among them. By concentrating on the value chains (where is value created, how is it transferred)—the relationship between the arts sector and the citizen, the relationship between artists and cultural institutions, and the relationship between the sector and the government—in effect, he invited the participants to sketch out an image of an arts sector that sits squarely in the societal midfield.

The ensuing discussions went straight to the core of the arts professions and their attitudes to collaboration. The arts often try to create a position that is slightly removed from society—as their public profile, but also as a deeply engrained identity that is strongly propagated through how arts education is handled, especially in the art academies. The classic educational model (described as *breaking down and rebuilding*) is not always healthy for the person in question, but also, it is structurally unsound as it stresses autonomy, not connection. This results in a sector-wide inability to collaborate among peers and with other parties in society. Some first collaboration principles that arose from the workshop and subsequent conversations are worth mentioning: (1) fair judgment (not too negative to one another, which can be harmful); (2) trust (within the sector and for building a trust relationship with the culture department); (3) all audiences have value, in solidarity, inclusivity—"you are welcome"; (4) involvement starts where the other is; (5) peer support—in the cultural sharing economy (the sector has great assets that are not fully used); and (6) public funding to make sure that all grants are about connecting and creating new relationships rather than quality in isolation.

The aim is to use collaborative projects based on these principles to influence the system. This can only be achieved through many interventions with a common purpose: This is a movement!

6.6 CREATING SPACE FOR MEANINGFUL TRANSFORMATION

The variety of approaches in the examples shows that this is a rich playing field, in which many different elements, relationships, and processes have to be brought together to create momentum and change. Although there are snippets of structure that these examples have in common, this is clearly not the place or the moment to talk about creating *the* method. That would be a gross oversimplification of the real-world issues and would be riddled with assumptions. In such a complex space, the practitioner is better served by building up the skills to navigate the paradoxical landscape. In the preceding cases, you saw some of the many different shapes that sector transformation and societal transitions can take—depending on the starting points, the role/position of the initiator, and the (expected) dynamics of the change process. There are many different ways of being a change agent, and they can come from anywhere. Apart from taking care of their own core activities, there is a sense that these agents of change are crystallization points that influence the broader system by inspiring/sparking changes in the practices of others. In terms of complexity theory, one would say that they operate as *attractors*.

It is also clear that agency is an issue and a point of attention for all of them; they have no set role within the current system, and people within the system may not feel empowered to engage with them. After all, engagement requires the people within the system to step out of business as usual practices. This can result in a bit of a vicious circle: inspiring conversations and lots of good will, but in the end, no action. We need courageous creators strive to make a difference in an overwhelmingly complex environment, people that are driven: They know this needs to happen for the greater good and have taken it upon themselves to drive the change, taking on the issues everybody sort of knows about but looks away from (Thriving Communities Australia) or that fall in the cracks between organizations (Bioto). Their deep commitment comes from their personal values, which they have taken to their professional lifeworlds. This requires a special type of leadership, one that creates a space for meaningful transformation.

7

HOW: THE STUDIO

I have yet to see any problem, however complicated, which, when you looked at it in the right way did not become still more complicated.
—Paul Anderson[1]

7.1 THE STUDIO

How can we respond to problem situations that are open, complex, dynamic, and networked—on a continuous basis? How can we create a space for deep change? What does it take? What are the mechanisms that make deep change happen, and how can we support those? As we are nearing the end of this book, we are well-stocked on models that help clarify and understand this challenge and have been gathering practices that can create deep change. Through the case studies, you have seen many ways in which we can move forward in concrete situations, as well as ways in which we can get stuck. In the process, we have also amassed an impressive list of demands that our response should address. It is time to bring all this together now and forge a way forward.

For reasons that will become clear later, we will call this elusive response a *studio*. Let's explore what it could be, building on what we know already:

WHAT SHOULD IT DO?

Looking at the game changers model, we know that such a studio should include the capacity to strategically spark and support reframing projects, as well as inform the reconsideration of the underlying paradigms of an organization (the field). The studio should be the engine room for ongoing change, ensuring the vitality of the organization. Since we introduced the original game changers model (figure 4.1), you have seen that the one-off arrow from the reframing project up to the field will not do: To create vitality, we need a continuous flow of ideas. There need to be structural links between the bottom-up and top-down processes.

WHERE SHOULD IT BE?
The studio should impact the middle level of the organization, in the space where we want the insights from the bottom-up and top-down processes to come together productively to create new practices and strategies, rather than clash. A studio is about exploring the unknown, and it should be structured around learning loops. To avoid clashes between these iterations and the linear delivery path of an organization, the studio should be located just outside of that critical path but be intimately connected.

WHAT IS IT?
To get at sense of how this might be shaped, we can look at the way creative disciplines like art and design have organized themselves. After all, artist studios and design studios are somehow structured to support creation, exploration, and change on a continuous basis—in contrast with the "classic" organizational model of the industrial firm, which is organized around exploitation.[2] The creative disciplines in themselves do not provide a ready-made answer for creating the deep and sustained change needed in times of transition, but their organizational principles and practices can be the inspiration and basis for developing ways of working that are fit for purpose. Note that we use the word *studio* here in the sense of a practice—as in architectural education, where people talk about "doing a studio."[3] A studio starts with a challenge and contains a set of different activities that unfold over time. This practice can be embodied in a physical space, but the crux is in the activities, rather than the space or the props.

HOW DOES IT WORK?
Leading architects, designers, and artists take great care to develop the intellectual (and physical) environment in which the design activities

of their agencies take place. They are very strategic about the intellectual, physical, and mental environments they create within their organization. These environments embody the culture of the company and nourish the inspiration and reflection that enables the particular kinds of projects that the firm excels in. These multifaceted environments are the locus where the themes and frames that the firm stands for are most clearly articulated and embodied, as well as explored, developed, and perhaps discarded over time. This underpins the manner of working in all the projects in the firm.

In the following passage, famed Singaporean architect Ken Yeang reflects on his office:

Any architect with a mind of his own, whether by design or default will produce an architecture which is identifiable to that architect . . . I had to study ecology, I had to study biology; that was the basis for most of my design work. I'm trying to develop a new form of architecture. We have this climatically responsive tropical skyscraper agenda and each project we try to see whether we can push an idea a little bit further. . . . I give every new member of staff the practice manual to read when they join. They can see not just past designs but study the principles upon which they are based. We work these out over time, over many projects.[4]

The agenda of the firm is very clear, and there is a set of very deliberate activities and working methods that support that agenda: "But in a project I have to be very dependent on my architects and each one of them has their own personal way of doing things, and I try to respect that so they are constantly improving and making things better, there is growth and they get motivated." There is a very sophisticated way of creating a balance between continuity and change within the design practice: "I do competitions more as an academic exercise. I treat competitions as research projects . . . . it motivates the office—gets them excited—lets the mind develop new thoughts and themes. I put all the drawings together and publish a book . . . look in this book, these were our competition drawings for Kuala Lumpur and people said 'how can you spend so much time doing drawings and so on' and I say 'it's research, it develops ideas.'" The projects and other activities like competitions, exhibitions, presentations, and publications are seen as part of a very explicit strategy for developing the practice into the future. Ken Yeang and other outstanding architects that were interviewed for this book influence what happens in their offices by overseeing the building and continuous development of the themes and repertoire of frames that together *make* the firm. This includes approaches to problem situations, strategies, particular knowledge, special skills, and a range of possible solutions that are all part of the common heritage. It contains statements on the kinds of knowledge and abilities that ensure projects are in line with the company's "philosophy." It also extends to the physical spaces in which the designers are working, the methods and tools they are expected to use, and human resource management. It captures the experience of the firm as it develops (resulting in the "common stories" and an overall narrative). All together, this constitutes the real and active intellectual capital of the firm. The term *capital* can be taken quite literally here: These experts are not approached by clients for their skills (these are widespread) but for their particular approach to design and the specific quality this can bring to the solution. Yet these firms only survive in a dynamic environment when they are dynamic constructions, when they are able to go through great changes over time.

Likewise, Jerry Hirshberg[5] describes how the Californian branch of Nissan Design was deliberately shaped by him to prioritize creativity, rather than a smooth and efficient "production" process. Taking the "creative priority" seriously requires a complete rethink of what an organization is and does. His principles include the following: (1) ensure creative abrasion by creating polarity in projects; (2) hire people in divergent pairs; (3) use tension as a springboard to create new insights; (4) always stress creative questions before creative answers; (5) regularly step back from the canvas and reflect; (6) stimulate failure and play (and cheating—fostering a culture of forgiveness and humor); (7) blur the disciplinary boundaries and foster intercultural creativity; (8) don't just focus on the core business, but do other things as well to diversify sources of inspiration; (9) trust intuition, and make the space and take the time to build it up (Hirshberg talks about "informed intuition"), and (10) use porous planning to cater for open learning processes.

From a creative practice perspective, all of these principles make sense; this is what it takes. Hirshberg holds up a mirror to organizations who say they want to be innovative yet try to achieve that within conventional organizational structures and linear processes that are not fit for the purpose (see appendix 1).

In his book *The Transdisciplinary Studio*,[6] Alex Coles takes an anthropological approach to describe the complex and multifaceted practices of four leading artists/designers in greater detail. Through multiple interviews with various staff members, he seeks deep insight into the high-level practices that keep such a studio both coherent and fluid. For the purposes of this book, we will concentrate on Studio Olafur Eliasson as an example:

Architecturally, Eliasson's Berlin studio is structured precisely so as to enable and promote this transdisciplinary model. On the top floor resides a school from which a Master of Fine Arts course that he leads is run, on the ground floor the work is fabricated, while the middle floors are divided between an office with architects, designers and model makers, and a space where his room-sized installations can be tested. The overall ambience of the studio is of a densely constructed think-tank in which artists, designers, architects, theorists and scientists collaborate to fashion new experiences and dialogues in the form of exhibitions, seminars and publications—all under the banner of Studio Eliasson.[7]

In addition to this studio in Berlin, Olafur Eliasson also has a small studio in Copenhagen that is not focused on project delivery but serves as a reflective space, and he also has a camper van in Iceland that he uses for landscape photography. All of these elements are inextricably linked in his oeuvre.[8] To quote Coles: "Instead of a machine, the studio has the sensibility of a living transdisciplinary organism in a constant state of mutation . . . Eliasson fluidly transfers a fundamental issue at play in the studio—the dialogical—to the work . . . with new workers perpetually being introduced into the studio and a constant stream of visitors, Studio Olafur Eliasson is able to produce an ever-widening range of works within the fields of painting, sculpture, design, photography, and architecture."[9] In an interview, Olafur Eliasson elaborates on this:

The methodological principles at play keep changing. This ensures that the studio doesn't become a static entity or a non-critical machine . . .

One of the most interesting collaborations for me . . . is the current one with the school upstairs. It's an entirely content-driven entity addressing questions that I am interested in, and a really crucial part of the studio right now, it's hard to imagine the studio without the school: the life of the Institute support and amplifies the diversity of the studio and vice versa. The school is very different ... the school puts me in a situation whereby instead of asking a question I'm assisting others to question—to co-question—what they are doing. A different kind of open-endedness comes from this that has a certain fragility to it.[10]

At the same time, he considers the studio to be purely an outcome of deeper, underlying processes—questioning Alex Coles's interest in the studio as a thing in itself:

Decisions about the structure of the studio were always content driven. In this sense, the studio has developed very organically—there has always been a good balance between input and output. I think there is a tendency to focus on its structure and form when talking about its development. But this seems a little abstract to me. The studio is never a primary topic, more a side product, and if I do think about it, it is always through content-related concerns ... it may be interesting to you as an object of study, but it doesn't really have a life of its own.[11]

Just as in the architectural practice of Ken Yeang, within the life of Studio Olafur Eliasson, exhibitions are not an outcome in themselves but seen more as testing grounds for development, the moment to expose the ideas of the studio to the wider world and invite comment. What Yeang, Hirshberg, and Eliasson are pointing toward are higher-level creative practices. They transcend the projects that creative activity is normally associated with, presenting a metalevel of practices for creating the infrastructure, the context for the practices and projects that sit within the philosophy of the firm—as well as the continued intellectual development across the projects.[12] In this chapter, we will combine all the lessons from the earlier chapters with what we know about these meta practices to come up with a structure for the studio.

The overall goal and organizing principle of a studio is systems vitality. What do we need to achieve that? We need to organize four types of studio activities:

- **Experimenting.** As an organization, we need to actively explore and learn as the world changes.
- **Learning.** We need to reflect on and draw lessons from these experiments, and also spread these lessons in our networks to inform change (and the development of the disciplines).
- **Communicating.** We need to show what we are doing and invite comments/feedback.

Figure 7.1 The studio model.

- **Growing.** The challenge of systems change means that we cannot remain the same ourselves. So in addition to the externally focused activities mentioned thus far, we also need to mirror these in a space of deep reflection, (personal and organizational) growth, and change.

These four types of studio activity can be organized into four spaces that stand in a dynamic relationship with one another: the *lab*, the *academy*, the *podium*, and the *temple* (see figure 7.1). Although there is no particular sequence to these activities (this depends on the situation and context of the organization), sustaining these activities in these four spaces is a prerequisite for the type of continuous change we associate with vitality. (Note that these elements can easily be recognized in the preceding examples—in particular, in Coles's description of Studio Olafur Eliasson.)

> **The lab** is the infrastructure for reframing and experimenting. In terms of the game changers model (see figure 4.1e, it strategically initiates the bottom-up experiments that create new practices within the organization, as well as feeds into the development of a new field—so the top-down processes are synchronized with the bottom-up ones. This is crucial: A system only really shifts when it shifts on every level. The lab is both the place of inspiration and exploration and the locus of the confrontation of ideas and dreams with reality.
>
> **The academy** is the infrastructure for learning within and outside the organization, as well as across the wider field. This is crucial

because in true systems change, it is not just organizations that will need to shift their practices, but whole professional fields that will need to reconsider what they do and redefine what they see as quality. For example, in the case of the agricultural crisis in the Netherlands (§ 6.2), whatever the precise outcome of the experiments and debates, it will in the future mean something else to be a farmer (moving away from maximizing production and toward more sustainable types of farming). This means that the education of farmers will also have to shift. Failing to do so would mean that through conventional schooling, we would continue to "copy" the old way of working into the new desired system. But building a new curriculum is a notoriously slow process, so the educational institutions of the key professions involved in the system will have to be closely involved in the experiments as they happen, picking up the new practices as soon as they emerge.

The podium is the infrastructure to ensure we change in constant open dialogue with the relevant context. Failing to do so could easily lead to new unquestioned assumptions creeping into the new practices, making them less than realistic and in the end creating risk (assumptions are a major cause of risk and failure). Experience has shown that it is good to set a strict rhythm for the podium activities; in creating a rhythm, the people working in the studio are continuously challenged ("What are we going to show?," "What are we going to do?," "Who should be there?"). This creates a continuous strategic discussion of what matters and of the nature of quality as the studio is developing. (In the project that we will describe in § 7.3, we settled on a six-month beat, so there is no real downtime). The podium is a dynamic self-portrait, open and extended out to the public, deliberately making the newly emerging practices vulnerable. It is staunchly future focused: Rather than "reporting" on what has been done, it is about preparing the ground for the activities in the time to the next podium moment.

The temple is the infrastructure for (personal and organizational) growth, anchoring the deep change and the new paradigms in the core of the organization and its people. The temple is a reflective, contemplative space, but it is also one of reckoning, making the change real on a personal level. This includes critical reflection on an existential level: Do the new practices the organization is developing make you feel alive (see § 8.1)?

These four spaces that make up the studio are all equally important; it is only when all are present and dynamically interrelated that there is systems vitality. The separate elements of the studio can be recognized in current activities and theories, often in isolation (learning organization, think tanks, skunkworks, etc.). But for second-order abduction (§ 2.4) to happen, these elements need to be present—all of them, all the time. This requires an effort and a commitment from the organization to creating these spaces: supporting them strongly but also holding on to them lightly so that the activities can remain fluid.[13]

7.2 THE STUDIO IS . . .

If we don't know how we can progress, we will need to *experiment*, *learn*, *discuss*, and *change*; these are the elements of the studio model. But this is all much easier said than done. The value of the studio model lies in the *how*, the collection and integration of practices that support these steps on all levels. The studio works right across the project level (framing; see chapter 3), the organizational level (game changing; see chapter 4), the sector level (paradigmatic shifts; see chapter 5), and societal transitions (see chapter 6), and we have already encountered the elements of the studio throughout the many case studies in this book. In this section, we will do a quick tour of the studio as a practice in order to emphasize the underlying thinking and concepts, highlighting elements that perhaps haven't had the attention they deserve in the earlier chapters. This is still a sketch: Although there are structures and principles that guide the workings of the studio, we will stay away from a proposing definite form. The shape things need to take really depends on the concrete problem situation or challenge (in agreement with Olafur Eliasson). A studio is content driven, so it is always *about* something. The case studies are much better at capturing how studio thinking works and how it can be shaped in very different environments. They show what a studio can do. We will structure a tour of eight snapshots of what makes the studio tick by starting each with the following statement: The studio is . . .

VITALITY

The studio is vitality.

The position and practices of the studio are shaped by its role in creating vitality (see figure. 7.2). The studio should initiate and inspire new reframing projects. The lessons from these projects can then be used to strategically challenge the organization's field: the paradigm that it sits within, as expressed in the narrative the organization lives, the qualities of the disciplines at play, and the (infra)structure that has been created to support (and perpetuate) the practices of the paradigm. The studio also plays a crucial role in syncing the bottom-up and top-down movement of ideas, the building and establishment of new practices. That is why the studio sits in the middle of the organization, where its ways are "set." The

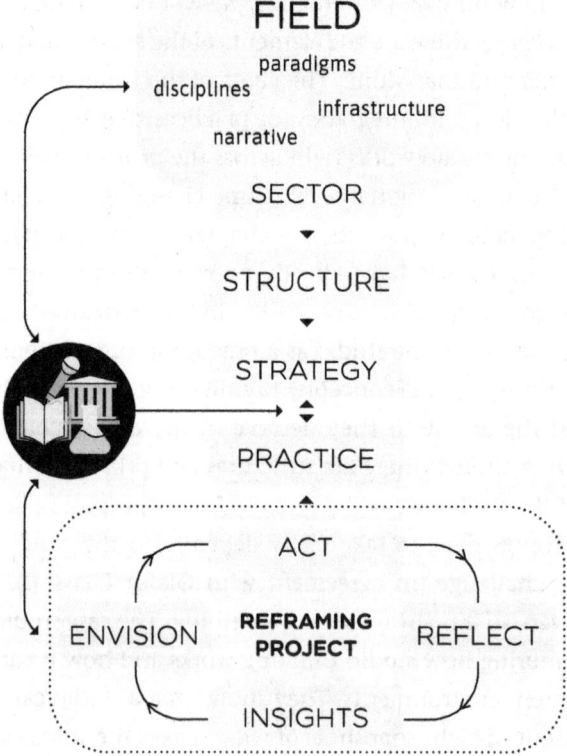

Figure 7.2 The position of the studio in the game changers model.

process of creating an initiative from first idea to realization and impact is a relay race that inevitably touches all parts of the organization; therefore, all of an organization should be represented in the studio practice. Some parts might be passive, in a support role, while others carry the initiative, but they should all be present. In this way, the studio connects the parts of the organization in new ways. The closer a studio can be to the line organization without compromising its freedom, the better.

A crucial aspect of that freedom is the right of the studio to challenge the certainties in the organization—using the lab, academy, podium, and temple to pick up signals in the real world and extending the scope of thinking beyond the confines of the day-to-day concerns. The studio is a little bit like a Jiminy Cricket, the conscience of the organization reminding it of its responsibilities in furthering a broader notion of prosperity— one that doesn't just deal with the here and now, but extends to the future and the *other* in the broadest sense of that word. The studio challenges assumptions and strategically initiates reframing projects to explore what practices are needed in the future and what the (structural) repercussions for the organization will be for adopting those. The studio is always a disturbance to the status quo. People that are wedded to business as usual may not like what the studio does, and it doesn't have positional power, but its independence, realism, transparency, and honesty should build a moral position and influence. The studio is also an irritant in the organization: hard to grasp, always unexpected, and at times activist in the way it operates. But the studio should always be interesting.

The studio is the place where an organization carries its bundle of overlapping frames (see § 6.3) and keeps them in tension: never resolved, never finished. The podium moments are incredibly important as they show the studio practice to the broader community. They create the dialogue around the studio and set its agenda for the next period. They also keep the studio dynamic: If something works, move on. The studio gives life to change. It *is* the vitality of the organization.

The openness of the studio works well with notions like open innovation and transdisciplinarity, and the studio easily reaches beyond the confines of the organization. After all, an organization is a structure to formalize activities and processes, but from a content perspective, these boundaries are quite arbitrary (they should be questioned constantly, in a networked world). You have seen that in frame creation, one of the crucial steps is to look at the broader field. The studio does the same, constantly searching for new perspectives and practices to move away from the old ones: moving far afield so that the organization can't fall back into those classical patterns. There is a treasure trove of practices out there. In that sense, it is much better for a studio not to go it alone; communities of practitioners that are each working on studios in their own context (a community like this has arisen around creative intelligence degrees; see appendix 6) are extraordinarily fruitful and exciting. They become an innovation ecosystem in their own right.

CONTENT

The studio is essentially content driven.

In the studio, content is central, while forms and practices are being questioned, undone, redesigned, created, tried, and discussed. You have seen this time and again in the case studies: Existing forms and practices had to be undone, and in the free space this creates, new forms and practices can emerge. For instance, in the A9 case study (§ 3.3), the current practices of the stakeholder managers (in the shape of organizing consultation evenings) had to be undone so that the temporary economy form could emerge. In the Kings Cross case study (§ 4.1), the police's law and order practice had to be loosened before the music festival frame, with all of its new forms and actions, could take root.

Organizations can become very focused on the forms and practices they have created for themselves over time and identify with these. For such an organization, the studio holds quite a different way of thinking that can be unsettling: Established/cherished forms and practices are questioned and discarded, with very little certainty about what will emerge in its place; initially, what we get in return are just more questions about what might be possible. On the positive side, for people in the organization, engaging with free-form conceptual thinking can spark a feeling of being liberated from the existing forms and practices, a true *freedom of thought* that wasn't there before.

The studio that is holding this thinking needs to be organized around abduction (just like Hirshberg organized his design agency around the creative priority). Olafur Eliasson alluded to this type of organizing when he said his Studio Olafur Eliasson has "no life of its own": Although it had a form, it had never been deliberately shaped as such; the form is just the result of purely content-driven decisions. That is exactly what makes it the space for deep change: The content is central in all thinking and all decisions. There is no striving to pin down a certain form or practices. On the contrary, there is a firm intention of not settling on its own shape. Studios are shapeshifters by nature. Not having a settled form is not the same as being in chaos; as you will see, there is a lot that can be said about the value to be achieved, the intent, the collaboration principles, and the external conditions that have to be taken into account. Yet there is a fundamental unformedness, a certain restlessness to a studio. The trick is to *organize* the studio practices without *formalizing* them or turning them into a bureaucracy.

This is counterintuitive to some people. In one of our projects, we saw this up close when a public sector organization that really wanted to adopt new practices and to become a true change agent for society faltered in its attempt because it had a very strong allergic reaction to unformedness. When a studio model was proposed, the organization never got away from its existing form; it tried to fit the fluidity (the "unform") of the studio within its existing structures and practices (rather than changing those). This is fundamentally impossible, and in the end the organization gave up. This is part of the great tragedy that some of our public sector organizations are living: They will continue to be part of a failing, broken system that is heading for a parliamentary enquiry (or a royal commission). The enquiry in turn will lead nowhere[14] because in its recommendations it will be aimed at fixing the existing forms (organizations) in the sector under review, rather than creating a space for deep change. They need a studio, they want one, but they can't accept it—yet.

MOVEMENT

The studio is ongoing movement.

The studio should always be changing. In a way it is very much like a *perpetuum mobile*: For centuries, scientists and engineers have been trying to create a frictionless machine that would just keep going, generating everlasting movement and energy (this is the engineering version of the alchemist's gold). Organizationally, the studio is the same; the paradox is that we want the studio to be very coherent, but avoid stability. And we want it to be integrated, yet the last thing we need is another organizational structure. We want to organize these specific practices without formalizing them, let alone creating a bureaucracy around them. Maybe we should be thinking about the studio as an inherently temporary phenomenon, a bit like Jean Tinguely's "self-destructing machines": forever disintegrating.[15] The studio is a space—not an innovation department, but a network of people that come together. It should involve people from across the organization and beyond. The quality of the relationships among the elements of the studio, and a shared sense of general direction (What are we moving away from? What do we explore? What do we want to move toward?) should be fostered in an open and informal space. There is only so much that can be organized in a studio; informal relationships are crucial as they are driven by inspiration and meaning. If we manage to get these relationships right, all the rest will follow (see the section on mentality ahead). Yet this lightness of touch is difficult to hold on to; the creation of fluidity is a never-ending task, as success and failure might both lead to stasis in their own way. We somehow have to avoid the establishment of a set way of working at all cost. How do we make a perpetuum mobile? Brilliant engineers have tried for centuries, but the laws of nature conspire against us; it can't be done. In trying to create an ever-changing, structured nonorganization, we are sinning against the laws of human nature, the deep-felt need for belonging and stability. It can't be done. But still, we have to keep doing it.

MENTALITY

The studio is a mentality.

It shares with creative fields like design a feeling that the world should not be taken at face value but that it can be reinvented, remade better. This requires an inquisitive nature, trying to understand why the man-made world is the way it is ("designer's eyes") coupled with an innate need to create and explore possibilities. Psychologically, the people involved should have a high tolerance for uncertainty, and socially, trust and safety in their relationships is absolutely crucial. If any of these are not present, they need to be tended to before the studio work can even start. In that sense, the studio is a mental space for deep change, which thrives on uncertainty, disturbance, the changing of the rules, and all the inspiration and vulnerability that comes with that. This space needs to be made.

A studio is as good as the quality of its relationships. The first step in the process of establishing a studio practice is to start a conversation about the principles we need to adopt to work together. The studio space consists of relationships that need to be minted and understood. These principles should be challenging, different enough from business as usual that nobody can fall back into their "normal" patterns of practice. They should be strongly anchored in people's positive drivers, especially those drivers that are normally not part and parcel of their professional lifeworlds. The principles should also be surprising, light, and humorous (see § 8.4 and appendix 5).

Normally, we hardly pay attention to the way we work together, and therefore we assume a certain type of relationship to be productive. The very act of sitting down together and discussing these various sets of remarkable principles sets the prospective studio participants up for the journey ahead. Taking the time to do this well guides and fosters a positive culture in the studio and beyond. Actually, more than just having a positive culture, a studio should be *fun*: Humor is important as it helps creates the lightness needed to deal with heavy, complex problem situations. Humor is often a play with expectations, which helps to break the ice and open up the dialogue to the possibilities of different frames. Hearing laughter in a studio meeting is always a good sign.

OPEN

The studio is open, complex, dynamic, and networked.

When looking for models of what a studio could and should be, the closest comparable concept in the domain of business and organizational models is open innovation.[16] Although the literature on open innovation is very tech oriented, the ethos and principles easily move across to studio thinking. Open innovation is an attitude that seeks to expand the horizon of an organization by learning from other organizations, sectors, and disciplines, and it is generous in return. It also seeks to avoid the myopia that can come from closing the shutters on an organization and holding on to its intellectual property for dear life. In the face of open, complex, dynamic, and networked problem situations, that approach just does not work anymore.

Still, the idea of this radical openness, deliberately paying it forward with unsure returns, does go against the grain for many people—especially in times of change, when there is very little basis for second-guessing what an eventual return might even look like. In first-order abduction, we can still guess in a fairly transactional way what we might expect. But in second-order abduction, we really cannot be sure where things will go, and we will need to keep our expectations open for a long-term give-and-take cycle. For people within an organization, this requires a license to explore and bring in practices that are further afield. Some creative agencies have these mechanisms in place and reward their people accordingly.[17] Open innovation is an attitude, and it should be everybody's business to be the eyes and ears of the studio. One can talk about the elephant in the room' to encourage people to express what is otherwise unsaid; the studio model is about going one step further and actively asking: "What elephants *should* be in the room?"

In the studio model, the podium gives shape to open innovation by creating an open dialogue about the work that is being done, as seen through many perspectives. It is the locus where other disciplinary practices can be brought in and transdisciplinarity can start to happen. The hypercomplex nature of transitions demands this open, dynamic, and flexible approach to navigate all the unknowns as the future unfolds. This is the only way to ensure long-term system vitality.

FUTURE

The studio is about the future.

This may seem like an obvious thing to say, but when we go to school, we learn thinking skills and doing skills based on the world as it is and how it was. Thus, we build up a relationship with the past (history and literature), with the world (geography, sustainability), with each other (culture), and with broader society (economics, citizenship). But we don't learn how to deal with the future. Yet that is what we are going to need most when we go out into the world. What is a healthy relationship with the future, anyway? When we think about the future, we seem to be caught in trying to "read" the developments in the world, but that is a passive way of dealing with the future.

How can we look ahead and engage with the future in such a way that we feel empowered? Riel Miller (UNESCO) talks about the skills to do this in terms of *future literacy*. He advocates for the creation of a new *science of anticipation*.[18] After all, even in our day-to-day decision-making, we are constantly anticipating what the world is going to be like, and our actions are guided by our expectations. In the social sphere, this even doubles in complexity when we try to take into account our expectations of what others might expect of us.

In Riel Miller's words:[19]

Exploratory futures are those aspects of the present that need to be discovered. Exploration is about "seeing" the present differently. . . . Exploring this dimension of the potential of the present is a delicate and ephemeral balancing act when compared to optimisation or contingency, and depends on the paradoxical, even contradictory task of building scaffolding that enables "rigorous imagining." . . . Exploration is not about the paths not taken—which are only the possibilities of the past brought to life by the present. Instead, it is about futures unimagined and hence a present that does not *yet* make sense.

He then distinguishes three types of explicit anticipation: optimization, contingency, and novelty:[20]

There is no way to outsmart the complexity of reality; unforeseeable novelty is a certainty. Instead, the approach should be to try and develop the capacity to use the future in a range of different ways, and not be limited by prediction or by narrow conceptions of a desired future. It is about being Futures Literate. . . . The foresight process must be designed using a threefold framework [a learning cycle] that pays equal attention to:

1. Narrative—developing sense-making frameworks and stories that are meaningful to the participants in the process and "targets" decision makers relevant to the process;
2. Collective intelligence—generating evidence through action research that uses imaginary futures to invent and create collaborative maps, enabling

all participants to bring their deep and specific knowledge into the "story";
3. Reframing—using "rigorous imagining" to develop and question the theories and models that define the variables and relationships, metrics and definitions being used to make sense of the present (note: pattern recognition/data mining is insufficient).

... The point is not to test present assumptions against some predictive future, but to use the future to question, unpack, invent what is going on and what is doable now. By increasing our capacity to improvise and be spontaneous, live with permanent ambiguity and novelty, [future literacy] frees us up to go beyond the predictable, and enables us to embrace complexity.

And as we have said before, there are different timescales of futures that work out completely differently in all of this: the short-term, small future is pretty much like the present, and immediate fixes are needed to change undesirable problem situations into better ones. The long-term, Large future (with a capital *L*) is full of words, ideas, and visions about where the world will and/or should go. The medium future is the hard one to grapple with: This is the battleground; this is where we should create strategies that give us a way to move from short-term and small to long-term and Large—and this where we are treading water. To navigate this medium-range issue (in time and in scope) is precisely why we need the studio. Within the studio practice, the lab and the podium most explicitly deal with the future. But future literacy should permeate all studio practices, all the time. More on this later.[21]

ACTION

The studio is a path to action.

Starting a studio practice cannot be captured in a set, step-by-step process. The variety of situations requires an equal variety of studios as content is always leading, and process and structure should follow. Yet there are some very general rules of thumb that have surfaced in our own practices that might be helpful in scaffolding early studio activities, presented here with the caveat that the upcoming case studies will give a much broader, more detailed, and real sense of what is required. Within the context of the master's program in creative intelligence and innovation (see appendix 6), we have developed three subjects in which the participants (midcareer professionals from many different disciplines) get three semesters to basically set up a bespoke studio within their own organizations. Those three semester-long subjects are as follows:

1. **Digging for paradigms.** In this subject, the participants first establish an archaeology of the current situation and practices within the organization, then look beyond the organization at the paradigms that dominate the sector and its key disciplines (and hold it in place). This step, in which they use open qualitative research methods like grounded theory and the Delphi method, leads to a mapping of the open and the hidden rules[22] as a stepping stone to deframing. Then they identify what practices most likely are going to be needed in the future and which of the current ones are going to be in the way. This defines the challenges for the studio and informs the strategic frame experiments of the next subject.

2. **Frame experiments.** In the second subject, these framing experiments are executed to test some of the assumptions from the first subject, as well as to explore possible paths forward for the organization. These frame experiments are set up to show what is going to be hard to change. It is not the objective to deal with these challenges and barriers just yet; for now, they are just noted as facts of life.

    At the same time, these framing experiments prepare the ground for future developments by involving a broad group of stakeholders within and outside the organization. This intervention starts to create a context for change by inspiring people and showing what is possible.

3. **Future-proof your organization.** In the third subject, we take a step back and ask: "What is needed to make this happen? What needs to change? What does an organization that is good at X look like?" This creates the profile of the studio and an agenda for the development of an innovation infrastructure within the organization.

On a very practical note: the fact that a studio can take so many shapes can make it difficult for people to get a grasp of what it is and what needs to be done. In an absolute worst-case workshop scenario, people can become completely fixated on the four spaces in the studio and not get much beyond discussing what should be in the lab, the academy, the podium, and the temple. To avoid this, we have used questions to help guide the discussion in such a workshop (see box 7.1). The answers to these questions help define the studio much more easily.

Box 7.1. The Studio Workshop Questions

LAB

Experimenting
What could work?
  How do we find out?
  What are we going to do?
  (Who/what/when?)

ACADEMY

Learning
What do we know?
  What do we want to know?
  What can we learn from the experiments?
  Who should know this?
  How can we reach them?
  What are we going to do?
  (Who/what/when?)

PODIUM

Discussing
How are we doing?
  What could be done better?
  What are we missing?
  What do other people think?
  What are we going to do in the next step?
  (Who/what/when?)

TEMPLE

Growing
What does this mean?
  (For me and for the organization?)
  What will I change?

QUALITY

The studio is all about quality.

The studio exists in the systems world, and though the studio practice is different from the way an organization normally operates, it should integrate with the world of systems and organizations to a degree if it is to be taken seriously. Therefore, the monitoring and measuring of the value created in the studio should be an integral part of its practice. But the peculiar nature of the studio—structured as it is around processes that are driven by content and shaped by second-order abduction—means that this needs some special attention. A studio can be measured, but not by common criteria. The point is that within a studio, quality is a discussion.

One example that has inspired us in this respect is Design Academy Eindhoven, one of the foremost design schools in the world. The agenda of the school is dominated by the fact that two times a year, it has a podium moment: the Salone del Mobile in Milan (March/April) and the Dutch Design Week (in October). Having to perform on these podiums is really hard work—and as soon as you have finished with one, the full attention needs to go to the next one, which is not many months away at all. This means that the whole community is *continuously engaged in a quality discussion*: "What are we going to show? Why? What is 'good'?" This is the best stimulus for achieving quality one can imagine.[23]

Often, in a fluid studio practice, people are worried about quality control: The appropriate response is that within an environment with so many unknowns, quality is not a simple measurement, but it is a discussion. All activities in the studio are about quality, about (re)defining it time and time again. Anybody who wants to know what the quality is can come in and take part in that discussion. The fundamental fluidity of the studio model requires a more active role than just measuring quality after the fact. Once things that are created in the studio practice have taken shape as a more formalized outcome, their quality can be measured. But in the studio practice itself, quality is participatory.

7.3 CASE: ATTRACTIVE, CLEAN, WHOLE, AND SAFE IN NEW-WEST

Amsterdam New-West is a greenfield extension to the city that was built in the 1960s to 1970s. It is dominated by social housing, mostly in low-rise apartment buildings, and has suffered from years of neglect. This particular project kicked off when some citizens in New-West were fed up with the litter and filth in public spaces and took action. A citizen-led initiative around garbage collection and cleanliness (the "Litter Revolt") led to the establishment of the "Attractive Clean Whole Safe" program, initiated and supported by the local government. Social designers were engaged to work on hotspots, like those we'll discuss in what follows.

A Market

The weekly market on Plein 40–45 is a crucial source of affordable goods and food for the whole area. But there have been long-standing complaints and conflicts around the after-hours cleanup, especially about the packaging materials (plastic waste) left behind. It took quite a bit of effort to establish communication between the stakeholders and discuss possible ways forward. In the end, a common budget was allocated, and the key parties (local residents, council, market stall holders) now discuss and decide together how to allocate this budget to new initiatives. Proud before-and-after pictures provide evidence that the situation on the ground has improved immensely.

A School

The street on which the neighborhood school stands is known locally as the "candy strip": There are problems with litter in public spaces. The school was built without a schoolyard, so pupils spill out onto the street during breaks and hang around after hours. Together, all parties have created an "experience map" (a map annotated with quotes) of the street. This has provided a basis for calling out antisocial behavior and has led to collaboration on a street party to demonstrate the value of the environment for everybody. For the residents, this also led to a closer understanding of the lifeworlds of the pupils and the pressures they are under (and the insight that, interestingly, the pupils initially didn't want to be involved in the cleanup because they associated it with compulsory community service). Close observation also led to the realization that a lot of the litter actually comes from the clientele of the two night shops in the street and not from the school at all.

An Industrial Area

This particular industrial area is built as a twenty-four-hour activity zone. It was discovered by youth during COVID lockdowns as a convenient place to hang out in their cars at night and do some street racing. This makes the workers in the area feel unsafe. Closer engagement helped allay some of these fears, and the parties are now looking for a location where the car recreation can happen without getting in the way of business.

An Area with Student Housing

This particular area of the city, close to a major railway hub, has always been a transit zone. People here are nomadic; the social structure is weak, and the public spaces look unloved and unkempt. A major problem is presented by the large student housing complexes, where household wares are dumped when students are moving out.

Completely in character, the initial call for participation in an initiative to create better green spaces in the neighborhood had no response at all. But when the initiators started doing guerilla gardening, this immediately attracted students and residents who that came to help (even in the pouring rain). This was the start of a growing local movement.

The social design approaches (experience maps, creative sessions) had great impact on a local level and sparked lots of new community engagement. Although these are exemplary social design projects in their own right, there is also an ambition on the part of the designers and local council to actually change the system. (On the system side, Amsterdam is divided into seven local government areas that are serviced by centralized departments, directly under the overall municipality. These departments are impressive organizations in their own right; greater Amsterdam has about nine hundred thousand inhabitants.)

The New-West local government area has taken the lead in trying to achieve systems change. But the system parties (centralized departments like garbage collection, for example) felt challenged by the citizens' initiatives and the results achieved in the hotspots. In terms of the game changers model, there was a real danger of exceptional-quality bottom-up projects not getting through to impact—and top-down models struggling to engage in a positive manner with this disturbance of business as usual (the first reaction is allergic). Internally, the centralized service departments are dealing with their own pressures (budget cuts, efficiency drives, pressure on human resources, etc.) and can't always engage with innovation and change.

A podium moment was set up for the two sides to meet. Introducing the game changers model to the discussion helped both camps, the bottom-up citizen initiatives and the top-down public service organizations, to recognize the situation, understand the issue, and realize that mutual learning needs to happen. After all, the bottom-up initiatives are unlikely to "replace" the existing systems; a lot of these local initiatives can only work because they sit close to the lived worlds of people and within their social spheres. As such, they don't scale, and perhaps they can only work in an informal manner (in terms of the studio, they can be organized but not formalized). For the system parties, the bottom-up initiatives do represent values that apparently have not been well represented in the system. If that is deemed unacceptable, then it needs to change—but how? This is where we need to think together about a way forward. One proposal in the workshop was to look at other organizations that have managed to embed these same values that have driven the citizens to action, and see what we can learn from those organizations in terms of practices, structures, and processes. For example, one of the values was helpfulness—which led to a comparison with the Automobile Association as an example of an organization that does manage to organize itself around this value. What does it do, and how does this compare to the practices of the municipality? (It starts with the fact that the Automobile Association picks up the phone when you call.) This served as a good, nonthreatening mirror and a source of inspiration for how things could be done differently.

In terms of the game changers model, this could be seen as a one-off intervention to change the narrative around the municipality departments (figure 4.1e) and introduce new practices that have been developed in the hotspot projects. But the problem is more systemic, and the ambition is to actually change the way the municipality operates, not just on a local level or in this problem arena, but more broadly. This needs a studio to create an ongoing movement. The parties decided to work together to reset the relationship (with the local government area as a crucial bridge between top down and bottom up, and a source of unwavering support).

In the next podium session, the stakeholders were brought together at an exhibition of the project work to date, hosted at the local government area offices. First participants were invited to look at the hotspot projects from a distance, as a phenomenon, and then in a second round the question was asked: What infrastructure would be needed to support this on a bigger/larger scale? What needs to change to make this happen? This helped frame the next steps: These included more conversations to draw the lessons from the existing hotspot experiments and involving more of the (missing) middle-management layer of the service organizations in the development of structural solutions.

The municipality realizes that this has to be part of a larger strategic movement toward what it calls *relational government*: creating a different relationship with the citizen and making the quality of that relationship central in the practices of the public sector organization. This requires the development of new practices and capabilities. This includes big shifts in culture and practices, like the adoption of a radical transparency: If there is an issue in the neighborhood, don't pull it into the public sector organization (as the problem owner) and shut yourself away with a problem to "solve" it for the citizen; instead, be transparent in your communication and open to input all along the way. The studio has been set up with a six-month rhythm of podium moments (sometimes workshops or dialogue sessions; sometimes an exhibition like the one mentioned earlier), and the next steps will involve setting the agenda for the academy: There needs to be some capability building on all sides to really make this happen, beyond the original initiators and hotspots.

In retrospect, this systems change project could have been sparked by just about anything and would have led to the same structural questions for the municipality. But rubbish is a good, very visible symptom of the state of the public space. From a citizens' initiative perspective, the interventions are clear and the results are immediately visible for everybody. From the side of the municipality, the issue of rubbish cuts through the organization in an interesting way: it includes departments like Planning (the architecture of public spaces), Maintenance, Enforcement, Garbage Collection, and Resources, and it touches on broader policy agendas in the circular economy (Amsterdam has embraced the "donut economy" thinking and is keen to implement this across the organization). The theme also brings up bigger questions, highlighting issues in the relationship between the central municipality and the local council areas, and it brings up some hidden skeletons, processes that should have worked, but in effect didn't; this can be painful, bad news, but these things need to be addressed to have an impact.

In the end, the studio needs to be about creating the relationships that make a neighborhood thrive. In the case of New-West, there was a bit of a lucky accident with remarkable people (on the side of the citizens and municipality) in just the right positions to make this happen. The local council played an important role as a catalyst for both the bottom-up and top-down movements: coming in from the side, like in figure 7.2, and synchronizing the movements when needed. Because of the apparent success of the Attractive Clean Whole Safe program, the municipality now wants it spread to other neighborhoods. The conventional rhetoric will talk about "rolling out" this program, which is a recipe for disaster—for two reasons:

- In design terms, the projects done in New-West are a prototype of a new way of working (and a proof of concept). There is a long road ahead to develop this from a prototype to a product. A prototype is a very handcrafted version: What is the minimal viable version that will help other people get on the same journey?
- What are the exact conditions that have made this work so well in New-West? These include the coming together of three remarkable people, the opportunity created by the local council to support the hotspot activities with time and attention, and the patience on its part to engage with the studio as an open way of working. That is crucial for the right things to have a chance to emerge. Also, on the citizens' side, New-West has proven to be a fruitful social space, and the garbage revolt has proven to be an ideal catalyst for getting people together. This will all not be the same in other areas of the city. The very unformedness of the original project also cannot be replicated; other people will see the shape the interventions have taken in New-West and can consider it to be a threat to their current practices—projecting their fears. Ideally, you'd want to start all over in these other neighborhoods, take a fresh approach to the real issues at play, and work with people to create ownership and empowerment. But this is hard. You can only have a first kiss once.

The podium moments of the New-West studio can be a gentle way to make others aware of what is happening and to look for the initiators that intuitively get it. This is a temple moment for the original crew: What does it really take to make this happen? Over time, there will be a need for more academy-type activity; you cannot assume that capabilities are just there, in the home-grown way that the New-West projects have developed over time. The synchronization of the three developments—(1) on a project level, (2) organizational change on a local and greater city level, and (3) the personal growth of key people that accompanies the development of new practices—needs to be monitored and managed closely. If one of these runs ahead, it may need to be slowed down. This is especially true for the project level; something is only a good idea when there is a context that can value it. If the organization isn't ready, press pause and do not present it yet. Above all, beware of the top-down rhetoric on "rolling out" a form; as ever, content should lead.

The pressure is on: This approach has received broad recognition and interest, and an opportunity for continuity has presented itself through National Program New-West—a twenty-year government initiative to elevate the neighborhood.

7.4 CREATING INNOVATION ECOSYSTEMS

The studio, as we have discussed it in this chapter, creates space for meaningful transformation in an organization or problem situation. You have seen that engaging deeply with the issues also leads to implications on a sector level (in the Amsterdam case study: adopting the "relational government" paradigm). But as said the big challenges we are facing in the world, the societal transitions, require yet a different setup. They cannot be approached directly: We need to muster the meaningful transformations we can create on a sector level and bring them together to achieve the big transitions. We will use the concept of an *innovation ecosystem* to describe the infrastructure needed to support systems change on this scale.

In principle, the studio elements and lessons are valid on this level too—an innovation ecosystem could be seen as a "Studio of Studios." However, the incredible complexity of transitions, and the fact that there is no clear ownership, brings additional challenges: (1) Who *initiates* an innovation ecosystem? Or is an innovation ecosystem something that should emerge naturally? (2) Innovation ecosystems develop across many stakeholders—raising the question of *configuration*: Who should be involved, in what way, and what roles should they play? And (3) how are we to deal with all of these developments across groups and organizations? How do we orchestrate these meaningful transformations, so they add up to an overall transition worth wanting? This is the question of *navigation*: how can we keep track of where we are and how we are doing. We will see that the art of bringing together these meaningful transformations in an innovation ecosystem is not so much about deliberately "shaping transitions" in a predetermined shape or form, but creating new overall value and meaning through open innovation (see § 7.5).

INITIATION OR EMERGENCE

How does an innovation ecosystem come about? Well, your hand can be forced: In the Amsterdam New-West example, a citizen 'uprising' worked as a catalyst for change, and the next case study will illustrate how a shift toward more sustainable industries forces the development of a new basis for regional thriving. In both these cases, pressures originating outside of the system created a clear and distinct impetus for change for the problem owner ("we can't go on like this"). Unfortunately, this also means that these transitions start quite late in the game; they are a reaction to things that are already going awry. The question is how we can be much more proactive, initiating an innovation ecosystem before the proverbial shit hits the fan. This is tricky because in transitions, there is no clear problem owner: Where can the initiative come from? And where should it land? It is hard to talk about such things in general, so let's consider a specific example: the much-needed transition in the care system. Care is a deeply human value and one of the drivers holding a society together.

The sheer scale of the need for care has led to the creation of many large organizations (service providers), together making up very complex systems that are bureaucratic, are hard to navigate for the people that need care, and are becoming unaffordable in the face of an aging population. Earlier attempts to make care more efficient and affordable has led to measures like privatization, the redistribution of money through "personal care budgets," and basically handing care back to society, expecting citizens to care for each other. This has had immense impact on people's lives: Informal caregiving can be a huge burden (research into people looking after chronically ill partners shows these carers reporting a quality of life rating of zero) and has unintended side effects, like taking people that are at the height of their productive careers out of the economy to care for ailing family members. The consensus is that this "participation society" has largely failed through a lack of proper support infrastructure for people to take on these added care tasks. So the care system still needs reimagining. In this book, you have seen promising projects and new types of organizations like Partners in Recovery (§ 4.3), Thriving Communities Australia (§ 6.5), Care Republic (§ 6.5) (and there are others, like the Redesigning Psychiatry program[24]) as great examples of radically different approaches. They prove that things can be done differently, and to great effect. What these programs have in common is that they all are based on providing empowerment/support for people that need care, challenging the idea that medical care is the model for all types of care.

The problem of waiting lists that do not ever go away is currently the trigger for a radical systems rethink. The medical care paradigm is organized pretty much as a problem-solving process: from intake to diagnosis, referral, and treatment. These different parts of the machine are connected in stage gate processes that ensure moments of quality control. Although the process of sickness that leads the process can be gradual and unpredictable, the system works in discrete steps—meaning that there always is a misfit between the development of the illness and the treatment response. There will *always* be waiting lists, because they are created by the system. This situation becomes dramatic when the system is overstretched: If a diagnosis is followed by a lengthy time on a waiting list before the treatment commences, chances are the diagnosis has slipped by that time and the treatment will be ineffective. In the medical care paradigm, the patient and their immediate carers have no agency in any of these processes. It is clear that we need to move away from medical thinking and develop a new paradigm that is appropriate to what care actually is, in society and in the lifeworlds of people. There is a wealth of projects around the world that are providing the evidence that things can be done differently, and better. These projects are starting to find one another. In places, we are close to a critical mass of people involved in this movement to cause it to self-ignite and get going. The pressure is on, and the innovation ecosystem is emerging. What is probably needed is a catalyst, a temporary sponsor (most likely to come from outside of the current system) to create the space so that deep change will finally happen.

CONFIGURATION

Who should be involved in the innovation ecosystem? In the transitions we have discussed before (and the one we will explore in the next section), it is clear that they range across all parties, coming together in the societal midfield. If we use the studio as a model for supporting innovation in a world of open, complex, dynamic, and networked problem situations, the innovation ecosystem can be seen as connecting the partners' studio practices—if you want, a *studio of studios* (to echo General McChrystal's *team of teams*). These studios need to be in a dynamic relationship with one another, complementing each other, leveraging off one another, and holding each other close across the differences.

In general, the movement that a studio goes through over time—from sketchy to more focused and precise—is even stronger here. Analogous to urban planning methodologies, we can see how an innovation ecosystem would have to work in layers, from small and general to bigger and ever more detailed, meticulously staged discussions to gather input to make decisions. More stakeholders are needed along the way as we move from content discussions to gradually approaching the creation of form. Thinking back to earlier cases of collaborative projects in this book, we can use the innovation ecosystem concept as a lens to consider what infrastructure was available to progress the change and what was lacking. In the Gouda case study in § 4.3, for instance, the project level could be supported well by the different partners. The collaboration between the partners was also supported (with some funding from the Arts Council), but the overall vision for the transition came from the university, and in retrospect it did not have a firm home in the field (at the top of the game changers model). The new narrative that the projects were working toward was there, but it was only supported by individuals rather than understood and supported by the organizations more broadly. When one of these remarkable individuals (the director of the museum) left, support dwindled across the board and the initiative was lost.

In the Amsterdam New-West case study, there was an interesting role for the local council as a catalyst providing crucial support and infrastructure for this development. It is definitely a stakeholder in the area, but not a direct player on the critical path in the problem situation between the citizens and the departments of the municipality. Positive results coming from the Attractive Clean Whole Safe initiative are good for the council, but it could have chosen to ignore this development; again, the commitment hangs on an inspired individual going the extra mile. The project would not have flourished without that individual's support; the hotspot projects would have been just as good, but they would have been stuck in the bottom-up process of the game changers model. These catalyst partners on the side might be crucial in supporting transitions across the board (see appendix 2).

In creating an innovation ecosystem, it is good to remind ourselves of the fact the societal transitions are not happening in isolation: They are happening in parallel (§ 6.1) and will impact the lifeworlds of people simultaneously. Our understanding of the (future) lifeworlds of people should guide the configuration of the innovation ecosystem. Ideally, an innovation ecosystem is built up out of studios dealing with the future of the various domains, coming together in discussions on the lifeworld (especially the lifeworlds of people who are vulnerable and might be left behind if we are not careful). In creating this studio of studios, we have found it useful to steer away from the usual way of defining sectors in our society (education, health, etc.), instead creating these studios by societal function—for instance, not education, but learning (which happens everywhere in society, and when you think of it, the formal education sector is only a small part of that); not health, but care; not agriculture, but food. This gets us closer to the values that need to be created (what actually matters) in the chain, while taking us away from the usual suspects in a sector and the pitfalls of the usual discussions. It creates the ground for a fresh and unexpected set of parties coming together around the issues. To populate these studios, we need pioneers in all these sectors to contribute. A community of innovative and committed pioneers from right across society, going across all sectors, is a real asset to broaden the repertoire of practices at play in the innovation ecosystem (see appendix 6).

NAVIGATION

Innovation ecosystems are complex configurations of multiple stakeholders, often organizations that are coming from completely different sectors, plus community groups and individuals, each with their own internal and external agendas and change processes. It is easy to lose track of what is happening. Yet we don't want to enforce a structure on what should fundamentally be fluid and shapeless for the emergence of new form, sense, and meaning to occur.

Where are we? What should the next step be? These questions are absolutely crucial in navigating this hypercomplexity. This is tricky; the quality of the innovation ecosystem lies in the quality of the connections and the quality of the dialogue. This often does require somebody to take on the role of a curator of the innovation ecosystem. This role can be supported by some helpful tools for creating overviews and shaping the right discussions. The reason is twofold: Through a lack of overview, the innovation ecosystem might be inadvertently slanted toward one or more stakeholders, sectors, or domains and fail to properly represent the breadth of the issues under consideration. And for the purpose of synchronizing the activities in the innovation ecosystem, we need to trace where parties are in their development, the nature/maturity of their discussions, and their readiness for the next steps.

Having said that, there is not a single matrix or canvas that can do justice to the complexity of a developing innovation ecosystem—yet in this book, you have seen a number of models that help position and trace where people are in their activities and thinking, and we can borrow practices from many different professional fields that all have had to develop their own ways of dealing with complexity (in a true transdisciplinary manner).

For instance, we have found it useful, for every major stakeholder, to regularly map the level and breadth of the discussion:

- **The level of discussion.** Where are they on the different layers of the practices model (action, method, principles, values)? This allows us to plot the depth of the discussions (Are they about methods? Principles?) and flag when there is a stakeholder that is not on the same page, so to speak. This is done by tracing how things are talked about and on which level, rather than what is said.
- **The breadth of the discussion.** How they are dealing with the elements of "broad prosperity"? This traces whether they concentrate on the now or on the future (short term, midterm, long term) and on which level they consider the other (from the immediate other to the global other).[25]

The models in this book all provide different ways to trace the development of the discussions; for instance, it can be useful to consider the locus of the discussion of the game changers model and trace the projects and relationships formed within the innovation ecosystem in the societal midfield model to ensure a good spread of parties across the different societal domains.

7.5 CASE: FUTURE HUNTER: SOCIAL CHANGE IN TIMES OF TRANSITION

To get a sense of the nature and dynamics of transitions, we will briefly consider two examples of regional transformation from the Netherlands before launching into the main case study on the Hunter innovation ecosystem.

The Case of Eindhoven: A City Reinvents Itself

For an example of a successful transition, we can consider the change that the city and region of Eindhoven, in the Netherlands, has experienced in the last twenty years. In the early 2000s, the giant consumer electronics firm Philips saw its markets shift to the point where it realized it was no longer fit for purpose. After a decade of reorganizations to keep the boat afloat, the firm decided to create spin-offs of its most successful new ventures, sell off its consumer electronics branches, and completely concentrate on the professional market in the medical domain. The industrial city of Eindhoven, which had literally grown up around the Philips factories and their need for workers, shifted very quickly into an open innovation model.[26] The now-abandoned factories were turned into creative hubs; high-tech firms were drawn by the well-educated workforce, and twenty years on the city is thriving like never before. The organization driving this transition is called *Brainport*;[27] it is a collaboration between private and public sector parties that has created the infrastructure for this new economic basis to emerge. Crucially, it has provided a clear focus (in this case, specializing in creating the hardware for the software revolution), financial support, and risk mitigation to attract key players to the region—and it has done so consistently for over twenty years. However, this great success also holds a cautionary tale: The industrial shift to a deep-tech innovation ecosystem has come with many new high-tech (engineering) jobs. Expats are pricing the local people out of the housing market, and this situation is expected to worsen dramatically as the authorities expect another seventy thousand high-tech vacancies over the next ten years.[28] In Eindhoven, there are now voices for more democratic control over this development. The main lesson to be learned here is that great economic success comes with great social upheaval—and that in terms of transitions, in the end, if it doesn't work for society, then it doesn't work at all. A second lesson would be that this social strife could have been avoided, to a degree, if the local education sector had kicked into gear earlier to educate the workers of the future. But educational change is slow, and all kinds of (financial) rules make it hard for parties like the Fontys University of Applied Sciences and Eindhoven University of Technology to scale up to meet the demand.

The Case of Chemelot: From Coal to Oil-Based Chemistry to . . .

Something similar is now happening at an oil-based chemical factory near Sittard, in the south of the Netherlands. When the coal mines closed in the early 1970s, Dutch State Mines (DSM) reinvented itself as a chemical/materials industry based on oil. Now that oil-based chemical products are declining and eventually coming to an end, shifting to bio-based chemistry is no mean task. The old mine site turned chemical factory has been renamed *Chemelot*,[29] and it has opened its gates to start-ups and experimental labs to use the facilities and profit from the chemical/process know-how and high safety standards. The open innovation approach is supported by a special organization called *Brightlands*.[30] The area now employs 8,500 people in seventy-five industrial companies and eighty materials-development companies—and, most importantly for the future, there are 1,200 students there now on a continuous basis. It is also one of the anchor points for a broader regional transformation; the surrounding countryside is now part of an IBA (*Internationale Bau Ausstellung*;[31] see appendix 5). Like Philips, the chemical industry complex is using an open innovation approach to engage in what is basically an act of creative self-destruction. This involves stepping back from the form things have taken historically and concentrating on content—a process of deconstructing, reinventing, and rebuilding differently. This is all built on a broad consensus, in industry and in society, that we can't go on like this. Creating this consensus is crucial: It means that new developments are not hampered by the need to fight the existing structures and can concentrate on creating space for learning to achieve deep change. What these transitions also show is that real systems change is a huge responsibility to take on, too much to bear for any one party. The precise consequences of a structural transition are hard to predict; this holds true if we consider each of them separately, but especially when they coincide, when transitions come together to influence the lived world of the citizen (a perfect storm). Conventionally, technological and economic development thinking would lead these kinds of change processes, and people's lives and society would be left to deal with the consequences. In this case, societal transformation should inform and guide the technical and economic change, rather than the other way around. Taking on these transitions also means taking on a large responsibility. After all, this is not about creating some improvements for an existing system, it is about creating a system that is fit for purpose in 2030, 2040, and beyond. To do so, we need to envisage what the values and needs of that future society will be. And who are we to decide? We will need to create a normative framework for the development of the new system. Just meaning well is not good enough.

Note that there are also differences between this and the previous case study. Eindhoven made a strategic choice early on to specialize in creating the deep-tech ecosystem that produces the hardware for the software revolution (becoming the hardware version of Silicon Valley). And it has stuck with that choice for more than twenty years, investing in it structurally through Brainport and other mechanisms. In contrast, the Chemelot complex is exploring whether its current core capabilities (ammonia, naphtha) might be too narrow a focus in the long run. The development of a bio-based chemical industry requires fundamental research and development, as well as the creation and scaling of new technology; consistency in infrastructure strategy is crucial, as is the development of a local base of skills, knowledge, and talent. This is early-stage open innovation in the true sense, and the best thing for now is to let a thousand flowers bloom, monitor the opportunities as they crystallize, and be ready to support the development from that point.

Now let's move to a transition that is very wide open: the case of Newcastle and the Hunter Valley in Australia.[32]

Future Hunter: Social Change in Times of Transition

The Port of Newcastle, in the Hunter region just north of Sydney, is the largest coal port in the world and proudly positions itself as "Australia's deepwater global gateway." Like many other ports and regions, it will need to shift away from a coal-based industry and infrastructure and find a role in a world that moves toward renewable energy. The port has set up a program for diversifying for the future and investing to support thriving communities, local jobs, and a prosperous Hunter region. Its centerpiece is the development of a 220-hectare Clean Energy Precinct on reclaimed land. The precinct is powered by a green energy infrastructure (one of Australia's biggest green energy zones is projected in the hinterland). The port has excellent facilities (with excellency in supply chain management) and is supported by a strong alliance of local stakeholders—including ones that are going through their own transitions, like a major mining company that is soon closing down one of the biggest coal mines in the country. The broad alliance of project partners includes clean energy producers; electricity infrastructure companies; stakeholders in gas network / power generation; heavy industry; traditional port activities like logistics, export, and bunkering; mobility and infrastructure providers; and local educational institutions.

The technical, industrial, and economic questions that are facing this innovation ecosystem of companies and institutions are formidable: What, for instance, should the role of hydrogen/ammonia be in this new economy? It could be a useful carrier of energy for the local industry, but exporting raw energy in the form of liquid hydrogen is a relatively low value-add proposition. Greater value could be created by new industries that capture the energy through added value in goods—or even in raw materials like steel and aluminum. But greater added value could also be created in new biochemical industries—for instance, through the use of algae to create complex carbohydrates. That requires an investment in new technology development and the creation of whole new industries, as well as an investment in infrastructure.

What type of industry could thrive if green energy was available in abundance? What type of industry could support a regional economy that is strong, sustainable, and inclusive? What type of industry could be supported by the local educational institutions so that the good people of Newcastle and the Hunter Valley can thrive in the new economy? Just asking the questions immediately gets us into the tricky realm of social transitions. Who are the current people in Newcastle and Hunter? Who will be the future people that the region will attract through its shift in activities? What will they want and need? And this also raises a red flag: We have seen that education is slow to shift, so they would need to start the educational change now or risk leaving people behind. The Eindhoven example has shown that if a transition doesn't work for society, it doesn't work at all.

To complicate matters, the city of Newcastle and the Hunter Valley are of course dynamic already, evolving in many ways. (1) Socially, we see a generational shift, with younger generations having completely different levels of education, jobs, and needs than their parents. (2) There are many new people coming into the area. During the COVID lockdowns, people from nearby Sydney discovered the beauty and lifestyle of Newcastle and Hunter and have flooded in. (3) This in turn has made housing much more expensive, making it harder for local young people to live in Newcastle. The challenge of this transition to creating a strong, inclusive, and sustainable economy and society for the region, in itself, is a break with the past. Historically, a lot of the wealth generated in Newcastle and Hunter flowed to business owners in Sydney and elsewhere. Value was always extracted from the region; the challenge going forward is to reverse this, to create value and hold on to it. So the central questions for Hunter are: How can the region transition? Transition toward what? What is a good idea? And, by the way, what *is* "good," in a transition, when everything is shifting? These are too many questions, with so many unknowns; this is not a problem that needs to be solved but is a development that needs to be given shape in meaningful transformations over a period of twenty years or more. The Port of Newcastle and the partners in the Hunter Innovation Network are taking on this challenge.

Before we can even begin to move forward, we have a first challenge to tackle: When we want to achieve systems change, we assume that there is a system to start with—but this is not often the case. After all, a system only hangs together when there are relationships and feedback loops. But the city of Newcastle and Hunter Valley together make up a huge area that has many communities, many industries, and many ways of looking at the world. If we want people to be involved in the discussions and help the balancing of values in this development, they should first develop the capacity to contribute. People contribute to these discussions from their lifeworlds, but when what they're asked is way beyond their social space (where they can weigh their own interests and needs against those of others), they tend to fall back to their immediate self-interest. In the IBA Parkstad regional development program mentioned in the Chemelot example, this was addressed by creating a multimedia environment (a cinema, "IBA scoop") that helped bring the region together in people's experience and view. In the case of Newcastle and Hunter, we will also need to create an immersive environment to help people get the feeling of the whole area at play (a state-of-the-art, virtual environment Bubble Games[33]).

The next phase will then be to configure the studio activity to support the reframing and the creation of a new narrative for Newcastle and the Hunter region, using a variant of the process outlined in § 7.1; this can be organized around societal domains as they are going through their transformations, specific problem arenas, or geographic areas within Newcastle and the Hunter region—whatever makes the most sense. It is vitally important that the studio or studios cover a societal terrain that is much broader than the industrial shift discussed previously; that is merely the spark to set this broader regional transformation project in motion (see figure 7.3). We

Figure 7.3 Visual map of an initial stakeholder workshop. *Source:* Nina Pirola, graphic scribe.

need to deal with the multiple transitions that are coming to the region in parallel, so we need a broad set of studio activities that deal with care, learning, mobility, and so on in the future. These studios naturally go across the various stakeholder groups; they should involve not only the companies and other usual institutional suspects (as in open innovation), but also a good cross-section of the societal midfield.

We are using a community of pioneers across these domains, covering the major shifts and always keeping our eye on the ball, on the changes that will impact the lifeworlds of people, so as not to leave people behind. These studios then are linked, coming together in a regional innovation ecosystem.

The reason that this differs from the § 7.1 process is that in this case we are dealing with regional transformation, rather than an organization or sector. But the elements of that model have their direct counterparts in regional transformation. The "hidden rules" of how things hang together in an organization or sector here correspond to the cultural norms, narratives, and shared history of the area. The reframing work in these studios has to be based on a keen understanding of the culture of the city and region as it is realized in objects, customs, stories, and rituals. The culture shows what values and meaning are important, now and in the future, and what are leverage points for the reframing and shaping of transitions. In this case, there is a strong can-do attitude; massive change has been part of the local history before, and there is a pride in having the grit to deal with that. But the flip side of this is that the region has in a sense become good at enduring change that was brought upon it by outside (economic) forces. The challenge going forward will be to shape its own future. Similarly, there are elements of the economic makeup that the region will have to move away from; the extraction-based economy and the low added value, also very much part of the culture, do not hold vitality for the future. The pressure is on to develop valuable and meaningful alternative pathways that are more attractive for the current and future community. Future strengths can be quite different; for example, knowing how to create a wholesome transition of a port is a valuable export product in itself. The Port of Newcastle can be a front-runner in a meaningful transformation that many ports, internationally, will have to find a shape for in the coming decade.

When we don't know yet how to progress, we will have to experiment. Open innovation allows us to remain broad in this approach and see what emerges as time goes by (studios and innovation ecosystems are open, complex, dynamic, and networked by nature; see § 2.1). Much can also be learned from the examples of Eindhoven and Chemelot; in uncertain times, open innovation is at least a good start. The opportunities are huge; as in the two Dutch examples, the move toward a less-polluting industry potentially opens up the large-scale economic monoculture that now dominates the port landscape to a much more diverse and interesting industrial landscape. All partners involved are aware of their responsibility and duty of care in shaping this long-term development and know that these great opportunities can only materialize when they involve and benefit the community in a meaningful way. Transitions are not singular changes: They require many initiatives and a strong support infrastructure to get around the many obstacles. The appropriate response to the overwhelming complexity of transitions is to build the capacity to navigate the complex and changing landscape. To develop vitality in the region, we first need to create the space for deep change.

7.6 AND THEN . . .

In chapter 7, the many lessons from the earlier chapters have been brought together in the frameworks of the studio and the innovation ecosystem. As we are nearing the end of the book, we need to take one more step back and talk about what really lies at the heart of deep change. You may have noticed that something has been missing.

8
DELIVERING DEEP CHANGE

When there are no clouds, the sun has to shine.
—The Christian mystic Meister Eckhart (ca. 1260–1328)[1]

8.1 FEELING ALIVE

These models and structures are meaningless unless they are acted upon by inspired people. If this isn't personal, then it isn't real. In his book *The Timeless Way of Building*, the architect and philosopher Christopher Alexander ponders what it is we strive for in life—what he calls the *quality without a name*: "The search which we make for this quality [the quality without a name], in our own lives, is the central search of any person and the crux of any individual persons story. It is the search for these moments and situations *when we are most alive.*"[2] This notion of feeling alive then is never defined in his book. That may seem problematic, but in fact it is not. Because feeling alive is so closely tied to our human nature, we can recognize it by intuition; we just know. And it prompts a good question to open up a deeper exploration of your own professional lifeworld:

> When did you feel most alive in your professional life?
>> What were the moments that really stood out?
>> What happened then?
>> What were the circumstances that made this happen?
>> What was it about?

And most importantly:

> What is it in *you* that was triggered?

The answer to this last question reveals things about your deeper self—your intrinsic motivation, what makes you tick, and what it is that you can bring to the world. The answer sits on a deep level that we normally don't think about. But we can access that level; deep down, we *know*. Engaging with this question is a great help in navigating the complex world of projects and jobs. Whatever we chose to do should create these moments of aliveness in us. If it does not, you should probably just leave, because there is no sense in staying. If you can't feel alive, then you won't be at your best and bring what you really have to offer into the world. This is doubly important for innovators: Innovation requires working with others, to help people get along, take them on the journey with you, and convince them of approaches, ideas, findings, and insights. For this, inspiration is our secret weapon. To be a true leader in your chosen field, inspiring others is what you need to do. This inspiration has to be real. One can only authentically inspire people when you are inspired yourself—when you feel alive.

At a deep level, this book is not about models or methods; it starts and ends with us, and it is all about being inspired to look and think and act differently. Maybe we have been approaching the creation of deep change the wrong way around, focusing on external structures and practices, when the spark to feel alive is inside of us. The strength and vitality of change initiatives are directly linked to the extent that they are connecting to the lifeworld, the extent to which they go back to what is meaningful and important for people. This inspiration is not about form; it is all about content: As we feel hemmed in by old forms, we need to throw them out and build a different, more fluid approach to the world and its challenges.

Making the ways of thinking in this book your own is not something to learn slowly and gradually. It is a sudden shift,[3] an epiphany, when everything we already know starts to make sense in a different way. Rodger Watson, who went on to codirect the Designing Out Crime Research Center, describes his journey and the moment it all clicked in his own words.

An Epiphany

I chose to work in the public service early in my professional career. I'd grown up in a loving family, with a single mother who struggled with mental illness and substance abuse. As the eldest child of five, I took on a lot of responsibility.

By my late twenties, I had found my dream job. I was a Crime Prevention Project Officer in the Department of Justice, working with local government to formulate their approaches to local crime issues. I was promoted, and I led projects in a reform agenda at the department. The projects were gold standard crime prevention projects, based on evidence-based initiatives that had demonstrated impact in other jurisdictions. My projects were nominated for public service awards, had mainstream media attention, and were generally seen as a new way of working. And yet, I felt uneasy. I was uneasy because I had looked deep into criminology. I could see that some of what we were doing and how we were working was straightforward. But some of the things we were facing were novel. There wasn't really anything in what I had learned in criminology that dealt with novelty in a productive way.

I went on secondment to the Designing Out Crime Research Center at the University of Technology Sydney. The center had been established under the Directorship of Kees Dorst as a partnership commissioned by the department. My brief was to engage with the center in a leadership role and provide advice as to whether the partnership should be continued. Very early in my secondment, I realized that I could see a different way of working in action. By using design as a way of thinking about complex crime issues, the team was developing a new practice. While I could see it in action, I couldn't do it right away. It took a few years before I became proficient.

One day, on my way home from work, I was walking through a park near my home. I was reflecting on the thinking behind this new practice, and I suddenly got it. It felt like a physical shift had happened in my brain. I realized that I had been educated to think in a particular way. I'd been taught to analyze an issue and to then draw from the evidence to formulate a response to the issue. But what we were doing at Designing Out Crime came at it from a different direction. We were forming an understanding of the issue, but rather than draw on the "evidence" to formulate a response, we were seeking to understand the deeper human values at play. From this understanding of values, we would then consider how these values can be realized, and from there what actions to take.

As a practitioner, I saw that this exponentially opened up the possibilities when formulating responses to crime issues. As an educator, I feel immense fulfillment when I am able to help someone move toward the same epiphany I had in the park that evening.

8.2 HOLDING CREATIVE TENSIONS

What is wisdom, in dealing with problems?

Problems are hard: They are a misalignment between how things are and how we want them to be. We don't like the tension that this brings. We love to "solve" problems so that the tension goes away. This is only natural, because a situation of tension between conflicting forces can take a lot of energy: not knowing what to do, mulling things over, going around in circles—and doubt is often seen as a weakness. There is a natural tendency, as persons, and by implication also as organizations or societies, to seek to get rid of these tensions.

But these tensions cannot and should not be resolved, because they are the source of creativity, and we need them to create the space for deep change. On a personal level, it would be a good start if we could just *hold* these tensions without directly acting on them (for the classically minded, this goes back to Aristotle: "Thinking starts when judgment is suspended"). But how can we deal with these inner tensions better? This question can be answered on three layers: in terms of thought, self, and action.

First, dealing with the tensions of thought requires what the physicist and philosopher David Bohm calls the *proprioception of thought*.[4] He proposes that we should develop this new sense (*proprioception* is basically the inner sense mechanism in your joints, which lets your body know where your limbs are without you looking at them). He observes that we make a grave mistake when we identify ourselves with our thoughts and feelings. In his view, thoughts and feelings happen more or less spontaneously, and we have a choice to accept them, by attaching significance and meaning to them—or to reject them. If you have a thought, you can look at that thought and say, "Where is this coming from? Is it coming from an old pattern that I want to get rid of? Or is it a thought that I would like to encourage and act upon?" The key point that Bohm makes is that you *are not* that thought; the thought is merely the result of a constellation of influences that together have created it in you. You don't have to identify with it at all! This special level of reflection liberates us from the yoke of habit in one fell swoop. Stepping away from identifying with your thoughts allows you to be much more flexible. Experiencing this true, ultimate freedom of thought (namely, the freedom of your own thoughts) is immensely empowering.

Second, this creates an opening to deal differently with the tensions of self; we can let go of the assumption that we need to identify with a single "self" that is coherent and consistent. Let's instead think this through from the standpoint that there is not one single inner self, but that we create multiple selves,[5] structured by the roles we play in life: as a partner, as a friend, as a professional, and so on. This is called a *bundle of selves*.[6] Our selves come together from our culture, our history, and from our life experiences. They can be very contradictory. Rather than forcing yourself into the straightjacket of this one consistent person, it is much more interesting to look at these tensions and say "I am all these different things, and these different things are all part of me." Then your character and true identity is defined by the *way* that you deal with these tensions. That is the basis of your own personal wisdom.

The third point concerns the world of action. These tensions are actually creative spaces: They spark new thoughts, frames, and actions. If you consider a tension to be a creative space, you wouldn't want to resolve it at all. But we can't be stuck in doubt forever either. Therefore, we need ways to temporarily resolve these tensions and choose a path to action. But in doing so, we have to make sure that we keep alive and even strengthen the path that was not chosen. We have to be able to rekindle the tensions and bring them up again. This enables us to challenge the course of action again and to rethink, as circumstances require (we have seen this thinking before in this book; this is why we need a bundle of frames as part of the studio infrastructure).

The space for deep change is created by tensions.

8.3 REFRAMING THE THINKING

The studio model as presented in chapter 7 on its own is not enough. It merely delineates four different spaces for different types of activities and puts them in dynamic relationships with one another (and in a rhythm). But quality in the studio comes from the depth that is created by inspired people. The studio therefore needs a specific culture, one that doesn't materialize in and of itself: It must be created. If not, we run the risk of falling back into the organizational reasoning patterns that were called out in chapter 2 (and will be again in appendix 1); causality and scientific rationality have such a strong gravitational pull. It is all too easy to slip back into problem-solving. To quote Walt Kelly's *Pogo*, "We have met the enemy and he is us."

The studio culture thrives when multiple perspectives (each with their own rationality) are explored in parallel. It thrives also on a lightness (a playfulness, far away from the pressures of evaluation and constant justification) and requires us being comfortable with high levels of uncertainty and unfinishedness. All of these cultural attributes are more or less the opposite of conventional organizational cultures. Where do these come from, and how can we ensure that we do things differently in the studio environment?

In a thoughtful exploration, Ford contrasts eight different ways in which Western societies have constructed meaning over the centuries.[7] He investigates these *fields of thought* systematically, through five questions: (1) What can we know through this field of thought? (2) How do we know (within this field of thought)? (3) What does this field of thought emphasize, and what does it neglect? (4) What does this field of thought conclude should I do? (5) Who am I, in this field of thought? (That is, what is the view of the human actor that underlies this thinking?)

For instance, in his chapter on scientific thinking, Ford characterizes this as a tendency to objectify the world, and by its central claim to rationality and its aim of establishing what is true.[8] Looking at this as a cultural phenomenon immediately opens up a can of worms: Rational thinking is inevitably based on mental models, which are not nearly as clear-cut and rational as they purport to be. What is the rationality behind reducing the complex economic system of a country to a single measure like the gross domestic product (GDP)? Just the mind-boggling simplifications needed to achieve such a grand abstraction alone make the exercise very questionable. Yet government policies that deeply influence people's lives are based on such figures and justified as being logical. (You don't have to look far to see the absurdity of this. For example, some years ago, Australia's GDP was greatly helped by the terrible bushfires and devastating floods as they led to more work for the building industry. The immense loss of value and deep human suffering simply was not part of the GDP equation.) Yet these measures are used as if they are a "true" representation of reality, logical and therefore unassailable. The claim of so-called logic is used to abrogate responsibility and avoid moral questions. Values that cannot be quantified or monetized are simply disregarded.

In contrast to this scientific rationalism, Ford brings up the role that myth plays in creating meaning, the way stories help us make sense of the world (after all, a lot of our knowledge is episodic). The clue to understanding a person's underlying pattern of thinking lies not so much in listening to *what* they say but in paying very close attention to *how* they say it, the metaphors and stories they use (see appendix 1). This explicit awareness of underlying thinking patterns also helps us steer away from old stories that perhaps do not serve us anymore. For instance, if we want to engage in "studio" type thinking we might need to wean ourselves off the deep-seated narrative of the hero's journey—a deep cultural pattern that we have literally grown up with (in fairy tales), and that is reinforced all the time (for instance, in Hollywood movies). The problem is that the classic hero's journey is very conflict-driven (rather than dialogue-driven), propagates a simple view of the hero as a lone actor (rather than a collective intelligence), and so on.[9] That is not what we need if we want to engage with open, complex, dynamic, and networked problem situations.

8.4 CREATING SPACE

Organizations need functionally defined relationships to scaffold their structure and run their processes. By definition, these relationships are about the efficient running of the machine, and they are not the ones we need for creation and change. Yet often people in organizations come to see these functional relationships as the only ones they need to have—resulting in organizations that are definitely less than the sum of their parts: very mechanized, unimaginative, inflexible, stuck, and almost dehumanized.

To create newness and vitality in an organization, it often will need to be enriched with other, new relationships that help people get beyond the habit of functional and transactional interactions. This is especially important when we see the world as comprised of complex, interlocking networks. Yet when we draw a network, we seem to naturally gravitate toward thinking and talking about the *nodes*—yet the nature and quality of the relationships is equally important, and perhaps even more important in determining the quality of the whole.

To create vitality, inspiration, and newness, these relationships should not fall back to a level where they are purely functional in the rationalist scientific management sense of the word. How can we keep ourselves and others from reverting to this type of behavior? One of the things we have learned to do in setting up a studio is to run a workshop early on to co-create the "new rules of the game" that aim at pulling people away from "normal" relationships—using the great sets of rules in appendix 5 as a jumping-off point. These workshop sessions can be hilarious (in holding a mirror to how we are working now), and at the same time they can be liberating, as people start to realize and think through what could be done differently if we just agree to do it. The creation of the new rules of the game naturally involves taking responsibility for your own side of the relationship, challenging yourself and the other to find a different dynamic. Taking care of this together creates a new bond between people. In our experience, these rules are often referred to later on and taken very seriously. They are very much needed; all of us have the tendency every to slip into the wrong (functional, transactional) mode, especially in times of stress. Then we do need to be reminded that the studio is a different space.

We can also look toward the cultures of other professions as a source of studio rules and practices by using them as a metaphor. Metaphors are interesting because they challenge our thinking and can inspire new directions; they are half-right (as they are based on features that both sides of the metaphor have in common) but also half-wrong, and they challenge our thinking precisely because of the differences. Considering these differences may lead us in fruitful directions and connect to rich fields of practice, far and wide. You will have noticed that as this book draws to an end, it moves from the firm ground of models to the opening of possibilities, suggestions for you to follow or decide to pass on. Here we are not looking for a dominant, all-encompassing metaphor for a studio, but just partial ones that connect well to an aspect of the studio and that may be good think with or to play with. With the richness of culture at our disposal, what practices can we pick up? Or better, which practices can inspire us to create new ones? Some of the metaphors that follow have proven useful in studio practice over time. Some are worked out a bit, to give a sense of their applicability and show the depth of the practices involved; others are perhaps more useful as source material for a "rules of the game" workshop, as outlined earlier. These are just (personal) suggestions; this is an incredibly open list, and your own rich and deep experience is the best source.

The metaphorical reasoning pattern is this: "Considering the studio *as if* it is . . ."

AS IF IT IS REHEARSING FOR A PERFORMANCE

A studio can be seen as a performative practice: It plays out over time, has characters, has conflict, and so on. The practices of putting together a performance as a group effort are especially interesting in the studio context. I have been drawing on the director's practices from Erik Vos,[10] who is a master in shaping a process of rehearsals to draw out a really authentic performance from his actors. Nothing is fluid or too easy in this process; for him, seamlessness and fluency are *not* signs of quality. He purposefully disturbs the actor's rehearsals by, for instance, asking them to improvise meetings between their characters, without referring to the text, or by asking them to do the whole play very quickly. The play then gradually comes together (emerges) by crystallizing around a collage of key scenes rather than a "story." The text of the play (classic theatre like Sophocles or Shakespeare) comes in later. Everything comes together and finds its shape quite late in the process—but all the steps before have prepared the ground for this happening (note that this is completely different from a blue planning approach). This keeps everybody on their toes: There is authentic panic among the actors, but also real presence.

AS IF IT IS A NATURAL PHENOMENON

We have already used the concept of an innovation ecosystem to describe complex, multistudio environments. Although the popular notion of an ecosystems brings associations with a state of natural harmony, balance, and stability, in biology this is not the case; ecosystems are dynamic, and they shift over time. There is a telling distinction between *savannah balance* and *insect balance*. In a savannah, elegant antelopes nibble on the grass—eating it but not killing it; the grass will regrow. The antelopes themselves are hunted by predators like lions, yet the lions can only capture the weaker antelopes, so their impact on the overall population is small. In effect, a sense of balance is maintained because the antelopes and the lions are both "inefficient" in how they eat. In the case of an insect balance, that is very different. For example, a small bug lands on an orchard full of orange trees in California, multiplies, and eats all the leaves, killing the trees. So the bugs also die. But a couple escape, find another orchard, and again create a population explosion. They are just very effective at what they do, and very efficient in doing so. The simile here is that the more effective we are in our interventions, the more we move to the insect balance of boom and bust, of building and total destruction.[11] This is close to the pattern we see in our society—for instance, in social media (with an ever-quicker cycle of crises that blow up and blow over). Metaphors from the natural world can be very rich; we have already implicitly used autopoiesis[12] to describe the mechanism behind ongoing system vitality.

AS IF IT IS A SPORTS TEAM

Sports metaphors are often and easily used in our societies, yet I hesitate to name them here. They do unlock many useful practices (about training, team spirit, cunningness and strategy, sacrifice, the alchemy of coming together in collaboration toward a common goal, the moral element of the written and unwritten rules of the game, etc.). However, sports metaphors can also emphasize competition, winning and losing, and a sometimes primitive form of leadership that harks back to the adversarial model 1 thinking (see appendix 1) that the studio is made to move away from.

AS IF IT IS A JAZZ PERFORMANCE

Jazz improvisation is a very sophisticated set of practices for creative collaboration. Barrett, in his book *Yes to the Mess*,[13] encapsulates the elements and variety of jazz improvisation practices in a list of six principles: (1) yes to the mess: develop affirmative competence; (2) performing and experimenting simultaneously: embracing errors as a source of learning; (3) minimal structure-maximal autonomy: balancing freedom and constraints; (4) jamming and hanging out: learning by doing and talking; (5) taking turns soloing and supporting: followership as a noble calling; and (6) leadership as provocative competence: nurturing double vision. Jazz improvising is already used as an extended metaphor for organizational change and a methodology considered for innovation consultants.[14]

AS IF IT IS GARDENING

This is becoming a classic metaphor in innovation literature as people seek new approaches to address complex systems. Gardening requires deep knowledge and commitment—and one cannot create directly but can only influence the result. Gardening is a process of tending, caring, and being in tune with the forces of nature.

AS IF . . .

We can continue to look at the studio through endless metaphors: as if it is a workshop/toolshed, as if it is a memory palace,[15] as if it is a yoga practice, as if it is a playground, a landscape, a journey, a quest, and so on—any metaphor will do, so long as it helps to make the studio as intense and fascinating as possible. Engaging with the studio should be the best part of any person's job.

8.5 CREATING DEEP CHANGE

On an individual level, the way we deal with the paradoxes and tensions of life is what we call our *character*; on a collective level, it is what we call our *culture*. There is a lot to be learned from cultural practices to inspire the development of a studio practice. After all, the studio way of working is deeply human, and elements of it have been articulated in many different ways over time.

I would like to draw a parallel with the way that Friedman, in his seminal introduction to the *Worlds of Existentialism* reader, describes existentialist thinking not as a specific philosophical movement, but rather as a natural human tendency (or as he calls it, a *temper*) that is part of all time. For him, the movement at the core of this existentialist temper is a reaction against the static, the abstract, the purely rational or the merely irrational *and toward* the concrete, emphasizing of personal involvement and engagement, action, free choice and commitment, with a strong commitment towards "authentic existence," taking the actual situation of the existential subject as the starting point of thought. He holds that this is a deep human tendency that always existed and has taken many forms over the centuries; he starts his existentialism reader with texts from Heracleitus, the Bible, and Hasidism, and takes it from there to the present day.[16]

Likewise, in proposing the studio model, I would like to claim *naturalness* rather than *newness*. Elements of the studio have always been around, and they have come together variously in different times. If pressed to extend the parallel with Friedman, I could characterize the studio temper (the "movement of thought") by stating that it locates the creation of value in the lifeworld of people, and foregrounds the importance of framing not as a singular activity, but as the continuous movement of considering of various essences in parallel. It foregrounds learning cycles, shying away from relying on linear thinking, rejecting conclusions and "resolutions"; instead, it holds on to tensions to create ongoing vitality in the system. Results are closer aligned to the dynamics of a collage than to a single and definitive outcome.

The thinking behind the studio is old too; it goes beyond the author. At its root is a combination of continental and analytic philosophy (all the way from phenomenology to pragmatism). This book stands in a long tradition that is carried by giants like Thomas Kuhn, Donald Schön, and Chris Argyris. What I have been able to add to their thinking is a new emphasis on creation rather than reflection as a driver for change, and the introduction of creative practices to create a path to impact. As ever, this project is unfinished, and I am sure others will keep adding their personal wisdom, giving life to the change we need.

And you know you're doing well if it makes you feel truly alive.

EPILOGUE: THERE'S ONE MORE THING

You are not good enough.
—Tyson Yunkaporta

This epilogue opens with a quote from Tyson Yunkaporta, Australian author and academic.[1] He gave the opening keynote for a symposium addressing the enormous disadvantage that indigenous Australians experience in their lives. Over the last twenty years and more, great people have been doing good projects—but in the end, there has not been much change in the statistics, which are still horrendous. Apparently, we have not managed to change the system. Tyson Yunkaporta's statement was a reminder that in such a desperate situation, impact is the *only* thing that counts. If the forces that keep the system in place are stronger than we are, it simply means we are not good enough.

In this book, we have seen that by creating space for deep change, we can deal with these open, complex, dynamic, and networked problem situations we face. In doing so, we take a fundamentally different route from the paradigm that we have inherited, the *rational problem-solving* that is deeply embedded in our ways of thinking, our disciplines, and our organizations. We need to radically step away and forget problem-solving, to go to the deep human values and meaning that underlie the problem situation and rebuild our thinking and practices from there. If we do this well, we can't go wrong. Ever. The case studies show that this really works in practice.

The inner strength of this approach comes from its clarity, the undeniable truth that surfaces the moment we are dealing with deep value and meaning—the simple realization that this is what it is really about.

Operating on this level of value and meaning also harnesses our shared humanity, the driver to break through barriers we have created for ourselves and move forward. It is such a force. Situations that were very problematic and stuck just melt away and shift when we approach them in this way. The studio builds the infrastructure and practices for reframing and learning, so that new narratives will emerge that can shift the organizations, disciplines, and sectors. Ongoing vitality springs from holding and nurturing the tensions in this system, continuously. The cases bear witness to the fact that this works, right across societal domains.

At the same time, I would agree with Kuhn (see § 5.1) that for now, the new paradigm is still worse than the old one; we are building the new thinking, still collecting the practices we need to create the repertoire and make it stronger. This is a movement. I hope the models and stories in this book provide both the spark and a backbone for a much bigger and richer development. We know we *can* do this, so we should.

Let's make sure we are good enough.

APPENDIX 1: WHY INNOVATION FAILS

Why does innovation fail, when facing the new open, complex, dynamic, and networked problem situations?

First, there is always the temptation to keep treating these problem situations as if conventional problem-solving will still work. People that misdiagnose a problem situation in this way might use words like:

- **"Of course . . ."** This phrase is a call to the authority of direct causality; of course *this action* will cause *that effect*. This rational stance is part and parcel of being a reasonable and responsible person. And of course we should follow best practices and work in an evidence-based manner. These phrases often hide a very narrow and limiting definition of rationality, and that the reasoning that is defended in this way can be based on some very questionable models of reality (see § 8.3). But these models are rarely questioned; they are well defended by posing as the bedrock of rational thinking. This is a logical fallacy.
- **"More research is needed . . ."** In complex problem situations, there often is a tendency to rely on the gathering of knowledge to find a way forward—preferably objective, scientific knowledge. This leads to lots of studying of the problem, with the assumption that knowing more about the problem somehow equates to solving it. This is not true.
- **"Why don't we just . . ."** The uneasy complexity of problem situations can be overcome through simplification. In the political arena, where complex sets of values of diverse groups of people have to be worked through, weighed, and discussed, the simplification that is offered by populists provides an easy (and easily understandable) way out. Especially when they conveniently blame "the other" for the very

existence of the problem in the first place. Remove "those people" and you remove the problem. This is wrong.
- **"Manage uncertainty . . ."** Complex problem situations are often experienced as a lack of control, and before you know it every uncertainty can be seen as a risk. But these are very different things: Risks are concrete expectations that can be managed—ran away from, if you will. But uncertainty can only be reduced by exploration; it something we have to move toward. Confusion between risk and uncertainty stifles the space for innovation and change.
- **"Surely, . . ."** We pride ourselves on being good problem-solvers, and culturally there is an absolute value placed on being "sure" as a professional, especially as a leader. This can result in pressure to provide clarity where there is none and to jump to conclusions/decisions. In such a culture, even the fact that there is doubt is not discussable.
- **"Not now . . ."** From the rational problem-solving paradigm, here is a deep-seated mistrust of creative, open reasoning processes like abduction. Sometimes it is grudgingly accepted that creative practices are needed, but they are then hemmed in and risk-managed in small projects—or given free reign, but not taken seriously, like a court jester. These differences are reflected in how people behave. When people say "we don't have time," they basically express that something doesn't fit into their problem-solving worldview. This is not an issue of time; this is an issue of valuing and respecting these practices. When people are maximally busy with rational problem-solving, and they do not value building new practices, there will *never* be time. But saying this is giving up on deep change—which in the end means giving up on engaging with the future. That is clearly not acceptable.

Second, even when there is no outright misdiagnosis, there are many ways in which organizations resist change and hold on to business as usual, even in the face of a clear and present need to change. Causes of innovation failure include:

- Innovation is sometimes misplaced within the structure of the organization, leading to what professionals at an innovation unit in a bank called "innovation theatre": their innovation unit was set up to generate ideas and develop products it then had to "sell" to the

organization—but the KPIs in the rest of the organization did not support the adoption of new ideas at all. This is pure lip service: Nothing ever gets implemented, and the well-meaning people in the innovation unit were a pretty depressed group. They basically had no job.
- Innovation can fail through a deep misunderstanding of the kind of thinking that is involved. Renowned strategic management scholar Gary Hamel points to what he calls "strategy development's dirty little secret; that within strategy development, there actually is no articulation of a creative process that can lead to new strategies."[1] These so-called innovation strategies claim to be grounded in solid analysis, every step of the way—but how can that work? If organizations only use reductive and analytical ways of thinking, they are simply not capable of creating new responses to their challenges.[2]
- We have seen before that when responsibility is spread very thinly in an organization, nobody is in a position to push forward with anything more than incremental change. There is just no agency anymore for the people in the organization. Good ideas that do progress have to be whittled down to almost nothing.
- Within a knowledge-driven innovation paradigm, there is an idea that doing research on problem to more fully understand it somehow equals solving it.[3] But of course all this knowledge about the problem in itself doesn't lead to new practice. There is zero impact. Nothing changes. Yet everybody has done the right thing.
- Innovation is limited to innovation projects—and though called *innovation* projects, they are often initiated to create quick fixes for immediate problems. These have nothing to do with real innovation.
- Innovation tends to be set up as a linear process, making it hard to build in the learning needed for real progress. That is how real innovation gets stifled.
- In the risk problem, the innovation system is set up in such a way that it only allows small projects to happen in order to reduce risk. Or the organization is set up in such a way that it only allows slow, incremental change. Anything quicker or more radical is considered dangerous (see the example in § 7.5).
- Many so-called innovation strategies we encounter in practice are deeply flawed in their inception, formulation, and implementation.

And some of them are just outright bullshit; they are just pretense. They are not a "missed opportunity," but harmful nonsense. That is a reason to become very, very angry.

Third, the organizational model itself could be flawed. This is the point made by Chris Argyris in his remarkable little book *Flawed Advice and the Management Trap*,[4] in which he calls out "model 1 organizations." The basic tenets of such an organizational culture are:

- Unilaterally define goals and try to achieve them.
- Maximize winning and minimize losing.
- Treat any change in goals as a sign of weakness.
- Minimize the expression of negative feelings; they show ineptness, incompetence, or lack of diplomacy.
- Make sure you are seen to be rational, objective, and intellectual. Suppress feelings.

Argyris argues that it doesn't make sense to try and address some of the flaws of model 1, because they run very deep and on its own ground, model 1 always wins; winning is exactly what it was made for. He holds that we need to move away from this thinking completely and create radically different, open, and empowering organizational environments. He calls this learning-centered paradigm "model 2." Its governing values are:

- Actions need to be based on valid and verifiable information.
- Decisions are based on free and informed choice.
- Actions need to be based on internal commitment (intrinsic motivation) rather than coercion.
- Include people in the design and implementation of action.
- Share control and decision-making.
- Ensure that conflicting views are surfaced.
- Encourage the public testing of evaluations and decisions.

POSTSCRIPT: WHY DOES INNOVATION FAIL?

In the few pages of this appendix, we have seen that there are many ways in which innovation can fail, and that there are many possible causes for innovation failure that are often deeply embedded in conventional organizational practices, cultures, structures and processes. Following such a diagnosis, there is a real temptation to start thinking about remedies to all of these "illnesses."

That is not what we have done in this book. To get to the root of the matter, we have called out the limitations of the underlying *rational problem-solving* paradigm and developed a fundamentally different way of approaching the open, complex, dynamic, and networked problem situations we face. To create a different path, we have more or less started from scratch, using abductive logic to build up an alternative rationality and approach to practice. It is important to stress here that the differences between the old and the new paradigm run very deep: they have a fundamentally different philosophical basis. Doing justice to this new "philosophy of practice" would require a different book. But I hope that throughout these chapters, the underlying ontology,[5] epistemology,[6] morality (Levinas, Camus), and view of the human actor[7] will have shone through.

APPENDIX 2: THE METASTUDIO

What can support studios and broader innovation ecosystems, structurally? This appendix offers some mini cases that explore different models, for inspiration.

THE GOVERNMENT ARCHITECT

There is an infrastructure needed to support transitions that otherwise fall between the cracks of the existing organizations, a metastudio, if you like. This could be modeled on the infrastructural support in the realm of the built environment that in some countries is provided by government architect. The office of the government architect traditionally has three functions: (1) leading a public discussion on the quality of public space and the built environment, (2) challenging the architectural profession, and (3) ensuring the government is a good patron and commissioner of public projects. Such an independent and authoritative position combining inspiration, learning, and structural support could be created for many of the broad transitions we are facing.[1]

TRANSITION CATALYST AND THE TRANSITION STUDIO

In the transition case studies, we have found that a specific (infra)structure is needed to drive the movement to create a path to impact. The systems world needs to change (e.g., energy transition), in closely synchronized movement with the changes on the human side, in communities and the lifeworlds of people. Experience has shown that neither the organizations nor the community are set up to deal with this type and

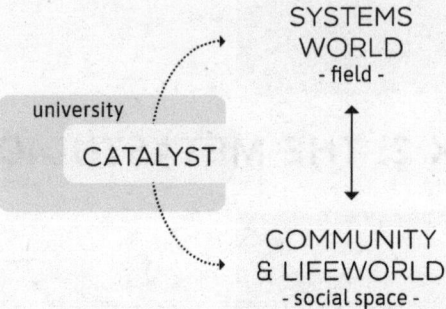

Figure A2.1 Positioning the transition studio.

level of innovation on their own, leading to resistance and lack of progress. There needs to be a third party that acts as a catalyst to set up the studio model in the first instance (e.g., in the Hunter transitions, the Port of Newcastle played this role; in Amsterdam New-West, it was the local council). A transition studio could also be catalyzed by a party with a long-term interest in societal thriving and vitality, inspired by a concrete transition or the moral imperative for inclusivity in the face of societal transitions—like philanthropic organizations. In addition, universities (and other higher education institutions) potentially play a crucial role in supporting true systems change (see figure A2.1); they provide a neutral convening space that stretches right across society, and any transition will require a change in the professions that shape the current paradigm in the systems world. Several of these transition studios running in parallel will create a rich and inspiring environment for innovators inside and outside the university; the cross-collaboration and cross-fertilization is especially important as it will start to capture the impact of these transitions, collectively, on the lived world of people and communities.

PONT

The PONT program partially fulfills that role: it is set up by the Dutch Ministry of culture as a three-year studio program to develop a common practice between designers and professionals in the public sector. In their own words:

The Public Design Practice (PONT in Dutch) creates a bridge between designers and public sector organisations. The program is based on a studio model, with learning and reflection at its core. It consists of five elements that inform, inspire and complement each other: the Practice, the Workshop, the School, the Temple and the Square. In this Public Design Practice, innovation that is created by developing new methods, structure and interventions, goes hand in hand with a constant search for (problems and opportunities) in the current collaboration between designers and the public sector. The *Practice* is central in this Studio model. Here, various current design projects for societal issues are closely followed and supported. This creates an experimental environment, in which we can learn from the current experiences and new approaches/interventions can be tested. At the same time, these projects are supported and coached (by "impact coaches"). In the *Workshop*, research is done into how we can better realise the potential of design for societal challenges. This is the basis for the development of new interventions to further the application of design approaches within the public domain, to support and improve them. At the *School*, the further education of designers, public servants and policy makers in public organisations is organised. The *Temple* is a space for intervision, contemplation and reflection. On the *Square*, various activities aimed at the interchange between designers, public sector workers and interested others are organised. This is the place to convene for thinking through and discussing the value of a design approach. These five parts together inform the professionalisation of the creative sector, and the creation of a context for the application of designerly approaches in the public domain. They provide a rhythm in which we can learn, create, reflect, share and deepen our insights. This process is called the "Public Design Practice."[2]

UN SDG DEVELOPMENT PLATFORMS

On a completely different scale, the United Nations, after endorsing the Sustainable Development Goals in 2015, tasked the UN Development Program with creating the environment and infrastructure for their attainment. The UN Development Program[3] developed a strategy to create 177 platforms in countries to do this, and it asked experts around the world to sketch what these platforms should consist of and how they should work. Our proposal (with Dick Rijken) in this space ran more or less along the same lines as the regional transformation in the Newcastle case study (§ 7.5): a studio model across sectors, involving the societal midfield, shaped around a learning cycle. The idea was to be very respectful of the many good initiatives that people are already creating and to limit the role of the UN to being a catalyst and providing an infrastructure for further development.

EDGEOF

In Shibuya in Tokyo, the Egdeof innovation building (a hive of socially oriented business initiatives like the Prosperity Exchange), set up by remarkable entrepreneur Daniel Goldman, contains studios, workshop spaces, labs, a podium, and a restaurant with a terrace on the top floor. There is a beautiful Japanese temple in the basement.

APPENDIX 3: PUBLIC SECTOR INNOVATION

In this appendix, I would like to host André Schaminée, the project leader of the highway tunnel project (chapter 3) and the nitrogen crisis project (chapter 6). He is a consultant and partner at TwynstraGudde in the Netherlands. Some years ago, we collaborated on a small booklet (commissioned by the Ministry of Agriculture, Nature, and Food Safety, as a result of the nitrogen project) to help understand the nexus between design thinking and public sector thinking and organizations. Within that practice-based document we formulated nine core lessons from our experiences to date, here translated in their entirety.

Experience has shown that the application of design thinking at times goes directly against some of the basic tenets of public sector organizations; for example, the complexity of the problem situation can easily result in pressure from the top to be in control at all times, which leads to a strong bias toward the cognitive approach. Paradoxical problem situations in which the sides are represented by different stakeholders might easily push the process toward one of negotiation. And the feeling of crisis in itself creates a pressure to move to concrete measures immediately, while the learning approach of design thinking needs time and space for exploration—and in design thinking, the need for emergence means we need (at least temporarily) to let go of control. This can make design thinking very vulnerable in public sector organizations. To help bridge the gap, we developed nine lessons for the public sector.

(1) Start from values and principles (i.e., framing).
(2) Don't confuse the design approach with others like lean, agile, or theory U (they are not unrelated, but they work out very differently).

(3) Give content and meaning to the roles in the collaboration (not transactional, but shaped around a learning approach).
(4) Make the process "A UFO": Attractive, Useful, Flexible, and Open (communication is key, right from the start).
(5) Connect bottom-up and top-down processes (create learning loops between the two).
(6) Build competencies within the public sector organization (do not underestimate the design expertise needed; just doing a design thinking workshop is not enough).
(7) Ask the experts: Realize that this process requires a combination of design expertise, public service expertise, and strategic expertise.
(8) Create long lines of engagement; this is not a project but a learning program.
(9) Realize that the design approach touches many in your organization: decision-makers, communication, and so on. Frontline staff are especially important, as they can be bridge builders to the lived worlds of the stakeholders.[1]

1. START FROM VALUES AND PRINCIPLES

In transitions, we set out on the road to a destination we don't know yet. And we need to bring a large number of very different stakeholders along on that journey. It would be wrong to propose a solution early on (jumping to conclusions) and start an innovation project that basically details it further. That may feel psychologically safe (we have something), but it is counterproductive as stakeholders tend to stick to their standpoints and dig in. Then the space to discover what should be the framing of the original question just evaporates. It is important to take the time to create such a space, by working from an intent (What is this really about? What is the meaning of this? What values are we trying to achieve?) rather than jumping to a solution. Such solutions are almost always rooted in the current frame, the current way of looking, and encapsulate existing standpoints and vested interests. The beauty of working from intent is that there doesn't need to be much debate; nobody has to change their mind to enter into the co-creation process. The co-creation process is about finding ways to work together on an issue, not about agreement. This all can feel very unsettling to directors and managers, even unsafe. Explaining the process of design thinking can help people feel a bit more at ease, but it remains a challenge.

2. DON'T CONFUSE THE DESIGN APPROACH WITH OTHERS

One of the barriers to introducing design thinking as a road to innovation is that people in an organization already have innovation approaches that they like (whether they are tested and tried or not). Design thinking is not the only new approach that has found its way to the public sector these last few years. Approaches like theory U,[2] lean,[3] and agile (scrum)[4] have been adopted, and they—like design thinking—seek to respond to a common problem: the fact that some organizations have become very technocratic/bureaucratic and have lost their edge and the power to innovate and change. What are the commonalities and differences between these? When should you use which approach? This is a difficult quandary, and one that is hard to answer to satisfaction; any comparison is bound to miss points and perhaps overstate others (straw man). Experts will easily find fault with a hasty analysis, as the method stands for a deep and rich landscape of practices, tools, and insights. And the quality of the result in applying them will always depend on the practitioner themselves and their ability to deeply understand the situation. A method is only an aid to the practitioner and never guarantees success. With these provisos in place, we do still need to address the question of which method to use, as it often arises in discussions with public sector organizations. We cannot avoid a quick characterization of the methods here, and hasten to apologize for the generalization it entails.

Theory U is not dissimilar to design thinking, but it focuses more on the personal level (personal development)—with less attention to actionable steps for teams and organizations. Lean eliminates process steps that do not add value (anymore). Agile combines thinking and doing in quick iterative steps, as an alternative to the classic approach of first thinking, then acting. Design thinking, as we are using the term here, is also an alternative to the classic project approach. But where lean and agile tend to move quickly to the producing of solutions, design thinking focuses on the problem situation. In complex problem arenas, it is crucial to first focus on the problem, understand it deeply, and frame it in novel and interesting ways before proceeding. The strength of design thinking lies in a clear process that takes the practitioner through several steps, away from the problem situation into the realm of value and meaning, to be creative on that deeper level and reframe before going back to scoping actions. But this is just a process, a backbone. The real strength of design thinking lies in the rich repertoire of methods, tools, and techniques that designers have developed to actually perform these steps and manage the transitions between them. Many other approaches miss this flesh on the bones. The design field has developed a rich repertoire of practices over the course of its long history.

3. GIVE CONTENT AND MEANING TO THE ROLES IN THE COLLABORATION

A key feature of transitions is that nobody has a complete overview of the whole problem area and that there is no clear problem owner. This makes the big issues of our time very hard to tackle. They are everybody's problem and therefore also nobody's problem. Take the energy transition, as it is to impact our houses: A lot of the responsibility for achieving this is to be organized on a local government area level (municipalities, etc.). But what happens behind the front door is still the owner's domain. The energy provider is responsible for the infrastructure (the grid). In social housing, the Department of Housing is basically the landlord. How do you organize such a disjointed system? In many countries, the responsibility for rolling out the energy transition is put on local government. But under pressure, they could be tempted to use the wrong repertoire. If they take the role of director, that easily sparks resistance. They should probably switch between such a directive role (the initiator sets the course), a partner role (collaboration to achieve a collective ambition), and being a facilitator (connecting the values and interests of the stakeholders into a common ambition). These roles then have to work in concert. Often, organizations have quite a bit of experience in the director and partner roles, but less so as a facilitator. That results in ad hoc approaches. Design thinking processes and practices can help build out the facilitation role.

4. MAKE IT "A UFO"[5]

In transitions, nobody has complete control over process or outcome. Public sector organizations will have to develop the ability to shift between roles, as discussed previously. The role of the facilitator is particularly important as an active driver of transition processes. To energize people and entice them to action, empathic research is key. It enables the public sector organization to show people how the process links to the values that are important to them and that they can shape the future shape these values will take. For this, we use the acronym A UFO; we have to make this Attractive (you want to be part of this), Useful (people feel they will benefit), Flexible (to let the future forms emerge), and Open (there is a low threshold to participation). One can create A UFO in several ways, such as through reflecting the results of the empathic research back to the stakeholders—and broader society—and ask, "Have we got this right or have we missed something?" Then we can invite people to give shape to the new frame. To seduce people into this space, the new frame needs to be expressed well so that people can have a sense of what this is going to look like in the future, but without too much detail. The detailing and implementation will have to be done in a genuinely open co-creative process.

5. CREATE LINKS BETWEEN TOP DOWN AND BOTTOM UP

In literature on organizational change, the distinction is often made between top-down and bottom-up approaches (between change that is initiated in the systems world of policy and organizations and change that is created from the lifeworlds of people). Organizing links and feedback loops between top-down and bottom-up developments is deemed important. In the past couple of years, there has been a shift in the public sector, toward looking more favorably on bottom-up initiatives and seeking to stimulate these (through grants, pilots, etc.). But a bottom-up movement can only survive and thrive when it is accompanied by strong and strategic top-down support. This is typical for transitions. To create progress, we need to create feedback loops between top down and bottom up, between the systems world and the lifeworld. The creation of these feedback loops is not traditionally part of what designers do. This is one of the areas where public sector thinkers and design thinkers will have to come together and develop a suite of new practices (see § 4.7).

6. BUILD COMPETENCIES IN YOUR ORGANIZATION

This type of systems change cannot be delegated to consultants; after all, the public sector organization is an integral part of the system, and it therefore also has to be an integral part of the transition. Several public sector organizations have invested in building up their knowledge and skills in design thinking by employing designers. Others choose to build up design capability within their existing staff, often by involving outside expertise from time to time. But often, these developments are not accompanied by a strategic drive to build this capability across the organization, unfortunately—and the design thinkers will become isolated. Design thinking needs to be part of an explicit program of organizational learning.[6] This learning extends from the subject matter at hand to the meaning of the learning for the practice of professionals and the whole organization (double loop learning). Clarity about the importance of learning, within and across organizations, will create a culture of inspiration, exploration, and reflection.

7. ASK THE EXPERT—TIMES THREE

The application of design thinking in transitions inevitably contains a number of expert moments, in which experience really counts. We will briefly point out three:

1. Within the design thinking process, much depth is attained through creative research into the deep human themes (values) that are at play and the generation of a fruitful and interesting frame. Experienced designers can help avoid a lot of unnecessary exploration in this step.
2. Public sector organizations know how to create (political) support for new frames, experiments, and solutions. This is where designerly thinking should take a step back and let the people that are good at negotiation carry the initiative forward.
3. Then there is the expertise needed to make sure the insights that come from frames and that experiments find their way toward the strategic choices that have to be made to support them. This expertise, on the nexus between bottom up and top down, will have to be developed jointly between designers and the professionals from within the organization.

8. DRAW LONG LINES

This is not an innovation project. Transitions require a sustained effort. This is a point of concern, because politicians and senior public sector managers tend to regularly change positions. And a design thinking program is not the kind of work where a new person can easily take up the role of his/her predecessor. Design thinking programs involve creating a deep connection between the stakeholders, on a professional but also on a more personal, more subjective level. Changing the players really sets back the game, more or less back to square one, and gets in the way of breakthrough developments. Often, but not always, there are moments in the whole process where it is possible to pass the baton without undue damage.

A longer transition program can also be influenced by political changes. Yet a program that is well underway, and well-supported by a wide range of stakeholders, is less vulnerable to interference. It would be foolish for a politician to go against the will of the people.

9. THE DESIGN APPROACH TOUCHES MANY IN A PUBLIC SECTOR ORGANIZATION

Design thinking programs are like relay races, rather than isolated innovation projects. They need to be, as the new practices they lead to in the end touch all parts of the public sector organization. But they do so in different ways:

- For decision-makers, the design thinking program pulls them away from negotiation into an much more open, explorative, learning process where the outcome is unclear and there needs to be space for making useful mistakes. This might feel unsafe to them, in particular because they are accountable for the way public money is spent. This often—understandably—leads to risk aversion. Unfortunately, risk management is also applied when it is counterproductive. In transitions, we just don't know what the new paradigm is going to be and how it is going to pan out. This means we need to be alert in distinguishing between risks (known effects that are undesirable) and uncertainties (unknown effects that help us learn about the future).

Through experiments, we learn our way to innovation. Risk we can run away from; uncertainties we need to go toward and investigate.
- The link to the lifeworlds of citizens is absolutely crucial in transitions. Bridge builders, public servants that have a foot in each camp—the systems world of public sector organizations and the lifeworlds of people—are very important in this. In their work, the tension between the systems world and lifeworld surfaces in a very concrete way. Empowering them to flag this and take action often leads to immediate insights and on-the-ground results. But these bridge builders are often quite far removed from the level of the organization where strategy is developed. To protect themselves from what they see as interference by the system, they often operate a bit on the periphery of the organization. Recognizing the importance of their role and creating a path for them to influence the practices across the organization will lead to much better transition processes.
- In the world of the public sector, communication is often defensive (avoiding reputation damage). That is at odds with the type of transition explorations we are talking about here. We have found that it can be liberating to be transparent and collectively not know. Citizens normally understand this, and being upfront and honest creates a much more equal playing field for collaboration.

In reflecting on these nine lessons, one cannot help but be impressed by the complex nature of the gap they are meant to bridge. Design thinking is very different from business as usual in public sector organizations. But that is of course exactly the reason to embark on this quest to connect the two.

APPENDIX 4: THEME ANALYSIS

In this appendix, I would like to host Dick Rijken, friend and longtime collaborator, who the reader will know from the Waterwolf project in Gouda (§ 4.3), the Pavillion rules (appendix 5), and the text on the professional lifeworld (§ 6.4). But his influence on the thinking in this book is much greater than that. In workshops and teaching we run together, Dick is a master in helping people understand the fine art of theme analysis. I am happy to step back and give him the text.

WHAT IS A THEME?

A theme is a dynamic psychological or social construct (with internal structure and dynamics), which can play a crucial role in motivating people to act in a situation. It exists in the domain of lived experience. This is crucial: A theme refers to something that can be experienced as such in life; fear and joy are human themes, but social cohesion is not. No one ever feels socially cohesive. Social cohesion needs to be broken down into different experience themes in order to be meaningful: people may *care about* each other, they may want to *feel at home* in their neighborhood, they may enjoy *feeling accepted* by others, and so on. Those are experience themes that relate to the more abstract notion of social cohesion.

Themes can also be used to understand personal experience when looking for the dynamics of meaning in a certain problem field. Meaning is never static; the desire and the attempt to make sense of life are dynamic processes that constantly change and unfold. Examples include fear, loneliness, feeling appreciated, and ambition. Often, groups of themes have interesting interrelationships (e.g., fear, risk-taking, forgiveness, and courage have many relationships). Themes are conceptual constructs with different psychological and social aspects that can be closely connected. The architecture of a theme can be done at a generic level: What other concepts is it related to (e.g., the relationship between fear and stress). But it is also useful to situate it in different contexts: How does it play out in a specific context that is different from the original context?

THEME ANALYSIS

Now we will discuss two aspects of theme analysis: what to look for (structure and dynamics) and how to actually investigate (sources of information, knowledge, and insight).

WHAT TO INVESTIGATE?

Themes can be analyzed in terms of their internal structure and in terms of their temporal dynamics. *Structure* refers to a network of meanings, concepts and other themes around a theme (e.g., fear is the opposite of hope; it is related to a perceived threat or to anxiety). *Temporal dynamics* refers to the way a theme develops over time (e.g., what causes someone to *become* afraid, what's it like in that moment to *be* afraid, what are the possible reactions to fear, how does one stop being afraid, what can possibly happen afterward).

1. STRUCTURAL ASPECTS OF THEMES

Themes are multifaceted. They can be spiritual, physical, social, and so on—and all that at the same time. The following is a checklist of different possible aspects of themes that can be investigated. The list does not pretend to be exhaustive, but it has served us well in many different situations. Consider the following aspects of a person's psychology and pay attention to how they are/may be related in terms of structural relationships: What influences what? Don't force anything; try to stick to obviously relevant factors.

SPIRITUAL

Does a theme relate to a person's essence or to deeply felt beliefs or values? For example, a problem like unemployment is not just a social or financial issue but can have deep effects on someone's sense of self or their purpose in life.

EMOTIONAL

What emotions are involved? How? Emotions are powerful components of themes. They drive people's actions and are often interrelated in complex ways. For example, if we want to deal with anger or violence, it is worth understanding possible relationships between emotions like fear, desire, frustration, and resentment as violence is often the end result of complex chains or emotional patterns that need addressing at earlier stages unfolding patterns; prevention in early stages is usually more effective than repression in later stages.

COGNITIVE

Look at mental models, knowledge, learning processes, thinking, and so on. Our beliefs, our knowledge, and our memories determine how we interpret the world, and people have different capacities for and styles of learning. Our ideas about the world strongly influence the way we perceive and experience it. It is important to understand the role of knowledge and mental models in a theme and to consider where and how learning can make a difference. For example, self-confidence, a positive outlook on the world, or knowledge in a certain domain can help a person to feel empowered to go out and act rather than sit down and complain. Anticipation can be an effective strategy to prepare for an experience. Knowing that anger is a natural part of a mourning process can help once it occurs. Many things can be consciously learned. The interplay between our thoughts and our emotions is strong, and this is something to look out for and work with.

MOTIVATIONAL

What personal goals are or can be involved? What drives people to do the things they do? At what level? Does a person want more money, or is money a means to an end like more freedom? Is money a source of social status? An event may trigger an emotion, which may trigger a set of actions, but there may be deeper reasons that go beyond superficial emotions. For example, frustration may cause a person to become angry, but at a deeper level there may be insecurity about one's ability to deal with certain challenges. Building confidence may then be more useful than finding ways to deal with frustration.

PHYSICAL

Does the theme have physical/biological aspects? Does the human body play a role? A theme like fear may have obvious physical features such as increased heart rate or sweating, but themes like insecurity or vulnerability may relate to a person's self-image of their body. Psychologists often use the concept of arousal as a container for a general sense of excitement, positive or negative. Hormones and neurotransmitters play an important role here: adrenalin, dopamine, serotonin, and so on. Once the body starts producing a certain hormone, its effect will linger for some time.

SOCIAL

How can social relationships affect the theme? This is a very important part of theme analysis: other people and what they mean to us. Not only are we social creatures, but a deeper insight into social structures can be a very fruitful starting point for interventions in later stages of design. Friends can provide help. Strangers can make people insecure. Peer pressure is always a force to be reckoned with. Recommendations from others can make us trust someone. The list is long, and this perspective is always worth investigating.

CONTEXTUAL

What external factors can have an effect on personal experience? Physical space? Specific events or circumstances? Time constraints? A feeling like anxiety may only occur in specific situations where much is expected from a person, whereas in other situations, the feeling may be absent even though the challenges are the same. The privacy of a home creates a completely different psychological space than the streets of a city or the board room of a company. Like social relationships, contexts can be redesigned and changed, so be alert!

2. THE DYNAMICS OF THEMES

How can the personal experience of a theme change over time, and through which causal relationships is this possible or plausible? How does intensity influence personal experience regarding the theme? A little bit of something may be irrelevant, but above a certain threshold, things can go crazy. Are there discontinuities, or is everything smooth and gradual?

Make a list of factors that have a negative or positive influence on a concept. Draw a rough flowchart-style diagram of how different factors relate to the theme in terms of modulating causal relationships. It should show crucial structure and dynamics in a simple way. Don't make it too complicated. The goal is group inspiration, not universal truth.

How does the theme develop? What happens before, during, or after the experience of the theme? What are factors that make it develop or change?

3. HOW TO INVESTIGATE THEMES

Themes can be researched in different ways. What follows is a list of methods that can be used. This list is not exhaustive. Any source that makes you feel you understand a theme better is a good source. In practice, the process of theme investigation is inherently constrained by time and teams. Any theme is worth years and years of study, but in reality you will only have weeks, days, or hours. The good news is that even a single hour or afternoon will produce results you feel you can work with. Also, when doing this with a team, you can divide tasks: one person looks at science, one person will interview people, and so on. You discuss the outcomes together. Again, even a one-hour discussion with your team will yield results and deeper understanding. It is important to realize that theme investigation is not a quest for truth, but for inspiration. We want to deepen our understanding and our empathy in order to create something new. Once we do that, we can test it to know if it makes sense.

SCIENTIFIC LITERATURE: EMPIRICAL

This is not always easy, as scientific literature tends to be very specialized. Searching databases for "ambition" will give thousands of results, and more specific search queries may be less useful for a more general understanding of a theme. But when a search is successful, it can be conceptually insightful, with roots in empirical research.

PHILOSOPHY: CONCEPTUAL

Philosophy can be a great starting point for some themes. Some philosophers literally devote most of their thinking to specific themes. Examples include alienation (Marx), otherness (check out http://discourseontheotter.tumblr.com), responsibility (Levinas), and so on.

ART (MUSIC, VISUAL ART, LITERATURE, FILM, AND MORE): EVOCATIVE

The arts are interesting because good artworks can give universal insight while being very concrete at the same time. Art is evocative; it makes you feel something, which can be a powerful addition to thematic analysis. For example, the film *The Dead* by John Huston is a mind-blowing excursion into the experience of loss.

FIELDWORK: CONTEXTUAL VARIATION

Examine the theme in a real-life context. This can be the context of investigation, but not necessarily. Other contexts may provide new kinds of insights or inspiration. In each case, the goal is to examine the theme as such, without paying attention to the original problem. Observe and talk to people!

PERSONAL EXPERIENCE

Consult your own experience or interview people about theirs. Have you ever experienced trust? What triggered it? What did it feel like? What were you thinking and feeling? What changed it? What did you do? How did the situation develop? Did other people play a role?

4. TIPS AND TRICKS

When there is little time for researching a theme, some of the preceding approaches are too time consuming. What generally works well in a group of people with one or two hours of time is to focus on personal experiences and focus on key concepts and relationships between them. Also, if there is online connectivity, try searching for quotes about the theme. For some reason, google queries that also include the word *art* yield very interesting results in very little time—for example, *ambition art quotes*.

Useful sites include the following:

http://quote.robertgenn.com/ (for art-related quotes about themes)

http://www.emotionalcompetency.com (has great flowcharts for themes like fear)

http://thesaurus.com/ (thesauri are always interesting starting points as they always show collections of related concepts; for more on this, and Dick's writings, please see https://leefwereldacademie.nl/; see also his earlier papers on design[1] and the framing work of his group at The Hague University of Applied Sciences[2])

APPENDIX 5: STUDIO PRINCIPLES

THE PAVILLION RULES

Dick Rijken established the Pavillion, a social design education studio for The Hague University of Applied Sciences. In setting it up, he developed these studio rules to set the expectations for anyone entering the space:

The Pavillion does research into a meaning-led approach to complex problems. This is fundamentally practice-based research: asking fundamental questions to (and about) practice. We approach social problems in various domains like safety, education or governance from an artistic mentality. We are looking for methods and techniques that enable students and professionals from various domains to work in such a meaning-centered way.

0. There are nine rules—No more, no less. Ten is too much and eight is not enough. This is rule number zero, so it doesn't count. All rules will be strictly enforced.
1. Only nice people [Fight Club]—We are working with passionate people, that also have a sense of humour and do not make things unnecessarily difficult. We are dealing with very serious problems, that can only be dealt with from a playful mindset. Nice people have a broad scope of interest, and they are always curious about what others are doing. Where possible, we help each other. Asking questions about the definition of "nice people" is not nice. The use of terms like "innovation," "management," "valorisation," "social cohesion," "implementation" etc is kept to a minimum. We will only use difficult words for difficult things. What we can say, we will say accurately and about all other things we remain silent.
2. It's about meaning [Yes Men]—Many complex problems are hard because they consist of people, organisations and their relationships. We are fascinated by technology, but will always search for the human and social meaning behind the questions, and use this approach to create new perspectives.

Nobody is waiting for us to come up with solutions that have no meaning. Meaning first—this is non-negotiable.

3. Nobody is the boss—Everything is allowed, in particular the things that cannot happen anywhere else. Everybody can do what they want and if this causes practical problems, then we solve those collectively. Everybody cleans up after themselves and makes coffee for others. There are no limits to the agreements we can reach. When in doubt, see rule 1.
4. Quality—Nothing is done sloppily. No spelling mistakes or typos. Everything can always be better, but the perfect is the biggest enemy of the good. We are never content, except when something is finished—then we are happy with what we have done, and the learnings we can take to the future. See rule 1.
5. Think big, do small . . . and doing is thinking—We never just solve a problem, but will always search for the bigger story around or behind the issue. We will publish all we can, once we are convinced we have learned something that would also be interesting for others. We are not very interested in abstract ideas about life in general, or other questions that cannot be resolved in a concrete manner. Everything we do is deeply thought through, and feasible in execution. Thinking is doing. We learn through experimenting, trying out and learn from our mistakes.
6. Taking responsibility—An idea is good when we can take it forward ourselves. If not, then not. Anybody who has a plan, takes care that it is implemented. If you have a great idea that should be implemented by others, you make sure they can do so. See rule 1.
7. Feeling and thinking: beautiful is good—We are working intuitively, but we know what we are doing (although this may take a while). Intuition is important for judging and deciding, and very useful as a starting point for incisive thought. When we show results, we make clear that feeling and thinking are equally valuable. In content and form. No bureaucratic language, but also no PowerPoints with pictures that do not add feeling to a bunch of keywords. In everything we do, we try to add beauty, even when that is not needed. Beauty is important. It doesn't arise on its own. That's why. See rule 1.
8. Take risks wherever you can—If you don't make mistakes, you are not really trying. Experimenting is doing first, and then learning. As long as nobody dies in the worstcase scenario, anything is possible. Lack of courage has caused us much trouble and prevented much good from happening. Saying sorry is appreciated, doing better next time is preferred. See 1.
9. From the outside in—Everything we do because of the potential meaning it has for the outside world. So we drag the outside world into the lab. Partners, users, stakeholders, all are equally welcome to participate in everything we do. If the outside world doesn't get it, or isn't ripe for it, we should explain better. We do not work on request (see rule 1 to 8).

BURNING MAN PRINCIPLES

These rules emerged bottom up from the practices of the Burning Man series of events, from the early days on a Seattle beach—a fascinating story in itself. The enormous scale of the events in the desert requires a deep level of common understanding and also organization, which is not easily achieved when the whole event is focused on freedom to experiment and creative expression. The nine rules ahead were created as a "cultural guide" to try and achieve this paradoxical result. The nine rules didn't really work that well, until the tenth rule was added by the founder. Then everything fell into place. Since then, these rules have allowed spin-off festivals across the globe that all manage to take part in the fantastic culture of Burning Man:[1]

1. Radical Inclusion—Anyone may be a part of Burning Man. We welcome and respect the stranger. No prerequisites exist for participation in our community.
2. Gifting—Burning Man is devoted to acts of gift giving. The value of a gift is unconditional. Gifting does not contemplate a return or an exchange for something of equal value.
3. Decommodification—In order to preserve the spirit of gifting, our community seeks to create social environments that are unmediated by commercial sponsorships, transactions, or advertising. We stand ready to protect our culture from such exploitation. We resist the substitution of consumption for participatory experience.
4. Radical Self-reliance—Burning Man encourages the individual to discover, exercise and rely on his or her inner resources.
5. Radical Self-expression—Radical self-expression arises from the unique gifts of the individual. No one other than the individual or a collaborating group can determine its content. It is offered as a gift to others. In this spirit, the giver should respect the rights and liberties of the recipient.
6. Communal Effort—Our community values creative cooperation and collaboration. We strive to produce, promote and protect social networks, public spaces, works of art, and methods of communication that support such interaction.
7. Civic Responsibility—We value civil society. Community members who organize events should assume responsibility for public welfare and endeavour to communicate civic responsibilities to participants. They must also assume responsibility for conducting events in accordance with local, state and federal laws.
8. Leaving No Trace—Our community respects the environment. We are committed to leaving no physical trace of our activities wherever we gather. We

clean up after ourselves and endeavour, whenever possible, to leave such places in a better state than when we found them.
9. Participation—Our community is committed to a radically participatory ethic. We believe that transformative change, whether in the individual or in society, can occur only through the medium of deeply personal participation. We achieve being through doing. Everyone is invited to work. Everyone is invited to play. We make the world real through actions that open the heart.
10. Immediacy—Immediate experience is, in many ways, the most important touchstone of value in our culture. We seek to overcome barriers that stand between us and a recognition of our inner selves, the reality of those around us, participation in society, and contact with a natural world exceeding human powers. No idea can substitute for this experience.

INTERNATIONALE BAU AUSSTELLUNG (INTERNATIONAL BUILDING EXHIBITION)

And in Germany, the idea of a lab is taken to a completely different scale by the Internationale Bau Ausstellung. This has been around for over one hundred years, from its inception in Darmstadt in 1902. Over this time, it has offered a format for urban planning—for instance, in the rebuilding of Germany after the war. More recently, it has served as a vessel for guiding the transformation of the Ruhngebiet, a heavy mining and industrial area, into a completely different, much more friendly, natural and cultural landscape.

In their own words:[2]

Over the course of 100 years, International Building Exhibitions have evolved into an experimental field for urban and regional development and have expanded their focus to include social, economic and environmental aspects, as well as public participation and the quality of processes. Each one acquired a significance beyond its time and place. There is no binding convention defining what an IBA is, what issues it should tackle or what organisational form it should take. It is precisely because each IBA has to invent itself from scratch that continuous quality assurance is essential, consolidating its value for for urban and regional development and making the experience gained useful. Despite the differences in the issues dealt with, the success of former IBA is based on similar qualities.

1. Each IBA focuses on the pressing challenges in architecture and urban and regional planning that arise from local and regional problems. They are

forward-looking, exploring questions of social change and focusing on regional developments that can be influenced by the design of spaces in urban and rural contexts.
2. IBA propose social blueprints for future ways of living and offer answers to social problems, not just through the design of buildings, but also through new ways of appropriating urban and rural spaces.
3. IBA arise from specific challenges: while the central themes of IBA are of necessity based on a specific issue and location, their relevance extends far beyond the local context.
4. IBA strive to develop model solutions to current or future problems—be they architectural, economic, environmental or social. By demonstrating the relevance of the issues, challenges and strategies on an international scale, they set in motion an ongoing debate in the context of wider social developments.
5. The actual buildings and projects are at the core of any IBA. However, IBA draw attention not only to the buildings, but also to the conditions in which they were created and the quality of the processes that contributed to them. By qualifying instruments and formats, each IBA aims to contribute to a new culture of planning and building.
6. IBA must be created with an international dimension—determining factors include the international relevance of their central issues and the resulting model projects, the involvement of external experts, outstanding contributions from abroad and the fact that their networking activities have international reach.
7. The concentration of intellectual, artistic and financial resources for a limited period of time makes IBA unique showcases for the exceptional. They are experimental research and development laboratories in which intense collaboration between experts and stakeholders, combined with their experience and success stories, can stimulate projects elsewhere.
8. IBA call for the courage to take risks. They are experiments with open outcomes that generate new ideas. They sometimes use provocation. Contentious issues and productive controversies are important aspects of planning culture. All stakeholders—especially public servants, politicians and the public—must be aware of this from the outset to facilitate initiatives that step outside the realms of standard practice and to generate widespread interest in the projects.
9. Each IBA needs sufficient autonomy and appropriate operative framework to be able to produce exemplary, generalizable solutions that can act as beacons of excellence. In place of established processes and tried-and-tested courses of action, IBA call for imaginative programmes, designs and organisational approaches, coupled with a degree of improvisation and the agility to respond quickly to unforeseen events.

10. IBA thrive on sharing their themes, ideas, projects and images of their built results with the world. They are both a forum and a stage for their participants, presenting their contributions and commitment to a national and international audience. Communication and presentation are essential.

THE DOGME RULES

The Dogme 95 movement produced some very raw and disturbing films. The rules were developed by von Trier and Vinterberg as a set of constraints and enablers to elevate authentic storytelling, acting, and the expression of deep themes in filmmaking. To this end, von Trier and Vinterberg produced ten rules to which any Dogme film must conform. They are referred to as their "Vow of Chastity":[3]

1. Shooting must be done on location. Props and sets must not be brought in. (If a particular prop is necessary for the story, a location must be chosen where this prop is to be found.)
2. The sound must never be produced apart from the images or vice versa. (Music must not be used unless it occurs where the scene is being shot.)
3. The camera must be hand-held. Any movement or immobility attainable in the hand is permitted.
4. The film must be in colour. Special lighting is not acceptable. (If there is too little light for exposure the scene must be cut or a single lamp be attached to the camera.)
5. Optical work and filters are forbidden.
6. The film must not contain superficial action. (Murders, weapons, etc. must not occur.)
7. Temporal and geographical alienation are forbidden. (That is to say that the film takes place here and now.)
8. Genre movies are not acceptable.
9. The film format must be Academy 35 mm.
10. The director must not be credited.

BRIAN ENO'S OBLIQUE STRATEGIES

Brian Eno has been using these strategies since the 1970s to insert creativity into situations where people are working together—originally for musicians in the context of the recording studio. It's useful to take up some of these cards (the set contains 103 cards) randomly as prompts to upset the business as usual way of working when that feels stale or risks getting stuck. Many of the very professional and brilliant musicians he worked with report having a love-hate relationship with these cards, but everyone admits that using these random cards does lead to results that are out of the ordinary. In the spirit of this use, we just picked a random number of random cards—and invite the reader to use these at random moments in their practice:[4]

> Swap instruments
> State the problem in words as clearly as possible
> Retrace your steps
> Slow preparation . . . Fast execution
> Work at a different speed
> Make an exhaustive list of everything you might do and do the last thing on the list
> Do we need holes?
> Use an unacceptable colour
> Take a break
> What wouldn't you do?
> Abandon normal instruments
> Decorate, decorate
> Are there sections? Consider transitions
> Once the search is in progress, something will be found

THE BOOK OF FIVE RINGS

The Book of Five Rings (1645) was written by Miyamoto Musashi, a legendary Samurai warrior in ancient Japan, at the very end of his life. These principles hold deep lessons that go way beyond sword fighting; they extend to strategic thinking and express a poetic philosophy of action. Here is a sample from the introduction to the book of the Void:[5]

When you appreciate the power of nature, knowing the rhythm of any situation, you will be able to hit the enemy naturally and strike naturally. All this is the way of the void. . . . There is timing in everything. Timing in strategy cannot be mastered without a great deal of practice . . . in all skills and abilities there is timing . . . all things entail rising and falling timing. You must be able to discern this. In strategy there are various timing considerations. From the outset you must know the applicable timing and the inapplicable timing, and from among the large and small things and the fast and slow timings find the relevant timing, first seeing the distance timing and the background timing. This is the main thing in strategy. It is especially important to know the background timing, otherwise your strategy will become uncertain. . . . All the five books are chiefly concerned with timing. You must train sufficiently to appreciate all this.

Musashi then goes on to formulate a set of principles:[6]

This is the way for men who want to learn my strategy:

    Do not think dishonestly
    The Way is in training
    Become acquainted with every art
    Know the ways of all professions
    Distinguish between gain and loss in worldly matters
    Develop intuitive judgment and understanding for everything
    Perceive those things which cannot be seen
    Pay attention even to trifles
    Do nothing which is of no use.

APPENDIX 6: MASTERING DEEP CHANGE

More than ten years ago, together with colleagues, I designed a creative intelligence curriculum for the University of Technology Sydney as a bachelor's degree program.[1] It is based on the model of transdisciplinarity that is also used in this book; the learning in this degree is not about combining disciplines but about becoming nimble in exchanging practices between them. After all, every discipline has a way to deal with complexity, create newness, and so on (see § 5.2), which are all equally interesting. That is why the curriculum is presented as a double degree across all twenty-seven disciplines of the university. Students study in a regular faculty (engineering, business, nursing, design) and in summer schools and winter schools, plus one year full time at the end when they can add a second bachelor's degree. The curriculum included summer/winter courses like Problems to Possibilities, Creative Practice and Methods, Past Present and Future of Innovation, Creativity and Complexity, Leading Innovation, Initiatives and Entrepreneurship, and Envisioning Futures. The final year is studio-based, in which students work together on long projects for partner organizations in subjects like professional practice at the cutting edge, new knowledge making lab, and speculative startup.

When this bachelor's program became a great success for the university, the inevitable decision arose to devise a master's program in this same space. But master's programs here are for mid-career professionals, so there was no way that a master's could mirror the bachelor's curriculum. We started from scratch, and in doing workshops with fifteen organizations we landed on a new model for the master of creative intelligence and strategic innovation.[2] This degree program for professionals is a flexible suite of online subjects, studios, and labs. Although the degree is suitable for individuals, ideally organizations should enroll groups of staff to strategically build innovation capability across their existing departments and disciplines—effectively building a studio. Some people will take the full master's degree to become the core innovation leaders; others can take separate subjects to build capability and support the innovation network.

Masterclass. This subject introduces the key concepts and, through a short project, creates strategic advice for an industry partner. This gives a sense of how the creation of deep change can be approached in practice.

Transdisciplinarity. This subject challenges the participants to think about their own discipline and work environment in terms of practices, interrogating patterns and assumptions that guide what is considered normal.

Fields of thought. In this subject we explore concepts, principles, practices, and methods from various disciplinary fields. These lenses and this depth of thought is then used to examine your own professional practice from different philosophical and pragmatic perspectives.

Complexity. This subject introduces ways to recognize, think, communicate, and act within complex systems, moving beyond problem-solving approaches.

Frame creation and co-evolution. This subject introduces the frame creation model and challenges the participants to explore a complex problem situation from within their own organization using the frame creation methodology.

Futures. This subject starts by questioning the assumptions that underpin the approaches to futuring and innovation in your discipline, and then moves on to articulating multiple alternative future landscapes for your professional field.

Future value and impact. This is a hands-on subject that introduces a very wide range of futuring methods from different fields. The participants experiment with these in creating possible future scenarios for their own sector and society more broadly, and explore how these can be used to drive positive change on a world scale (sustainable development goals).

Networks and ecosystems. In this subject, we introduce methods and tools for creating networks of committed people: What does it take to create a studio and/or innovation ecosystem?

Changing minds. This subject introduces various theories and models to detect elusive patterns of practice that can inhibit change, and examines a range of practices to overcome these.

Theory of change. Here we examine the various theories, principles, and methods of organizational change, devise speculative strategies for creating change, and critically assess the applicability of these approaches in your own work. Then the challenge is to create your own theory of change.

Creative practices and methods. In this subject, participants explore creative practices and tools from across many professional domains to generate, discover, and explore new ideas, insights, and solutions.

Studios. In studio subjects, participants come together to collectively take on a complex real-world challenge for a partner organization and apply, trial, and experiment with the concrete methods and tools you have gained through other subjects within the studio environment.

Bespoke labs. For a brief description, see § 7.2.

A key outcome of this program is a collaborative community of committed innovators (past and current participants). They come from many different fields and have together learned and worked to create space for deep change. They are a formidable group of people that I would trust with any problem situation. They create impact. They are a movement in themselves.

APPENDIX 7: MAKE YOUR OWN COLOR OF CHANGE

To end with a challenge: In chapter 5, the five colors of change were introduced, and many of the case studies in this book can serve as illustrations of the real-world dynamics between them. Yet there is a nagging doubt that in using the five colors as a lens to look at change, we might be missing something. After all, in creating the studio model, we have put *creation* of new practices centrally as a driver for change, positioned in the middle of the organization (see § 7.2). But creation as such doesn't really figure very prominently in the original model by Vermaak and de Caluwé. So the question is, if this is an additional color of change, what would it be? Take a look at the matrix in table A7.1 and consider how you would fill in the question marks in the last column. Make (or mix) your own color of change!

Table A7.1 The five colors of change at a glance—and there is more

	YELLOW-PRINT negotiation	BLUE-PRINT rational and planned	RED-PRINT motivation and attention	GREEN-PRINT learning and development	WHITE-PRINT dialogue and self-organizing	???
something changes when you …	bring common interests together	think first and then act according to plan	stimulate people in the right way	create setting for collective learning	create space for spontaneous evolution	???
in a/an	power game	rational process	process of exchange	learning process	energizing process	???
and create …	a feasible solution, a win-win situation	the best solution, a brave new world	a motivating solution, the best "fit"	a solution that people develop themselves	a solution that catalyzes initiatives	???
interventions such as …	forming coalitions, changing top structures	project management, strategic analysis	assessment and reward, social gatherings	gaming and coaching, open systems planning	open space meetings, self-steering teams	???
are led by …	facilitators who use their own power base	experts in the field, project managers	HRM experts, managers who coach	facilitators who support people	sense makers who engage themselves personally	???
and target …	positions and context	knowledge and results	procedures, inspiration, and atmosphere	setting and communication	patterns and meanings	???
the outcome is …	unknown and shifting	defined and guaranteed	outlined but not guaranteed	envisioned but not guaranteed	unpredictable but not aimless	???
and ensured by …	policy documents, power balances, loyalties	benchmarking and monitoring	personnel systems and healthy relationships	a learning organization	self-organization and dialogue	???
the pitfalls in …	daydreaming and lose-lose outcomes	ignoring external and irrational aspects	smothering and conflict avoidance	excluding no one and lack of action	superficial understanding, laissez-faire attitude	???

Source: Hans Vermaak and Léon de Caluwé. "The Colors of Change Revisited: Situating and Describing the Theory and Its Practical Applications," in *Research in Organizational Change and Development*, vol. 26, edited by Debra A. Noumair and Abraham B. Shani (Emerald Publishing Limited, 2018).

ACKNOWLEDGMENTS

I would like to thank the people that I have encountered on my academic journey over the years. I have traveled with colleagues, collaborators, and critical friends from TU Delft, TU Eindhoven, and the University of Technology Sydney (UTS). At UTS, I have had the good fortune to encounter management that supported me and created a space for exploring deep change: Sue Rowley, Desley Luscombe, Attila Brungs, and Roy Green, among others. Their trust has been extraordinary and allowed me to build the prototypes of the research centers, degree programs, and studios that culminate in this book.

I would like to thank the people doing the real work behind the many projects that have always been my main source of inspiration, and I hope that inspiration travels on to you, the reader. The terrific people from the case studies and all the organizations involved (named in the case study descriptions) are the real stars of the book. Theory is nice, but the fact that you have actually done it, created the deep change, is what builds the story and what matters in the world. A very special thank you to some of the headline acts: the practitioners and academics at the Designing Out Crime Research Center: Rodger Watson, Douglas Tomkin, Linsday Asquith, Lucy Kaldor, Lucy Klippan, Rohan Lulham, Tasman Munro, Mieke van der Bijl, and many others. The projects and insights live on! For the Amsterdam New-West case study: Peter van der Vliet, Zinzi Stassen, Nadia Najibi, and the team. Rene van der Veer and Thijs Ewalts (Bioto), Christina Luzi (the education revolution), Jeroen van Erp (the Kunsten 92 initiative), André Schaminée, Dick Rijken, Iris van Genuchten, Marieke von Berg, Fides Lapidaire, and Jip Geven (nature versus agriculture). Roy Green and Simon Byrnes and team (Port of Newcastle), Dick Rijken and the team from The Hague University of Applied Sciences (the Waterwolf project). Dennis Lohuis (Zorgvrijstaat), Ciara Sterling, and Katrina Moore (Thriving Communities Australia), and many others.

The sad side of writing a book lies in all the projects, models, and insight that ended up in the bin—not because they were less in any way, but they just didn't quite fit. There are so many more stories to tell. My deepest apologies. I hope to do justice to you later, in other talks and publications. You are not forgotten.

Translating this thinking into new transdisciplinary degree programs, the bachelor of creative intelligence and innovation and the master of creative intelligence and strategic innovation: Louise McWhinnie, Tanja Golja, Rodger Watson, Katrina Moore, Barbara Doran, and all the people that have contributed to these programs over the years.

The thinking behind this book is very much a group effort. Deepest gratitude to my "united brains": Dick, Peik, Rene, Willem, André, Rodger, and Emile. It is very special to have a close group of critical friends that live this philosophy so intensely. And it is great to see this thinking gaining momentum; we need a movement of people who are inspired and committed to working together in creating these spaces.

My academic journey on this path started with Nigel Cross, and it was Douglas Tomkin who ignited the flame of practice-based research. They generously shared their experience and wisdom, almost as the "letters to a younger self." I am dedicating this book to them, good friends and old masters.

Paulien is my source of unconditional love, support, and deep change. This is the last book, I promise.

NOTES

CHAPTER 1

1. Rudolf Ritsema and Shantena Augusto Sabbadini, *The Original I Ching Oracle or The Book of Changes: The Eranos I Ching Project* (Watkins Media Limited, 2018).

CHAPTER 2

1. Lewis Carroll, *Through the Looking Glass* (Penguin Books, 1965; originally published in 1872).

2. Ludwig Wittgenstein, *Philosophical Investigations* (John Wiley & Sons, 2009), § 133.

3. Donald Schön, *The Reflective Practitioner* (Basic Books, 1983).

4. For a more extensive description, see Kees Dorst, *Frame Innovation—Create New Thinking by Design* (MIT Press, 2015).

5. For a case study where this plays out, see § 4.1. See also Kees Dorst and Rodger Watson, "There Is No Such Thing as Strategic Design," *Design Studies* 86 (2023): 101185.

6. David J. Snowden and Mary E. Boone, "A Leader's Framework for Decision Making," *Harvard Business Review* 85, no. 11 (2007): 68.

7. As laid out in André Schaminée and Kees Dorst, *Design thinking binnen de overheid: Effectiever werken aan transitievraagstukken* (Twynstra Gudde, 2021).

8. Roland van der Vorst, *De toekomst is eindeloos* [The future is endless] (Ten Have, 2023).

9. For an extensive case description, see Dorst, *Frame Innovation*, 3, 173.

10. Horst W. J. Rittel and Melvin M. Webber, "Dilemmas in a General Theory of Planning," *Policy Sciences* 4, no. 2 (1973): 155–169.

11. See Rob Wetzels, *Handreiking voor agendabepaling bij duurzaam ondernemen* (Nyenrode Business School, 2016); George T. Ainsworth-Land and Beth Jarman, *Breakpoint and Beyond: Mastering the Future-Today* (Harper Business, 1992); and Paul Cilliers, *Complexity and Postmodernism: Understanding Complex Systems* (Routledge, 2002).

12. Derk Loorbach, "Transition Management for Sustainable Development: A Prescriptive, Complexity-Based Governance Framework," *Governance* 23, no. 1 (2010): 161–183.

13. Thomas S. Kuhn, *The Structure of Scientific Revolutions* (University of Chicago Press, 1997; originally published in 1962).

14. Based on Geert Mak, *An Island in Time: The Biography of a Village* (Random House, 2010).

15. Hubert L. Dreyfus, *What Computers Still Can't Do: A Critique of Artificial Reason* (MIT Press, 1992).

16. Bert Bongers, *Understanding Interaction: The Relationships Between People, Technology, Culture, and the Environment: Volume 1: Evolution, Technology, Language and Culture* (Auerbach Publications, 2021).

17. Kees Dorst and Nigel Cross, "Creativity in the Design Process: Co-evolution of Problem–Solution," *Design Studies* 22, no. 5 (2001): 425–437.

18. Tua A. Björklund, "The Dynamics of Proactive Striving-Initiating and Sustaining Development Efforts in Product Design and Entrepreneurship" (PhD thesis, Aalto University, 2015).

19. Please note that for this approach we are heavily indebted to the work of Norbert Roozenburg, as partly presented in Norbert F. M. Roozenburg and Johannes Eekels, *Product Design: Fundamentals and Methods* (Wiley, 1995). This work adapted and extended the original work by Peirce to think through a "logic of design."

20. See Dreyfus, *What Computers Still Can't Do*; and George Lakoff and Mark Johnson, *Philosophy in the Flesh: The Embodied Mind and Its Challenge to Western Thought* (Basic Books, 1999). See also Dorst, *Frame Innovation*, chap. 7.

21. John R. Searle, *Rationality in Action* (MIT Press, 2003); and Searle, "The Intentionality of Intention and Action," *Cognitive Science* 4, no. 1 (1980): 47–70.

22. Kuhn, *Structure of Scientific Revolutions*.

23. For a more comprehensive overview, see Kees Dorst, *Notes on Design: How Creative Practice Works* (BIS Publishers, 2017).

CHAPTER 3

1. As quoted by Nigel Cross in Cross, "The Method in Their Madness: Understanding How Designers Think" (valedictory lecture at TUDelft, 1996).

2. Manfred A. Max-Neef, "Foundations of Transdisciplinarity," *Ecological Economics* 53, no. 1 (2005): 5–16.

3. See Stanley McChrystal et al., *Team of Teams: New Rules of Engagement for a Complex World* (Penguin, 2015); see also § 5.2.

4. See § 5.4; see also Kees Dorst, "Mixing Practices to Create Transdisciplinary Innovation: A Design-Based Approach." *Technology Innovation Management Review* 8, no. 8 (2018): 60–65. For an application in education, see appendix 6.

5. Richard Rorty, "Foucault and Epistemology," in *Michel Foucault* (Routledge, 2017).

6. Note that we are concentrating on frames here in the context of action, not to be confused with the notion of framing as it is used in rhetoric (Hans de Bruijn, *The Art of Political Framing: How Politicians Convince Us That They Are Right* [Amsterdam University Press, 2019]). There a frame is a communication device, used in a political arena to manipulate and influence a discussion, often to silence opponents. But when we talk about framing here, it is about finding new ways forward in a vexed problem situation.

7. See Dorst, *Frame Innovation*. A further twenty project cases can be found in Kees Dorst et al., *Designing for the Common Good* (BIS Publishers, 2016).

8. Dorst, *Notes on Design*.

9. For a more detailed description, see André Schaminée, *Designing With and Within Public Organizations: Building Bridges Between Public Sector Innovators and Designers* (BIS Publishers, 2018).

10. Similar to Tom Kelley, *The Art of Innovation: Lessons in Creativity from IDEO, America's Leading Design Firm* (Currency, 2001).

11. For a great set of methods for this crucial step, see appendix 4.

12. Bryan Lawson and Kees Dorst, *Design Expertise* (Routledge, 2013).

13. See https://waag.org/en/article/toolkit-public-civic-collaboration/.

CHAPTER 4

1. Walt Kelly, *Pogo: We Have Met the Enemy and He Is Us* (Simon and Schuster, 1972).

2. For a more detailed description of this project and its outcomes, see Kees Dorst, "The Core of 'Design Thinking' and Its Application," *Design Studies* 32, no. 6 (2011): 521–532; Dorst, *Frame Innovation*; and Dorst et al., *Designing for the Common Good*.

3. City of Sydney. *Late Night Management Areas Research Project* (Parsons Brinckerhoff for City of Sydney, 2011); and City of Sydney, *Submission to the Joint Select Committee: Sydney's Night-Time Economy* (City of Sydney, 2019).

4. Deloitte, *ImagineSydney* (NSW Government, 2019), http://images.content.deloitte.com.au/Web/DELOITTEAUSTRALIA/%7B725ffb22-cab6-47f4-9958-37305087ba5e%7D_20190211-cit-imagine-sydney-play-report.pdf.

5. Clover Moore, "Summer Trials to Improve Sydney's Late Night Economy," Minute by the Lord Mayor, City of Sydney, July 25, 2011.

6. Christian Bason, *Leading Public Sector Innovation* (Policy Press, 2010).

7. Andréina Seijas and Mirik Milan Gelders, "Governing the Night-Time City: The Rise of Night Mayors as a New Form of Urban Governance After Dark," *Urban Studies* 58, no. 2 (2021): 316–334.

8. See, for instance, City of Sydney, *Submission to the Joint Select Committee*.

9. Treasury NSW, *NSW 24-hour Economy Strategy: A New State of Night* (NSW Government and 24-Hour Economy, 2020), https://www.investment.nsw.gov.au/assets/Uploads/files/Sydney-24-hour-Economy-Strategy.pdf.

10. Ralph D. Stacey and Douglas Griffin, eds., *Complexity and the Experience of Managing in Public Sector Organizations* (Routledge, 2007); Ralph D. Stacey, Douglas Griffin, and Patricia Shaw, *Complexity and Management: Fad or Radical Challenge to Systems Thinking?* (Psychology Press, 2000); Nynke Tromp and Paul Hekkert, *Designing for Society: Products and Services for a Better World* (Bloomsbury Publishing, 2018); and Dick Rijken et al., *Het Echte Werk, van Waterwolf naar FC de Omslag* (Haagse Hogeschool, 2011).

11. Paul Hekkert and Matthijs Van Dijk, *Vision in Design—A Guidebook for Innovators* (BIS Publishers, 2011).

12. Based on the classic model of experiential learning: David A. Kolb, *Experiential Learning: Experience as the Source of Learning and Development* (FT Press, 2014).

13. Charles Leadbeater and Jennie Winhall, *Building Better Systems: A Green Paper on System Innovation* (Rockwool Foundation, 2020).

14. See Schaminée, *Designing With and Within Public Organizations*; and Bec Paton and Kees Dorst, "Briefing and Reframing: A Situated Practice," *Design Studies* 32, no. 6 (2011): 573–587.

15. Bason, *Leading Public Sector Innovation*.

16. As in the "playing field," after Bourdieu. See Michael Grenfell, *Pierre Bourdieu: Key Concepts* (Routledge, 2014).

17. See Joris Luyendijk, *Swimming with Sharks: My Journey into the World of the Bankers* (Guardian Faber Publishing, 2015). In this ethnographic account, he shows how the banks do what all the other banks are doing.

18. Rik Braams et al., "Understanding Why Civil Servants Are Reluctant to Carry Out Transition Tasks," *Science and Public Policy* 49, no. 6 (2022): 905–914.

19. Mieke van der Bijl-Brouwer and Rodger Watson, "Designing for the Deepest Needs of Both Public Service Consumers and Providers; Innovation in Mental Health Crisis Response," in *Proceedings of ICED15: Vol 1: Design for Life*, edited by Christian Weber et al. (Design Society, 2015).

20. Peik Suyling, Diana Krabbendam, and Kees Dorst, eds. *More than 8 Design Ideas for the Integrated Living of Mentally Handicapped People in Society* (Ministry of Health Wellbeing and Sports, The Hague, 2005).

21. Rijken, *Het Echte Werk*, 28; author's translation.

22. The project's name, *Waterwolf* (literally, "water wolf"), refers to the threat of a flood, a wave that comes in and changes everything.

23. Schaminée, *Designing With and Within Public Organizations*.

CHAPTER 5

1. Ger Groot, *Twee zielen. Gesprekken met hedendaagse filosofen* (SUN, 1999); author's translation.

2. Kuhn, *Structure of Scientific Revolutions*.

NOTES

3. Quoted in Kuhn, *Structure of Scientific Revolutions*, 151.

4. Quoted in Kuhn, *Structure of Scientific Revolutions*, 151.

5. Kuhn, *Structure of Scientific Revolutions*, 157.

6. Kuhn, *Structure of Scientific Revolutions*, 155.

7. Kees Dorst, Rodger Watson, and Barbara Doran, eds., *Reinventing Strategic Innovation: Create Deep Change* (BIS Publishers, 2025); and UTS, "Meet the Teacher Taking a Fresh Approach to Education," an interview with Christina Luzi, *Postgrad Blog*, August 23, 2023, https://www.uts.edu.au/study/postgraduate/why-uts/news/meet-teacher-taking-fresh-approach-education.

8. Barbara Doran, Rodger Watson, and Diana Vo, *Creative Reboot* (BIS Publishers, 2021).

9. Howard Gardner, *Changing Minds* (Harvard Business School Press, 2006).

10. McCrystal et al., *Team of Teams*.

11. Steve Diller, Nathan Shedroff, and Darrel Rhea, *Making Meaning: How Successful Businesses Deliver Meaningful Customer Experiences* (New Riders, 2005).

12. Léon de Caluwé and Hans Vermaak, *Learning to Change: A Guide for Organization Change Agents* (Sage, 2003); Hans Vermaak, "Planning Deep Change Through a Series of Small Wins," *Academy of Management Proceedings* 2013, no. 1: 10947; and Hans Vermaak and Léon de Caluwé, "The Colors of Change Revisited: Situating and Describing the Theory and Its Practical Applications," in *Research in Organizational Change and Development*, vol. 26, edited by Debra A. Noumair and Abraham B. Shani (Emerald Publishing Limited, 2018).

13. Note that Vermaak and de Caluwé chose to assign colors to these modes of change because this creates a palette of neutral words in this contested arena. The use of the color names was originally inspired by the concept of the blueprint as the ultimate planning tool.

14. Chris Argyris, *Flawed Advice and the Management Trap: How Managers Can Know When They're Getting Good Advice and When They're Not* (Oxford University Press, 2000).

15. Lon Barfield et al., "Interaction Design at the Utrecht School of the Arts," *ACM SIGCHI Bulletin* 26, no. 3 (1994): 49–86.

16. See appendix 6 and the method cards from twenty-five disciplines.

17. Julia Kristeva, *Strangers to Ourselves* (Columbia University Press, 2024).

18. Kees Dorst, "Analysing Design Activity: New Directions in Protocol Analysis," *Design Studies* 2, no. 16 (1995): 139–142.

19. See Hugh Lawson-Tancred, ed., *The Art of Rhetoric* (Penguin, 1991).

20. Richard Buchanan, "Declaration by Design: Rhetoric, Argument, and Demonstration in Design Practice," *Design Issues* 2, no. 1 (1985): 4–22.

21. For more on this, see Dorst, *Frame Innovation*, beginning on page 137.

22. David Bohm, *On Dialogue* (Routledge, 2013).

23. Lindsay Asquith et al., "Design+ Crime: Introduction to a Special Issue of Crime Prevention and Community Safety," *Crime Prevention and Community Safety* 15 (2013): 169–174.

24. Donald Weatherburn and Stephanie Ramsey, *Offending over the Life Course: Contact with the NSW Criminal Justice System Between Age 10 and Age 33* (NSW Bureau of Crime Statistics and Research, 2018).

25. Rohan Lulham et al., "The Risk of 'a Cold Conservatism' in Correctional Facility Design: The Case for Design Innovation," *Advancing Corrections Journal* 1 (2016): 12–25.

26. Rohan Lulham et al., *Intensive Learning Centre Building Evaluation* (Designing Out Crime, 2015).

27. Anton Nemme et al., "A Product System for Meaningful Work, Rehabilitation, and Social Well-Being in Correctional Contexts," in *Maintaining Social Well-Being and Meaningful Work in a Highly Automated Job Market*, edited by Shalin Hai-Jew (IGI Global, 2020).

28. Roahn Lulham, "Does Design Matter? An Environmental Psychology Study in Youth Detention," in *The Palgrave Handbook of Prison Design*, edited by Dominique Moran et al. (Springer International Publishing, 2022).

29. Lucy Kaldor and Rodger Watson, "Improving Wellbeing for Victims of Crime," in *Proceedings of the International Conference on Engineering Design*, ICED, 2015, 1 (DS 80-01), 381–390.

30. Tasman Munro, "Appreciative Co-design: From Problem Solving to Strength-Based Re-authoring in Social Design," in *Future Focused Thinking—DRS International Conference*, edited by P. Lloyd and E. Bohemia (Design Research Society, 2016), https://doi.org/10.21606/drs.2016.271.

31. Rodger Watson, "Designing for the Common Good; Emergent Practices and Contemporary Challenges" (PhD thesis, University of the Arts London, 2025).

32. Luyendijk, *Swimming with Sharks*.

33. Michael McGann, Tamas Wells and Emma Blomkamp, "Innovation Labs and Co-production in Public Problem Solving," *Public Management Review* 23, no. 2 (2021): 297–316; and Michael McGann, Emma Blomkamp, and Jenny M. Lewis, "The Rise of Public Sector Innovation Labs: Experiments in Design Thinking for Policy," *Policy Sciences* 51, no. 3 (2018): 249–267.

34. See Mariana Mazzucato and Rosie Collington, *The Big Con: How the Consulting Industry Weakens Our Businesses, Infantilizes Our Governments, and Warps Our Economies* (Penguin, 2023).

35. Henry Mintzberg, "Managers Not MBAs," *Management Today* 20, no. 7 (2004): 10–13.

CHAPTER 6

1. This is the sentence Bert Mulder sometimes used at the end of his talks about the changing role for public sector organizations in the networked society, as discussed in a private conversation with the author.

2. See Pierre Bourdieu et al., *The Weight of the World: Social Suffering in Contemporary Society* (Wiley, 1999); and § 7.4.

3. Derk Loorbach and Jan Rotmans, "The Practice of Transition Management: Examples and Lessons from Four Distinct Cases," *Futures* 42, no. 3 (2010): 237–246; emphasis added.

4. See Loorbach, "Transition Management for Sustainable Development"; and Derk Loorbach, Jan Rotmans, and René Kemp, "Complexity and Transition Management," in *Complexity and Planning* (Routledge, 2016).

5. For instance, see Rick Bosman et al., "Carbon Lock-out: Leading the Fossil Port of Rotterdam into Transition," *Sustainability* 10, no. 7 (2018): 2558.

6. This is what Michel Foucault (*Archaeology of Knowledge* [Routledge, 2013]) terms their *cultural residue*.

7. After Loorbach, "Transition Management for Sustainable Development"; Schaminée, *Designing With and Within Public Organizations*; and Braams et al., "Understanding Why Civil Servants Are Reluctant."

8. Luyendijk, *Swimming with Sharks*.

9. Bansi Nagji and Geoff Tuff, "Managing Your Innovation Portfolio," *Harvard Business Review* 90, no. 5 (2012): 66–74.

10. From André Schaminée, *Werken aan transities* [Working on transitions] (Twynstra Gudde, 2023).

11. Paul Tullis, "Nitrogen Wars: The Dutch Farmers Revolt that Turned a Nation Upside Down," *The Guardian*, November 16, 2023, https://www.theguardian.com/environment/2023/nov/16/nitrogen-wars-the-dutch-farmers-revolt-that-turned-a-nation-upside-down.

12. Dorst, *Frame Innovation*; Schaminée, *Designing With and Within Public Organizations*; and see chapter 3.

13. Herbert A. Simon, "The Structure of Ill Structured Problems," *Artificial Intelligence* 4, no. 3–4 (1973): 181–201.

14. Note that the societal midfield differs from the quadruple helix (bringing together science, policy, industry, and society) or quintuple helix (university, industry, government, public, and environment) approaches, which are focused on knowledge exchange; here we are instead concerned with the exchange of practices.

15. Anton Zijderveld, *The Waning of the Welfare State* (Routledge, 2018).

16. Garrett Hardin, "The Tragedy of the Commons," in *Environmental Ethics*, by John Benson (Routledge, 2013).

17. Mariana Mazzucato, "The Entrepreneurial State," *Soundings* 49, no. 49 (2011): 131–142; and Mazzucato, *Big Con*.

18. As discussed earlier. See also Dorst, *Frame Innovation*, 116.

19. Lucy Suchman, *Plans and Situated Actions: The Problem of Human-Machine Communication* (Cambridge University Press, 1987).

20. Riel Miller, *Transforming the Future: Anticipation in the 21st Century* (Taylor & Francis, 2018).

21. Max van Manen, *Researching Lived Experience: Human Science for an Action Sensitive Pedagogy* (Routledge, 2016).

22. Rutger Bregman, *Humankind: A Hopeful History* (Bloomsbury Publishing, 2020).

23. Dick Rijken, https://leefwereldacademie.nl/.

24. Dorst et al., *Designing for the Common Good*.

25. Victor W. Hwang and Greg Horowitt, *The Rainforest: The Secret to Building the Next Silicon Valley* (Regenwald, 2012).

CHAPTER 7

1. As quoted in Bryan Lawson and Kees Dorst, *Design Expertise* (Routledge, 2013).

2. Frido Smulders, "Get Synchronized: Bridging the Gap Between Design and Volume Production" (PhD thesis, TU Delft, 2006).

3. Lawson and Dorst, *Design Expertise*.

4. All the designer's quotes are from Lawson and Dorst, *Design Expertise*.

5. Jerry Hirshberg, *The Creative Priority: Driving Innovative Business in the Real World* (Harper Collins, 1998).

6. Alex Coles, *The Transdisciplinary Studio* (Sternberg Press, 2012).

7. Alex Coles, "Designart." *Art Monthly*, no. 334 (2010): 10.

8. Olafur Eliasson, *Experience* (Phaidon, 2022).

9. Coles, *The Transdisciplinary Studio*, 61–76 and 167–208.

10. Coles, *The Transdisciplinary Studio*, 200.

11. Coles, *The Transdisciplinary Studio*, 192.

12. Unfortunately, both education and academic research in these creative disciplines overwhelmingly focus on the processes and practices *within* projects, and on the critique of outcomes (as things-in-themselves). The higher (meta) level of practices that these top professionals talk about is largely uncharted territory—although in professional literature, we can find interviews and books by practitioners that do refer to this knowledge and these practices. For example, consider these writings on architecture: Harma Horlings and Noel van Dooren, *Design Lessons from Practice: Professionals Reflecting on Design Processes* (Amsterdam Academy of Architecture, 2020); and Michiel Spaan, *The Wandering Maker* (Architectura & Natura, 2019). And on theatre, consider Erik Vos, *Herinneringen van een regisseur—een wereld van beeld en verbeelding* (International Theatre and Film Books, 2014). These texts are worth their weight in gold as it is exactly these practices that organizations from many fields need to learn from to create the space for deep and ongoing change.

13. Renske Bouwknecht, *PONT De Publieke Ontwerppraktijk* [The public design practice] (Ministerie van OCW, 2023). See www.ontwerpendeaanpak.nl.

14. Watson, "Designing for the Common Good."

15. Pontus Hultén and Jean Tinguely, *Jean Tinguely: A Magic Stronger than Death* (Abbeville Press, 1987).

16. Henry W. Chesbrough, *Open Innovation: The New Imperative for Creating and Profiting from Technology* (Harvard Business School, 2003).

17. Robert I. Sutton and Thomas A. Kelley, "Creativity Doesn't Require Isolation: Why Product Designers Bring Visitors 'Backstage.'" *California Management Review* 40, no. 1 (1997): 75–91.

18. Riel Miller, "Embracing Complexity and Using the Future," *Ethos* 10, no. 10 (2010): 23–28.

19. Miller, "Embracing Complexity and Using the Future," 25.

20. Miller, "Embracing Complexity and Using the Future," 26–28.

21. OECD, *Systems Approaches to Public Sector Challenges: Working with Change* (OECD Publishing, 2017), http://dx.doi.org/10.1787/9789264279865-en.

22. Jane Bower, Elisabeth Crabtree, and William Keogh, "Rhetorics and Realities in New Product Development," in *Hidden Versus Open Rules in Product Development*, edited by Jurg Thölke, Gerard Loosschilder, and Frido Smulders (TUDelft Faculty of Industrial Design Engineering, 1996).

23. Dick Rijken, https://leefwereldacademie.nl/.

24. Sophie Holierhoek, "Redesigning Psychiatry: A Strategic Repertoire to Stimulate Transition in the Mental Healthcare Sector" (PhD thesis, TU Delft, 2020); and Femke de Boer, Nynke Tromp, Sander Voerman, Matthijs van Dijk, Beatrijs Voorneman et al., *Redesigning Psychiatry* (Reframing Studio, 2016).

25. See https://longreads.cbs.nl/monitor-of-well-being-and-sdgs-2021/trends-in-well-being/.

26. Hans Horsten, *The City that Creates the Future* (Lecturis, 2016).

27. See Brainport's website at https://brainporteindhoven.com/int/.

28. A. Georges L. Romme, "Against All Odds: How Eindhoven Emerged as a Deep-tech Ecosystem," *Systems* 10, no. 4 (2022): 119.

29. See Chemelot's website at https://www.chemelot.nl/homeen.

30. See the Brightlands website at https://www.brightlands.com/en/brightlands-chemelot-campus.

31. See the Internationale Bau Ausstellung information at https://www.internationale-bauausstellungen.de/en/iba-memorandum/; see also IBA Parkstad's website at https://www.iba-parkstad.nl/; and the IBA Parkstad: IBA Scoop website at https://www.iba-parkstad.nl/projecten/c-city-iba-scoop/.

32. Kees Dorst, Rodger Watson, and Simon Byrnes, "Future Hunter: Social Change in Times of Transition," in *DTRS 14: The Role of Design in Shaping Sustainable Futures*, edited by Ulrika Florin et al. (Malardalen University Living Lab Press, 2024).

33. Froukje Sleeswijk-Visser and Jeroen van Erp, "Let's Step into Each Other's Worlds: Designing for Local Transformation Processes," in *ServDes 2023: Entanglements and*

Flows: Service Encounters and Meanings: Conference Proceedings, edited by Carla Cipolla et al. (ServDes, 2023).

CHAPTER 8

1. Maurice S. Friedman, *The Worlds of Existentialism: A Critical Reader* (Humanities Press, 1964).

2. Christopher Alexander, *The Timeless Way of Building* (Oxford University Press, 1979); emphasis added.

3. Jiddu Krishnamurti, *The Book of Life: Daily Meditations with Krishnamurti* (Penguin Books India, 2001).

4. Bohm, *On Dialogue*.

5. Douglas R. Hofstadter, *I Am a Strange Loop* (Basic Books, 2007).

6. Evan Thompson, *Mind in Life: Biology, Phenomenology, and the Sciences of Mind* (Harvard University Press, 2010).

7. Dennis Ford, *The Search for Meaning: A Short History* (University of California Press, 2007).

8. Ford, *The Search for Meaning*, 93–111.

9. Syd Field, *The Screenwriter's Workbook: Exercises and Step-by-Step Instructions for Creating a Successful Screenplay*, rev. ed. (Delta, 2006).

10. Vos, *Herinneringen*.

11. Paul Colinvaux, *Why Big Fierce Animals Are Rare: An Ecologist's Perspective* (Princeton University Press, 1979).

12. Humberto R. Maturana and Francisco J. Varela, *The Tree of Knowledge: The Biological Roots of Human Understanding* (New Science Library/Shambhala Publications, 1987).

13. Frank Barrett, *Yes to the Mess: Surprising Leadership Lessons from Jazz* (Harvard Business Review Press, 2012).

14. Rick Spann and Simon Martin, *Re-sounding: Introducing an Alternative Metaphor for Organisational Change* (Taos Institute Publications, 2021); and Hans Boutellier, *The Improvising Society: Social Order in a World Without Boundaries* (Eleven, 2013).

15. Frances A. Yates, *Art of Memory* (Routledge, 2013).

16. Friedman, *Worlds of Existentialism*, 3–15.

EPILOGUE

1. He is known for books like the following: Tyson Yunkaporta, *Right Story, Wrong Story: Adventures in Indigenous Thinking* (Text Publishing, 2023); and *Sand Talk: How Indigenous Thinking Can Save the World* (Text Publishing, 2019).

APPENDIX 1

1. Gary Hamel, "Opinion: Strategy Innovation and the Quest for Value," *Sloan Management Review* 39, no. 2 (1998): 7–14.

2. James Carlopio, *Strategy by Design: A Process of Strategy Innovation* (Palgrave Macmillan, 2010).

3. Rodger Watson and Kees Dorst, "Pragmatism, Design and Public Sector Innovation: Reflections on Action," in *DRS2022: Bilbao*, edited by Dan Lockton et al. (Design Research Society, 2022).

4. Argyris, *Flawed Advice and the Management Trap*.

5. Van Manen, *Researching Lived Experience*.

6. Rorty, "Foucault and Epistemology."

7. Thompson, *Mind in Life*.

APPENDIX 2

1. Rodger Watson, Who Framed the Government Architect?: Cultural Residue, and a Role for Design in Reshaping Organizations," in *DTRS 14: The Role of Design in Shaping Sustainable Futures*, edited by Ulrika Florin et al. (Mälardalen University Living Lab Press, 2024).

2. See https://www.depubliekeontwerppraktijk.nl/.

3. United Nations Development Group, *Mainstreaming the 2030 Agenda for Sustainable Development* (UN, 2017); and United Nations Development Programme, *UNDP Strategic Plan, 2018–2021* (UN, 2017).

APPENDIX 3

1. André Schaminée and Kees Dorst, *Design thinking binnen de overheid: Effectiever werken aan transitievraagstukken* (Twynstra Gudde, 2021).

2. Otto Scharmer, *Theory U: Learning from the Future as It Emerges* (Berrett-Koehler Publishers, 2009).

3. Eric Ries, *The Lean Startup: How Today's Entrepreneurs Use Continuous Innovation to Create Radically Successful Businesses* (Crown Currency, 2011).

4. Ken Schwaber and Jeff Sutherland, "The Scrum Guide," *Scrum Alliance* 21, no. 1 (2011): 1–38.

5. The term *A UFO* (in Dutch, *ONAF*, meaning *unfinished*) is a concept developed by Twynstra Gudde and Matching Futures.

6. Peter Senge, *The Fifth Discipline: The Art and Practice of Learning Organization* (Doubleday, 1990).

APPENDIX 4

1. Dick Rijken, "Design Literacy: Organizing Self-Organization," in *Open Design Now*, edited by Bas van Abel et al. (BIS, 2011); and Dick Rijken, *The Future Is a Direction, Not a Place* (Netherlands Design Institute, Sandberg Institute, 1994).

2. Jos van Leeuwen et al., "Finding New Perspectives Through Theme Investigation," *Design Journal* 23, no. 3 (2020): 441–461; and Jos van Leeuwen et al., "Thematic

Research in the Frame Creation Process," in *Service Design Geographies: ServDes.2016*, edited by Nicola Morelli, Amalia de Gotzen, and Francesco Grani (ServDes, 2016).

APPENDIX 5

1. See https://burningman.org/about/10-principles/.

2. See https://www.internationale-bauausstellungen.de/en/iba-memorandum.

3. See https://as.vanderbilt.edu/koepnick/WorldCinema_f02/materials/Dogme_Vow.htm.

4. See https://www.brian-eno.net.

5. Miyamoto Musashi, "The Way of Strategy," *FMR*, no. 54 (1992): 142.

6. Miyamoto Musashi, "The Way of Strategy," *FMR*, no. 54 (1992): 144.

APPENDIX 6

1. This program was designed with Tanja Golja and Louise McWhinnie. For more information, visit https://www.uts.edu.au/study/transdisciplinary-innovation/undergraduate-courses/creative-intelligence-and-innovation.

2. This program was designed with Rodger Watson and Katrina Moore. For more information, visit https://www.uts.edu.au/about/td-school/creative-intelligence-and-strategic-innovation.

BIBLIOGRAPHY

Ainsworth-Land, George T., and Beth Jarman. *Breakpoint and Beyond: Mastering the Future-Today*. Harper Business, 1992.

Alexander, Christopher. *The Timeless Way of Building*. Oxford University Press, 1979.

Argyris, Chris. *Flawed Advice and the Management Trap: How Managers Can Know When They're Getting Good Advice and When They're Not*. Oxford University Press, 2000.

Asquith, Lindsay, Kees Dorst, Lucy Kaldor, and Rodger Watson. "Design+ Crime: Introduction to a Special Issue of Crime Prevention and Community Safety." *Crime Prevention and Community Safety* 15 (2013): 169–174.

Barfield, Lon, Willie van Burgsteden, Ruud Lanfermeijer, Bert Mulder, Jurriënne Ossewold, Dick Rijken, and Philippe Wegner. "Interaction Design at the Utrecht School of the Arts." *ACM SIGCHI Bulletin* 26, no. 3 (1994): 49–86.

Barrett, Frank. *Yes to the Mess: Surprising Leadership Lessons from Jazz*. Harvard Business Review Press, 2012.

Bason, Christian. *Leading Public Sector Innovation*. Policy Press, 2010.

Björklund, Tua A. "The Dynamics of Proactive Striving-Initiating and Sustaining Development Efforts in Product Design and Entrepreneurship." PhD thesis, Aalto University, 2015.

Bohm, David. *On Dialogue*. Routledge, 2013.

Bongers, Bert. *Understanding Interaction: The Relationships Between People, Technology, Culture, and the Environment: Volume 1: Evolution, Technology, Language and Culture*. Auerbach Publications, 2021.

Bosman, Rick, Derk Loorbach, Jan Rotmans, and Roel Van Raak. "Carbon Lock-out: Leading the Fossil Port of Rotterdam into Transition." *Sustainability* 10, no. 7 (2018): 2558.

Bourdieu, Pierre, Alain Accardo, Gabrielle Balazs, Stephane Beaud, and Francois Bonvin. *The Weight of the World: Social Suffering in Contemporary Society*. Wiley, 1999.

Boutellier, Hans. *The Improvising Society: Social Order in a World Without Boundaries.* Eleven, 2013.

Bouwknecht, Renske. *PONT De Publieke Ontwerppraktijk* [The public design practice]. Ministerie van OCW, 2023.

Bower, Jane, Elisabeth Crabtree, and William Keogh. "Rhetorics and Realities in New Product Development." In *Hidden Versus Open Rules in Product Development*, edited by Jurg Thölke, Gerard Loosschilder, and Frido Smulders. TUDelft Faculty of Industrial Design Engineering, 1996.

Braams, Rik B., Joeri H. Wesseling, Albert J. Meijer, and Marko P. Hekkert. "Understanding Why Civil Servants Are Reluctant to Carry Out Transition Tasks." *Science and Public Policy* 49, no. 6 (2022): 905–914.

Bregman, Rutger. *Humankind: A Hopeful History.* Bloomsbury Publishing, 2020.

Buchanan, Richard. "Declaration by Design: Rhetoric, Argument, and Demonstration in Design Practice." *Design Issues* 2, no. 1 (1985): 4–22.

Carlopio, James. *Strategy by Design: A Process of Strategy Innovation.* Palgrave Macmillan, 2010.

Carroll, Lewis. *Through the Looking Glass.* Penguin Books, 1965. Originally published in 1872.

Chesbrough, Henry W. *Open Innovation: The New Imperative for Creating and Profiting from Technology.* Harvard Business School, 2003.

Cilliers, Paul. *Complexity and Postmodernism: Understanding Complex Systems.* Routledge, 2002.

City of Sydney. *Late Night Management Areas Research Project.* Parsons Brinckerhoff for City of Sydney, 2011.

City of Sydney. *Submission to the Joint Select Committee: Sydney's Night-Time Economy.* City of Sydney, 2019.

Coles, Alex. *The Transdisciplinary Studio.* Sternberg Press, 2012.

Coles, Alex. "Designart." *Art Monthly*, no. 334 (2010): 7–10.

Colinvaux, Paul. *Why Big Fierce Animals Are Rare: An Ecologist's Perspective.* Princeton University Press, 1979.

Cross, Nigel. "The Method in Their Madness: Understanding How Designers Think." Valedictory lecture at TUDelft, 1996.

de Boer, Femke, Nynke Tromp, Sander Voerman, Matthijs van Dijk, and Beatrijs Voorneman. *Redesigning Psychiatry.* Reframing Studio, 2016.

de Bruijn, Hans. *The Art of Political Framing: How Politicians Convince Us That They Are Right.* Amsterdam University Press, 2019.

de Caluwé, Léon, and Hans Vermaak. *Learning to Change: A Guide for Organization Change Agents*. Sage, 2003.

Deloitte. *ImagineSydney*. NSW Government, 2019. http://images.content.deloitte.com.au/Web/DELOITTEAUSTRALIA/%7B725ffb22-cab6-47f4-9958-37305087ba5e%7D_20190211-cit-imagine-sydney-play-report.pdf.

Diller, Steve, Nathan Shedroff, and Darrel Rhea. *Making Meaning: How Successful Businesses Deliver Meaningful Customer Experiences*. New Riders, 2005.

Doran, Barbara, Rodger Watson, and Diana Vo. *Creative Reboot*. BIS Publishers, 2021.

Dorst, Kees. "Analysing Design Activity: New Directions in Protocol Analysis." *Design Studies* 2, no. 16 (1995): 139–142.

Dorst, Kees. "The Core of 'Design Thinking' and Its Application." *Design Studies* 32, no. 6 (2011): 521–532.

Dorst, Kees. "Describing Design: A Comparison of Paradigms." PhD diss., Delft University of Technology, 1997.

Dorst, Kees. *Frame Innovation: Create New Thinking by Design*. MIT Press, 2015.

Dorst, Kees. "Mixing Practices to Create Transdisciplinary Innovation: A Design-Based Approach." *Technology Innovation Management Review* 8, no. 8 (2018): 60–65.

Dorst, Kees. *Notes on Design: How Creative Practice Works*. BIS Publishers, 2017.

Dorst, Kees, and Nigel Cross. "Creativity in the Design Process: Co-evolution of Problem–Solution." *Design Studies* 22, no. 5 (2001): 425–437.

Dorst, Kees, Lucy Kaldor, Lucy Klippan, and Rodger Watson. *Designing for the Common Good*. BIS Publishers, 2016.

Dorst, Kees, and Rodger Watson. "There Is No Such Thing as Strategic Design." *Design Studies* 86 (2023): 101185. https://doi.org/10.1016/j.destud.2023.101185.

Dorst, Kees, Rodger Watson, and Simon Byrnes. "Future Hunter: Social Change in Times of Transition." In *DTRS 14: The Role of Design in Shaping Sustainable Futures*, edited by Ulrika Florin, Karolina Uggla, Hasse Henningsson, Lasse Frank, and Björn Westling. Mälardalen University Living Lab Press, 2024.

Dorst, Kees, Rodger Watson, and Barbara Doran, eds. *Reinventing Strategic Innovation: Create Deep Change* (BIS Publishers, 2025).

Dreyfus, Hubert L. *What Computers Still Can't Do: A Critique of Artificial Reason*. MIT Press, 1992.

Eliasson, Olafur. *Experience*. Phaidon, 2022.

Field, Syd. *The Screenwriter's Workbook: Exercises and Step-by-Step Instructions for Creating a Successful Screenplay*, rev. ed. Delta, 2006.

Ford, Dennis. *The Search for Meaning: A Short History*. University of California Press, 2007.

Foucault, Michel. *Archaeology of Knowledge*. Routledge, 2013.

Friedman, Maurice S. *The Worlds of Existentialism: A Critical Reader*. Humanities Press, 1964.

Gardner, Howard. *Changing Minds*. Harvard Business School Press, 2006.

Grenfell, Michael. *Pierre Bourdieu: Key Concepts*. Routledge, 2014.

Groot, Ger. *Twee zielen. Gesprekken met hedendaagse filosofen*. SUN, 1999.

Hamel, Gary. "Opinion: Strategy Innovation and the Quest for Value." *Sloan Management Review* 39, no. 2 (1998): 7–14.

Hardin, Garrett. "The Tragedy of the Commons." In *Environmental Ethics*, by John Benson. Routledge, 2013.

Hekkert, Paul, and Matthijs Van Dijk. *Vision in Design—A Guidebook for Innovators*. BIS Publishers, 2011.

Hirshberg, Jerry. *The Creative Priority: Driving Innovative Business in the Real World*. Harper Collins, 1998.

Hofstadter, Douglas R. *I Am a Strange Loop*. Basic Books, 2007.

Holierhoek, Sophie. "Redesigning Psychiatry: A Strategic Repertoire to Stimulate Transition in the Mental Healthcare Sector." PhD thesis, TU Delft, 2020.

Horlings, Harma, and Noel van Dooren, eds. *Design Lessons from Practice: Professionals Reflecting on Design Processes*. Amsterdam Academy of Architecture, 2020.

Horsten, Hans. *The City That Creates the Future*. Lecturis, 2016.

Hultén, Pontus, and Jean Tinguely. *Jean Tinguely: A Magic Stronger than Death*. Abbeville Press, 1987.

Hwang, Victor W., and Greg Horowitt. *The Rainforest: The Secret to Building the Next Silicon Valley*. Regenwald, 2012.

Kaldor, Lucy, and Rodger Watson. "Improving Wellbeing for Victims of Crime." In *Proceedings of the International Conference on Engineering Design*, ICED, 2015, 1 (DS 80-01), 381–390.

Kelley, Tom. *The Art of Innovation: Lessons in Creativity from IDEO, America's Leading Design Firm*. Currency, 2001.

Kelly, Walt. *Pogo: We Have Met the Enemy and He Is Us*. Simon and Schuster, 1972.

Kolb, David A. *Experiential Learning: Experience as the Source of Learning and Development*. FT Press, 2014.

Krishnamurti, Jiddu. *The Book of Life: Daily Meditations with Krishnamurti*. Penguin Books India, 2001.

Kristeva, Julia. *Strangers to Ourselves*. Columbia University Press, 2024.

Kuhn, Thomas S. *The Structure of Scientific Revolutions*. University of Chicago Press, 1997. Originally published in 1962.

Lakoff, George, and Mark Johnson. *Philosophy in the Flesh: The Embodied Mind and Its Challenge to Western Thought*. Basic Books, 1999.

Lawson, Bryan, and Kees Dorst. *Design Expertise*. Routledge, 2013.

Lawson-Tancred, Hugh, ed. *The Art of Rhetoric*. Penguin, 1991.

Leadbeater, Charles, and Jennie Winhall. *Building Better Systems: A Green Paper on System Innovation*. Rockwool Foundation, 2020.

Loorbach, Derk. "Transition Management for Sustainable Development: A Prescriptive, Complexity-Based Governance Framework." *Governance* 23, no. 1 (2010): 161–183.

Loorbach, Derk, and Jan Rotmans. "The Practice of Transition Management: Examples and Lessons from Four Distinct Cases." *Futures* 42, no. 3 (2010): 237–246.

Loorbach, Derk, Jan Rotmans, and René Kemp. "Complexity and Transition Management." *Complexity and Planning*. (2016): 177–198.

Lulham, Rohan. "Does Design Matter? An Environmental Psychology Study in Youth Detention." In *The Palgrave Handbook of Prison Design*, edited by Dominique Moran, Yvonne Jewkes, Kwan-Lamar Blount-Hill, and Victor St. John. Springer International Publishing, 2022.

Lulham, Rohan, Kevin Bradley, Douglas Tomkin, Jessica Wong, and Kiran Kashyap. *Intensive Learning Centre Building Evaluation*. Designing Out Crime, 2015.

Lulham, Rohan, Douglas Tomkin, Luke Grant, and Yvonne Jewkes. "The Risk of 'a Cold Conservatism' in Correctional Facility Design: The Case for Design Innovation." *Advancing Corrections Journal* 1 (2016): 12–25.

Luyendijk, Joris. *Swimming with Sharks: My Journey into the World of the Bankers*. Guardian Faber Publishing, 2015.

Mak, Geert. *An Island in Time: The Biography of a Village*. Random House, 2010.

Maturana, Humberto R., and Francisco J. Varela. *The Tree of Knowledge: The Biological Roots of Human Understanding*. New Science Library/Shambhala Publications, 1987.

Max-Neef, Manfred A. "Foundations of Transdisciplinarity." *Ecological Economics* 53, no. 1 (2005): 5–16.

Mazzucato, Mariana. "The Entrepreneurial State." *Soundings* 49, no. 49 (2011): 131–142.

Mazzucato, Mariana, and Rosie Collington. *The Big Con: How the Consulting Industry Weakens Our Businesses, Infantilizes Our Governments, and Warps Our Economies.* Penguin, 2023.

McChrystal, Stanley, Tantum Collins, David Silverman, and Chris Fussell. *Team of Teams: New Rules of Engagement for a Complex World.* Penguin, 2015.

McGann, Michael, Emma Blomkamp, and Jenny M. Lewis. "The Rise of Public Sector Innovation Labs: Experiments in Design Thinking for Policy." *Policy Sciences* 51, no. 3 (2018): 249–267.

McGann, Michael, Tamas Wells, and Emma Blomkamp. "Innovation Labs and Co-production in Public Problem Solving." *Public Management Review* 23, no. 2 (2021): 297–316.

Miller, Riel. "Embracing Complexity and Using the Future." *Ethos* 10, no. 10 (2010): 23–28.

Miller, Riel. *Transforming the Future: Anticipation in the 21st Century.* Taylor & Francis, 2018.

Mintzberg, Henry. "Managers Not MBAs." *Management Today* 20, no. 7 (2004): 10–13.

Moore, Clover. "Summer Trials to Improve Sydney's Late Night Economy." Minute by the Lord Mayor, City of Sydney, July 25, 2011.

Munro, Tasman. "Appreciative Co-design: From Problem Solving to Strength-Based Re-authoring in Social Design." In *Future Focused Thinking—DRS International Conference*, edited by P. Lloyd and E. Bohemia. Design Research Society, 2016. https://doi.org/10.21606/drs.2016.271.

Musashi, Miyamoto. "The Way of Strategy." *FMR*, no. 54 (1992): 138–144.

Nagji, Bansi, and Geoff Tuff. "Managing Your Innovation Portfolio." *Harvard Business Review* 90, no. 5 (2012): 66–74.

Nemme, Anton, Berto Pandolfo, Roderick Walden, and Stefan Lie. "A Product System for Meaningful Work, Rehabilitation, and Social Well-Being in Correctional Contexts." In *Maintaining Social Well-Being and Meaningful Work in a Highly Automated Job Market*, edited by Shalin Hai-Jew. IGI Global, 2020.

OECD. *Systems Approaches to Public Sector Challenges: Working with Change.* OECD Publishing, 2017. http://dx.doi.org/10.1787/9789264279865-en.

Paton, Bec, and Kees Dorst. "Briefing and Reframing: A Situated Practice." *Design Studies* 32, no. 6 (2011): 573–587.

Ries, Eric. *The Lean Startup: How Today's Entrepreneurs Use Continuous Innovation to Create Radically Successful Businesses.* Crown Currency, 2011.

Rijken, Dick. "Design Literacy: Organizing Self-Organization." In *Open Design Now*, edited by Bas van Abel, Lucas Evers, Roel Klaassen, and Peter Troxler. BIS, 2011.

Rijken, Dick. *The Future Is a Direction, Not a Place*. Netherlands Design Institute, Sandberg Institute, 1994.

Rijken, Dick, Ton Korver, Arnoud Odding, and Karin Potting. *Het Echte Werk, van Waterwolf naar FC de Omslag*. Haagse Hogeschool, 2011.

Ritsema, Rudolf, and Shantena Augusto Sabbadini. *The Original I Ching Oracle or The Book of Changes: The Eranos I Ching Project*. Watkins Media Limited, 2018.

Rittel, Horst W. J., and Melvin M. Webber. "Dilemmas in a General Theory of Planning." *Policy Sciences* 4, no. 2 (1973): 155–169.

Romme, A. Georges L. "Against All Odds: How Eindhoven Emerged as a Deeptech Ecosystem." *Systems* 10, no. 4 (2022): 119.

Roozenburg, Norbert F. M., and Johannes Eekels. *Product Design: Fundamentals and Methods*. Wiley, 1995.

Rorty, R. "Foucault and Epistemology." In *Michel Foucault*. Routledge, 2017.

Schaminée, André. *Designing With and Within Public Organizations: Building Bridges Between Public Sector Innovators and Designers*. BIS Publishers, 2018.

Schaminée, André. *Werken aan transities* [Working on transitions]. Twynstra Gudde, 2023.

Schaminée, André, and Kees Dorst. *Design thinking binnen de overheid: Effectiever werken aan transitievraagstukken*. Twynstra Gudde, 2021.

Scharmer, Otto. *Theory U: Learning from the Future as It Emerges*. Berrett-Koehler Publishers, 2009.

Schön, Donald. *The Reflective Practitioner*. Basic Books, 1983.

Schwaber, Ken, and Jeff Sutherland. "The Scrum Guide." *Scrum Alliance* 21, no. 1 (2011): 1–38.

Searle, John R. "The Intentionality of Intention and Action." *Cognitive Science* 4, no. 1 (1980): 47–70.

Searle, John R. *Rationality in Action*. MIT Press, 2003.

Seijas, Andréina, and Mirik Milan Gelders. "Governing the Night-Time City: The Rise of Night Mayors as a New Form of Urban Governance After Dark." *Urban Studies* 58, no. 2 (2021): 316–334.

Senge, Peter. *The Fifth Discipline: The Art and Practice of Learning Organization*. Doubleday, 1990.

Simon, Herbert A. "The Structure of Ill Structured Problems." *Artificial Intelligence* 4, no. 3–4 (1973): 181–201.

Sleeswijk-Visser, Froukje, and Jeroen van Erp. "Let's Step Into Each Other's Worlds: Designing for Local Transformation Processes." In *ServDes 2023: Entanglements and*

Flows: Service Encounters and Meanings: Conference Proceedings, edited by Carla Cipolla, Claudia Mont'Alvão, Larissa Farias, and Manuela Quaresma. ServDes, 2023.

Smulders, Frido. "Get Synchronized: Bridging the Gap Between Design and Volume Production." PhD thesis, TU Delft, 2006.

Snowden, David J., and Mary E. Boone. "A Leader's Framework for Decision Making." *Harvard Business Review* 85, no. 11 (2007): 68.

Spaan, Michiel. *The Wandering Maker*. Architura & Natura, 2019.

Spann, Rick, and Simon Martin. *Re-sounding: Introducing an Alternative Metaphor for Organisational Change*. Taos Institute Publications, 2021.

Stacey, Ralph D., and Douglas Griffin, eds. *Complexity and the Experience of Managing in Public Sector Organizations*. Routledge, 2007.

Stacey, Ralph D., Douglas Griffin, and Patricia Shaw. *Complexity and Management: Fad or Radical Challenge to Systems Thinking?* Psychology Press, 2000.

Suchman, Lucy. *Plans and Situated Actions: The Problem of Human-Machine Communication*. Cambridge University Press, 1987.

Sutton, Robert I., and Thomas A. Kelley. "Creativity Doesn't Require Isolation: Why Product Designers Bring Visitors 'Backstage.'" *California Management Review* 40, no. 1 (1997): 75–91.

Suyling, Peik, Diana Krabbendam, and Kees Dorst, eds. *More than 8 Design Ideas for the Integrated Living of Mentally Handicapped People in Society*. Ministry of Health Wellbeing and Sports, The Hague, 2005.

Thompson, Evan. *Mind in Life: Biology, Phenomenology, and the Sciences of Mind*. Harvard University Press, 2010.

Tromp, Nynke, and Paul Hekkert. *Designing for Society: Products and Services for a Better World*. Bloomsbury Publishing, 2018.

Treasury NSW. *NSW 24-Hour Economy Strategy: A New State of Night*. NSW Government and 24-Hour Economy, 2020. https://www.investment.nsw.gov.au/assets/Uploads/files/Sydney-24-hour-Economy-Strategy.pdf.

Tullis, Paul. "Nitrogen Wars: The Dutch Farmers Revolt that Turned a Nation Upside-Down." *The Guardian*, November 16, 2023. https://www.theguardian.com/environment/2023/nov/16/nitrogen-wars-the-dutch-farmers-revolt-that-turned-a-nation-upside-down.

United Nations Development Group. *Mainstreaming the 2030 Agenda for Sustainable Development*. UN, 2017.

United Nations Development Programme. *UNDP Strategic Plan, 2018–2021*. UN, 2017.

BIBLIOGRAPHY

UTS. "Meet the Teacher: Taking a Fresh Approach to Education." An interview with Christina Luzi. *Postgrad Blog*, August 23, 2023. https://www.uts.edu.au/study/postgraduate/why-uts/news/meet-teacher-taking-fresh-approach-education.

van der Bijl-Brouwer, Mieke, and Rodger Watson. "Designing for the Deepest Needs of Both Public Service Consumers and Providers; Innovation in Mental Health Crisis Response." In *Proceedings of ICED 15: Vol 1: Design for Life*, edited by Christian Weber, Stephan Husung, Gaetano Cascini, Marco Cantamessa, Dorian Marjanovic, and Monica Bordegoni. Design Society, 2015.

van der Vorst, Roland. *De toekomst is eindeloos* [The future is endless]. Ten Have, 2023.

van Leeuwen, Jos P., Dick Rijken, Iefke Bloothoofd, and Eefje Cobussen. "Finding New Perspectives Through Theme Investigation." *Design Journal* 23, no. 3 (2020): 441–461.

van Leeuwen, Jos P., Dick Rijken, Iefke Bloothoofd, Eefje Cobussen, Bram Reurings, and Rob Ruts. "Thematic Research in the Frame Creation Process." In *Service Design Geographies: ServDes.2016*, edited by Nicola Morelli, Amalia de Gotzen, and Francesco Grani. ServDes, 2016.

van Manen, Max. *Researching Lived Experience: Human Science for an Action Sensitive Pedagogy*. Routledge, 2016.

Vermaak, Hans. "Planning Deep Change Through a Series of Small Wins." *Academy of Management Proceedings* 2013, no. 1 (2013): 10947.

Vermaak, Hans, and Léon de Caluwé. "The Colors of Change Revisited: Situating and Describing the Theory and Its Practical Applications." In *Research in Organizational Change and Development*, vol. 26, edited by Debra A. Noumair and Abraham B. Shani. Emerald Publishing Limited, 2018.

Vos, Erik. *Herinneringen van een regisseur—een wereld van beeld en verbeelding*. International Theatre and Film Books, 2014.

Watson, Rodger. "Designing for the Common Good; Emergent Practices and Contemporary Challenges." PhD thesis, University of the Arts London, 2026.

Watson, Rodger. "Who Framed the Government Architect?: Cultural Residue, and a Role for Design in Reshaping Organizations." In *DTRS 14: The Role of Design in Shaping Sustainable Futures*, edited by Ulrika Florin, Karolina Uggla, Hasse Henningsson, Lasse Frank, and Björn Westling. Mälardalen University Living Lab Press, 2024.

Watson, Rodger, and Kees Dorst. "Pragmatism, Design and Public Sector Innovation: Reflections on Action." In *DRS2022: Bilbao*, edited by Dan Lockton, Sara Lenzi, Paul Hekkert, Arlene Oak, and Juan Sádaba. Design Research Society, 2022.

Weatherburn, Donald James, and Stephanie Ramsey. *Offending over the Life Course: Contact with the NSW Criminal Justice System Between Age 10 and Age 33*. NSW Bureau of Crime Statistics and Research, 2018.

Wetzels, Rob. *Handreiking voor agendabepaling bij duurzaam ondernemen*. Nyenrode Business School, 2016.

Wittgenstein, Ludwig. *Philosophical Investigations*. John Wiley & Sons, 2009.

Yates, Frances A. *Art of Memory*. Routledge, 2013.

Yunkaporta, Tyson. *Right Story, Wrong Story: Adventures in Indigenous Thinking*. Text Publishing, 2023.

Yunkaporta, Tyson. *Sand Talk: How Indigenous Thinking Can Save the World*. Text Publishing, 2019.

Zijderveld, Anton. *The Waning of the Welfare State*. Routledge, 2018.

INDEX

Abduction, 23, 25, 143, 170, 212
 first-order, 23
 second-order, 24, 26, 36, 56, 167, 174
Abstraction, 19, 20, 64, 128, 138, 142, 143
 in design research (case study), 19–20
Academic hospital, 124
Agriculture (case studies), 9–10, 130–137
Amsterdam New-West (case study), 179–184
Anticipation, 69, 146
 the science of, 175–176
Archaeology, 38, 41, 44–45, 177
Argumentation, 97, 111
Assumptions, 10, 63, 109, 127, 158, 175, 176

Balance, 13, 14, 17, 68, 161, 205
Best practices, 10, 21, 114
Bird-watching, 109
Body as a system (case study), 17
Bottom-up change, 77–80, 83, 90, 103, 123, 138, 160, 181

Capability building, 88, 90
Causality, 18, 23, 211
Challenges, 10, 101, 122, 129, 143, 184
Change agent, 91, 151, 158
 biodiversity (case study), 155–156
 care republic (case study), 153–155
 cultural sector (case study), 157

 thriving communities (case study), 151–153
Changing minds, 101
 being wrong (case study), 102
Chaos, 13, 14
Character, 201
Coherence, 94, 127
Collage, 205, 208
Colors of change model, 107–110, 249–250
Complexity, 8, 11–16, 30, 63, 113, 143, 144, 245
Complex problems, 11, 13, 237
Complicatedness, 8, 12–13, 23
Confusion, 11, 212
Context, 8, 19, 38, 41, 48–49, 79, 144
Copernicus, Nicolaus, 22
Creative intelligence, 33, 124, 176
Creative practice, 26, 38, 109, 162, 164, 208
Crime prevention, 25, 82
 epiphany (case study), 198–199
 street robbery (case study), 25–26
Crisis, 13, 129, 221
Cultural sector
 as a change agent (case study), 86–89
 transforming the practices of (case study), 157
Curriculum development (case study), 102
Cynefin model, 11–13, 15

Deduction, 20–21, 24–25
Deep change, 30, 97, 122, 143, 159, 173, 198, 201
Defense (case study), 31–32
Design agency, 170
Design process, 19
Design projects, 181, 219
Design thinking, 109, 111, 221–228
Designing Out Crime Research Center, 117–118
  counterterrorism bin (case study), 34–35
  criminal justice system (case study), 118
  entertainment district (case study), 71–76 (*see also* Kings Cross)
  prison learning centers (case study), 118–119
  suicide prevention (case study), 150
  victim support (case study), 119–120
Detective novel, 22–23
Diagnosis, 186, 214
Dialogue, 110, 117, 166, 174, 189, 200, 203
Disciplinary matrix, 96, 127, 144
Disciplines, 117, 112, 124, 160, 209, 245
  development of (case study), 115
Discussion, 117, 166, 179, 189
Dissipative system, 13–15

Education
  for game changers, 245–247
  paradigms of (case study), 97–100
Eliasson, Olafur, 163–164, 167, 171
Emergence, 111, 112, 146, 185, 221
Empathy, 111, 233
Essence, 208
Existentialism, 207
Experience, 68, 201, 204, 226
Expertise, 30, 63, 64, 68, 144, 222
Exploration, 7, 25, 34, 160, 212

Farming (case study), 9–10
Field, 38, 41, 50–61, 63, 79–81, 91–93, 117, 122–123, 159–160, 170
  of thought, 202
Frame, 33–37
Frame creation
  method cards, 44–61
  process model case study, 39–42
  process models, 37–39
Frame communication (case study), 116
Frame innovation, 4, 37
Frames, 38, 41, 54–55
Framing, 33–36
Fruitfulness, 69
Future literacy, 174
Futures, 38, 41, 56–57

Game changers model, 76–83, 91, 103, 159, 168
Gouda (case study), 86–89

Hierarchy, 31, 104, 110
Hunter innovation ecosystem (case study), 192–196

I Ching, 1, 17
Identity, 114, 201
Improvisation, 206
Induction, 21–23, 25
Innovation, public sector, 221–228
Innovation ecosystem, 184–190
Innovation failure, 211–215
Innovation infrastructure, 79, 97, 117, 137, 139, 142, 164–166, 184, 210
Innovation projects, 18, 77, 213, 222
Inspiration, 165, 172, 198, 203
Integration, 38, 41, 60–61, 167
Interaction design (case study), 112–113
Intuition, 62, 162, 197, 238
Iteration, 64, 160

Kings Cross (case study), 71–76, 78, 80, 89–90, 140, 170

INDEX

Kuhn, Thomas, 93–97, 103–104, 127, 138, 210

Leadership, 82, 158, 206
Learning loops/cycles, 77, 112, 132, 135, 142, 160, 219, 222
Library, 87, 99
Lifeworld, 148, 153, 156, 188, 198, 208
  personal, 149, 155, 225
  professional, 144, 197
  professional (case study), 148–149
Logic, 2, 19–26, 72, 95–97, 110, 143, 202, 215

Meaningful transformation, 83, 90, 129, 157–158, 184
Mental health system (case study), 83–86
Mentality, 12, 25, 172, 237
Metaphor, 203
Misdiagnosis, 128
Motivation, 90, 104
  beautiful day at work (case study), 106
  intrinsic, 59, 61, 88, 104–106, 154, 198, 214

Narrative therapy, 120
Navigation, 146, 184, 188
Nitrogen crisis (case study), 130–137
Novelty, 175
Novice, 68

Objectivity, 111
Open innovation, 169, 173–174, 184
  Brainport Eindhoven (case study), 190–191
  Chemelot (case study), 191–192
  Port of Newcastle (case study) (*see also* Hunter innovation ecosystem)
Organization, 71–92
  formal, 108, 120, 141, 171–172, 179
  informal, 108, 153–156, 172
  structure, 77–81, 97, 103, 126–127
Ownership, 129, 139–140, 184

Paradigm, 93–124, 159, 168, 209
  current, 22, 79, 177
  new, 94–96, 166
  shift in, 22, 91, 138–139, 167
Paradox, 7, 38, 41, 46–47, 89, 130–134, 172, 207
Peirce, Charles S., 23
Perception, 37, 62, 79
Phenomenology, 51, 208
Planning and control, 32, 109, 120
Positive drivers. *See* Motivation, intrinsic
Practice model, 29–33
Pragmatism, 208
Priming, 116
Principles, 29–32, 113. *See also* Studio principles
Problem arena, 68, 69, 132
Problem formulation, 63
Problem holder, 136, 144
Problem owner, 10, 136, 144, 182, 185, 224
Problems, 7–28
  open, complex, dynamic and networked, 8–11, 19, 26, 142, 173–174
  wicked, 13
Problem situation, 7–23, 26, 31–39
Problem-solving, 12, 16–18, 23, 25–26, 91, 95, 109, 201, 209
Proprioception of thought, 200
Public space (case study). *See* Amsterdam New-West

Quality, 63, 114, 166, 173, 179, 201
  without a name, 197

Rationality 21, 32, 111, 201–202, 215
Reasoning patterns, 19–26, 143, 205
Reflection-in-action, 34, 64
Reflection-on-action, 34
Reframing, 34, 76–81, 165, 169, 176, 201

Regional transformation (case study). *See* Hunter innovation ecosystem
Relational government, 182, 184
Repertoire
 of actions, 30, 224
 of frames, 146, 162
 of practices, 109, 188
Resilience, 151
Resolution, 208
Rhetoric, 117
Risk, 128, 166, 212–213, 228

Scale, 2, 91, 109, 132, 138, 181, 184, 239
Schön, Donald, 33–35, 62
Selves, 200–201
Social enterprise, 42
Social space, 137, 148, 194
Societal discussion, 76, 80, 133
Societal midfield, 139–140, 157, 186, 219
Solutions, 1, 16–18, 63, 162
Stakeholders, 8, 16, 48–51, 57, 59, 68, 146, 184, 221
Strategy, 78, 243–244
 evidence-based, 10, 120, 211
Strategy formulation, 78–82, 213, 228
Studio, 159–196
Studio environment, 202, 247
Studio model, 165–167
Studio principles, 161–163, 173, 206, 237–244
Synchronizing, 2, 83, 90, 123, 189, 217
System, 11–18, 193
System border, 89, 158
System change, 89, 123, 129, 143, 148–149, 165–167, 184, 191
System vitality, 17, 150–151, 174, 206, 210

Team of teams (case study), 103–104
Tension, 162, 169, 199, 201

Themes, 38, 39, 41, 52–55, 63, 69, 146–147, 161–162
 theme analysis, 229–235
Top-down change, 78–81, 83, 90–91, 103, 117, 123, 160, 165, 225
Train (case study), 13
Transdisciplinarity, 33, 111–116, 169, 174, 245
 Bose (case study), 111
 exchanging practices (case study), 113–114
Transformation, 38, 41, 58–59, 123, 128–129, 195
Transitions, 126–143, 150, 190–195, 217, 224–225
 X-curve model of, 126, 138–139
Transport (case study), 142–143
Trust, 82, 90, 150, 173
Truth, 25, 35, 105, 209, 233
Tunnel construction works (case study), 39–42

Value, 20, 23–24, 26, 29–33, 36, 63, 68, 72, 144, 146–149, 179, 208
Village shop (case study), 14–16
Vitality, 17, 136–137, 149–151, 160, 168–170, 198, 203, 208, 210

Wisdom, 199–201, 208

Kees Dorst is James Wei Visiting Professor at Princeton University and Professor of Transdisciplinary Innovation at the University of Technology Sydney. He is considered one of the lead thinkers developing the field of design, valued for his ability to connect a philosophical understanding of the logic of design with hands-on practice. As a bridge-builder between these two worlds, his writings on design as a way of thinking are read by both practitioners and academics. He has written several best-selling books in the field: *Understanding Design* (2003, 2006), *Design Expertise* (with Bryan Lawson, 2013), *Frame Innovation* (2015), *Designing for the Common Good* (2016), *Notes on Design: How Creative Practice Works* (2017), and *Reinventing Strategic Innovation: Create Deep Change* (with Rodger Watson and Barbara Doran, 2025). Over the years, he has developed his focus on the use of designerly ways of thinking outside the traditional design domains—in particular, as applied to the problems of the new networked society. He has developed a set of methodologies to support these processes, experimenting with them in practice through the research centers and degree programs he has founded.

Publisher contact:
The MIT Press
Massachusetts Institute of Technology
77 Massachusetts Avenue, Cambridge, MA 02139
mitpress.mit.edu

EU Authorised Representative:
Easy Access System Europe, Mustamäe tee 50,
10621 Tallinn, Estonia
gpsr.requests@easproject.com

Printed by Integrated Books International,
United States of America